EDITOR'S CHOICE II

Small presses have long been the seedbed of fine American writing. As these presses continue to grow in size and significance, they are becoming the most important source of high quality contemporary writing both by established and younger authors.

—*Frank Conroy*, former Director of the Literature Program, National Endowment for the Arts

The Spirit That Moves Us Press was the first to publish in English, in the U.S.A., a collection of poetry by the 1984 Nobel Laureate in literature, Jaroslav Seifert—a year before he won the Prize.

In 1985, the editor and publisher of *The Spirit That Moves Us*, Morty Sklar, was awarded an Editor's Grant from the Coordinating Council of Literary Magazines.

SPECIAL OFFER: Order the first *Editor's Choice*, which was indexed in *Granger's Index to Poetry*, at the reduced price of only $7.50 + $1.50 pstg. (501 pp; includes essays and autobiographical notes by the authors and nominating publishers), and you'll have, with *Editor's Choice II*, a set which spans 18 years, from 1965-1983.

Subscribe to *The Spirit That Moves Us* (ISSN 0364-4014) and gain a 20% discount off cover prices, and free postage. Write for our complete, descriptive catalog.

The Contemporary Anthology Series:

No. 1—*The Actualist Anthology*
No. 2—*Cross-Fertilization*
No. 3—*Editor's Choice* (1980)
No. 4—*The Spirit That Moves Us Reader*
No. 5—*Nuke-Rebuke*
No. 6—*Editor's Choice II*
No. 7—*Men & Women* (1988)

The Outstanding Author Series:

No. 1—o.o.p.
No. 2—*The Poem You Asked For,* by Marianne Wolfe
No. 3—*The Farm In Calabria,* by David Ray
No. 4—*The Casting Of Bells,* by Jaroslav Seifert (1984 Nobel Laureate)
No. 5—*How In The Morning,* by Chuck Miller (1988)

Order direct or from the following:

Distributors: Bookslinger, Inland Book Co., Small Press Distribution, Bookpeople, Publishers Group West, the distributors, Baker & Taylor.

Library jobbers: Baker & Taylor, Blackwell North America, and many others.

The Spirit That Moves Us is a member of the Coordinating Council of Literary Magazines.

EDITOR'S CHOICE II:

Fiction, Poetry & Art from the U.S. Small Press

EDITED BY MORTY SKLAR & MARY BIGGS

Selections from nominations
made by the editors of independent,
noncommercial literary presses and magazines,
of work published by them
from 1978 to 1983.

**The first *Editor's Choice*
(indexed in *Granger's Index to Poetry*), covered
the period from 1965 to 1977,
and included essays.**

The Spirit That Moves Us Press

Iowa City, Iowa : 1987

3

Acknowledgements

Coverphoto by Richard E. Loftis; reprinted from *Chouteau Review*, Volume 5, No. 2—1982, edited by David Perkins.

Acknowledgement is made, with gratitude, to the following, for grants awarded in partial support of this publication:

The National Endowment for the Arts, a federal agency
The Iowa Arts Council, a state agency.

Appreciation is expressed also to the following, for donations of services or cash: John Hesse, Zephyr Copies, Technigraphics, Iowa State Bank, Charles de Prosse, Baskin Robbins (downtown I.C.), Walt Ellinwood, Frohwein's, Norma Vogel, Jack Jackson, Ann Struthers, John O. Cline, Selma Sklar, David Edelberg, John Hayek.

With reference to Marge Piercy's "Six Underrated Pleasures": This poem was nominated, and accepted by us, prior to its subsequent publication in her book, *My Mother's Body*, which made it to press before *Editor's Choice II*. Permission to reprint it here is also given by Alfred A. Knopf, Inc., copyright 1985 by them.

Number 6 of The Contemporary Anthology Series

This book is offered to subscribers to *The Spirit That Moves Us* (ISSN 0364-4014) as Volume 8, No. 2.

The first *Editor's Choice* (1980) was indexed in *Granger's Index to Poetry*. *The Spirit That Moves Us* is indexed in: *The American Humanities Index*; *Index of American Periodical Verse*; *Index to Periodical Fiction*.

Typesetting, design & layout by Morty Sklar.
Manufactured in the U.S.A. by Thomson-Shore, using acid-free Warren's Olde Style paper. The clothbound editions are Smyth-sewn.

Library of Congress Cataloging-in-Publication Data:

Editor's choice II.

   (The Contemporary anthology series ; no. 6)
   Issued also as The Spirit that moves us, v. 8, no. 2.
   Includes indexes.
   1. American literature—20th century. 2. Little
presses—United States. I. Sklar, Morty, 1935-
II. Biggs, Mary. III. Title: Editor's choice 2.
IV. Title: Editor's choice two. V. Series.
PS536.2.E35 1987   810'.8'0054   86-20352
ISBN 0-930370-23-6 (alk. paper)
ISBN 0-930370-24-4 (pbk. : alk. paper)
ISBN 0-930370-22-8 (signed A-Z : alk. paper)

Mary Biggs dedicates this collection,
with gratitude, to two of her former teachers,
Lyle Glazier and Theodore Adams.

Morty Sklar dedicates this book,
with great appreciation, to Leonard Randolph,
former Director of the Literature Program, National Endow-
ment for the Arts, for his seminal efforts
and accomplishments in developing programs
in support of literary publishing.

PREFACE

Morty Sklar

What's not here: 1) Works which were not nominated; 2) Works we liked for which we had no room; 3) Works we liked whose authors or nominators we'd already accepted (the exception to using only one piece per nominating press or magazine was where, of the two pieces used, one was written and the other visual); 4) Works we liked for which we could not get permission to reprint.

Mary Biggs' and my collaboration for *Editor's Choice II* was a happy accident, one of those elements which makes small-press publishing as exciting and interesting as living itself. I had received a manuscript from Mary, from Chicago, and as time went on we corresponded and found that we liked each other's work and each other. I thought Mary could be an ideal co-editor for the second *Editor's Choice*. She was energetic and enthusiastic, and was also a literary magazine editor (of *Primavera*). And she was a woman, which I felt would lend a good polarity to the selection process.

Had we not shared a mutual respect and been more interested in and excited by literature, excellence and human expression than in the bolstering of our egos or the protection of a narrow idea of art, this collection could not have come to be as fine as we feel it is, a book not engineered for commercial high-success, but one that our readers could enjoy, and of which our contributors and nominating presses and magazines could be proud.

The Small Press has changed a lot since publications were produced by letterpress, which limited the size, print-run and general bookstore distribution of them, and restricted the publication of prose. The "mimeo revolution" of the 1950s and 1960s resulted in part from the means of production becoming available to more people, as photocopying machines replaced mimeograph machines in offices, and the mimeograph machines became available cheaply. Typesetting machinery also became affordable when commercial publishers and printers began using photo-typesetting equipment (I typeset the text of this book with an IBM electronic Composer, an $8,800 machine which cost me $1,200). At the same time, some commercial printers set themselves up to efficiently handle "short-run" jobs, which enabled the publication of a thousand or less copies of a book at an affordable price.

But technology is merely the enabler. Mechanized typesetting and printing equipment have not caused writers or publishers to be more, or less, creative. The spirit of small-press publishing has thrived regardless of the available technology. As the large commercial publishers have for the most part been cutting back on poetry and fiction, the Small Press has more and more taken up the slack. If cost were not a consideration, *Editor's Choice II* could easily have consisted of ten 500-page volumes.

It seems remarkable now that when we started this project, Morty and I rarely discussed what the second *Editor's Choice* would, ideally, be. We were governed not by expressed standards or aesthetic preferences but rather by unspoken assumptions that turned out to be justified.

With great daring, given that we had met only once, we assumed seamless sympathy and affection between us; a mutual commitment to the arts and the independent press that would be strong enough to sustain us through the reading of 2,400 poems and stories and the study of hundreds of graphics, which we did with a shared passion for originality, feeling, and freedom in creation, and a repugnance for the uninspired. Which is not to say that we always agreed. Communicating mostly by mail, we often shot first beseeching, then furious, missives back and forth between Iowa City and Chicago. "I can't figure out why you like this guy!" Morty exclaimed about one of my favorite poets. "Because he is one of the greatest living poets, *that's* why," I retorted— perhaps overstating it a bit in my outrage. Or: "Are you *serious?*" I would demand of some choice Morty had made. "You can't *possibly* be *serious.*"

As I'd expected, and I think Morty hadn't, our disagreements often turned on our experiences as people of different sexes. That we resolved these, stubborn as both of us are, is a near-miracle that was brought about through our mutual trust and respect.

Although we were not constrained by any preconceived ideas of what this anthology should contain, we did hope it would reflect a broad spectrum of thoughts and life experiences in our society and others. To that end, we encouraged submission of work from editors with widely varying tastes and audiences, though we did nothing to assure equal (or proportional) space. Valid as that may be in other areas of endeavor, I believe it to be fatally compromising in the arts.

All I can promise is that the work you are about to experience evoked honest response from me. It moved me, surprised me, excited me, or made me laugh—struck me immediately, viscerally ("Yes, yes, *I want this one*"), or at first struck me not at all, but worked its way into my life as day after day I found it echoing in my mind until, after many re-readings, I knew that I must have it. Everything here—whether created by woman or man, gay or straight, young or old, Black or White or Asian or Native, North American or resident of another continent, traditionalist or experimentalist, much-maligned "academic" or not—everything here speaks to me; it breathes.

Colleen McElroy breathes in these pages, and Hilda Morley, Jack Anderson, Steve Kowit, Judy Grahn, Jane Rule, hattie gossett, Bukowski, Koertge, Stafford, Seifert...

I love this book and hope that you will, too.

The Writers & Visual Artists

We regret having insufficient space to publish notes on the contributors and presses/magazines. Please refer to the Directory of American Poets & Fiction Writers *(Poets & Writers, Inc.) and* The International Directory of Little Magazines & Small Presses *(Dustbooks). Send us a s.a.s.e. if you need more help.*

Dannie Abse
Fernando Alegria
Dorothy Allison
Benny Andersen
Jack Anderson
Dick Bakken
Barbara A. Banks
Jim Barnes
Lynda Barry
Richard Behm
Wendell Berry
James Bertolino
John Biggers
Roger Bower
Luke Breit
Donna Brook
Edith Bruck
Charles Bukowski
Michael Rink Cameron
Ernesto Cardenal
Andrea Carlisle
Wilfredo Q. Castano
Kathleen Childers
Bruce Cutler
Lloyd Davis
Charlotte De Clue
Donna Dennis
William Dickey
Douglas Dusseault
W.D. Ehrhart
Harley Elliott
Frank Espada
Martin Espada
Ruth Feldman (tr.)
Dumile Feni
Paul Fericano
Carol Flint
Steven D. Foster
Pat Therese Francis
Stephen Fredman (tr.)

Hattie Gossett
James Grabill
Judy Grahn
Richard Grayson
Linda Gregg
Sachiko Hamada
James Hazard
David Henson
Tony Hoagland
Anselm Hollo (tr.)
Mary Gray Hughes
Roberta Israeloff
Paul Jagasich (tr.)
Tim Jeffrey
Don Johnson
Michael Kenna
Brandon Kershner
Anna Kiss
William Kloefkorn
Ronald Koertge
Nicholas Kolumban (tr.)
Peter Korniss
Steve Kowit
Kala Ladenheim
Joanne Leonard
Richard Loftis
Phillip McCaffrey
Jo McDougall
Colleen McElroy
Thomas McGrath
Dennis Moler
Cristian Montecino
Robin Morgan
Hilda Morley
W.C. Morton
Clyde Munz
Leonard Nathan
Bill Nelson
Naomi Shihab Nye
Tom O'Grady (tr.)

Don Olsen
Jim Pallas
Marge Piercy
Suzan Pitt
Jurek Polanski
Patricia Rahmann
Victoria Rathbun
Judy Ray
Annie Rogers
John Rosenthal
Jane Rule
Randee Russell
Pentti Saarikoski
Lynn Saville
Jaroslav Seifert
Joe Smith
R.T. Smith
Thomas R. Smith
Michael Spence
William Stafford
Barbara Stafford-Wilson
Barbara Cech Stahl
Les Standiford
Sue Standing
D.E. Steward
Frank Stewart
Jeff Tagami
Michael Tarachow
Alexander Taylor (tr.)
Robert Taylor, Jr.
D. Thrapp
William Tunberg
Ron Wallace
Marianne Ware
Shelley White
Steven F. White (tr.)
Dennis Williams
Bill Wilson
Susan Wood

The Presses & Magazines

Annex 21
Appolyon Press
Beloit Poetry Journal
Bilingual Review/Revista Bilingue
Black Jack
Black Mountain II Review
Blue Cloud Quarterly
Bluefish
Callaloo
Calyx
Carolina Quarterly
Carolina Wren Press
Carpenter Press
Chase Avenue Press
Chouteau Review
Cincinnati Poetry Review
Conditions
Confrontation
Coyote Love Press
Crazyhorse
The Crossing Press
Cumberland Journal
Curbstone Press
Dacotah Territory
Dog Ear Press
Doris Green Editions
Epoch
Fedora
Gargoyle
Ghost Pony Press
Graywolf Press
Greenfield Review Press
Hanging Loose
Helicon Nine
Hiram Poetry Review
The Iowa Review
I. Reed Books
Juniper Press
Kalliope
Kitchen Table: Women of Color Press
Lame Johnny Press
Latin American Literary Review Press
Lightworks
Long Haul Press
Luna Tack
Magazine
Manhattan Review
Matrix Press
McFarland & Co.
Memphis State Review
Midatlantic Review

Milkweed Chronicle
Mississippi Mud
Modern Poetry Studies
The Naiad Press
New CollAge Magazine
New England Rev./Bread Loaf Qrtly.
New Kauri
New Letters
New Rivers Press
Nit & Wit
North American Review
North Point Press
O.ARS
Oink!
Open Places
Ox Head Press
The Paper
The Pawn Review
Pentagram Press
Pig In A Pamphlet
Pig Iron
Pikestaff Forum
Pinchpenny
Poet & Critic
Poetry Flash
Poor Souls Prs./Scaramouche Books
Primavera
Puckerbrush Review
Pudding Magazine
Puerto Del Sol
Punk
The Real Comet Press
Release Press
River Styx
Samisdat
Second Coming
Sing Heavenly Muse!
The Spirit That Moves Us Press
Tamarisk Press
Telescope
13th Moon
Thunder's Mouth Press
Toothpaste Press
TriQuarterly
Unicorn Press
Wild Mustard Press
Wisconsin Academy Review
The Wormwood Review
Yarrow
Zephyr Press

CONTENTS

photograph by Judy Ray; *New Letters*, Vol. 45, No. 2—1978
James McKinley, Editor (David Ray at time of publication)

Dennis Williams
I F

New Kauri, No. 8—1983
Will Inman, Editor

for Duncan Robertson

if a lot of people are laughing
it seems funnier
if yr. mother & father don't like you it makes
more difference than if nobler & more intelligent folks
think yr. fine
if a lot of people study it especially at the university
it seems more profound
if prizes are given, especially for dead people, it seems worthwhile
if more people are interested it seems more important
up to a point
of diminishing returns
for vested interests, so the world
will have room
for only a few
tyrants of its attention span
for the rest it is of no consequence
that we saw God in the bloody wreckage
of our lives, cries not sprinkled with the holy water of social
self consciousness are not song, so the committee begs you do not sing
too long, and do not expect to be invited
to places where yr. loneliness might want you to stay too long
& remind us too much of the pain we're in, rather
go out in the desert
place stones in a circle
call it tomb of the unknown poet, notice
how the sky begins to form around them
and yet to the rest of the world
this is a solitary
& unforgiven act.
Fuck the world
and its inferiority complex.
Let the record show
I sd. this here and nobody
of any importance
gave a shit.

Jane Rule
IN THE ATTIC OF THE HOUSE

The Naiad Press; *Outlander* (1982), by Jane Rule
Barbara Grier, Editor

Alice hadn't joined women's liberation; she had only rented it the main floor of her house. It might turn out to be the alternative to burning it down, which she had threatened to do sober and had nearly accomplished when she was drunk. Since none of the four young women who moved in either drank or smoked, they might be able to save Alice from inadvertence. That was all. And the money helped. Alice had not imagined she would ever be sixty-five to have to worry about it. Now the years left were the fingers of one hand. She was going to turn out to be one of the ones too mean to die.

"I'm a lifer," she said at the beer parlor and laughed until her lungs came to a boil.

"Don't sound like it, Al. If the weed don't get you, the traffic will."

"Naw," Alice said. "Only danger on the road is the amateur drunks, who can't drive when they're sober either. I always get home."

The rules were simple: stay in your own lane, and don't honk your horn. Alice was so small she peered through rather than over her steering wheel and might more easily have been arrested as a runaway kid than a drunk. But she'd never caught hell from anyone but Harriet, rest her goddamned soul. Until these females moved in.

"Come have a cup of tea," one of them would say just as Alice was making a sedate attempt at the stairs.

There she'd have to sit in what had been her own kitchen for thirty years, a guest drinking Red Zinger or some other Koolade-colored wash they called tea, squinting at them through the steam: Bett, the giant postie; Trudy and Jill, who worked at the women's garage without a grease mark under their fingernails; Angel, who was unemployed; young, all of them, incredibly young, killing her with kindness. Sober, she could refuse them with, "I never learned to eat a whole beet with chopsticks," or "Brown rice sticks to my dentures," but once she was drunk and dignified, she was caught having to prove that point and failing as she'd always failed, except that now there was the new test of the stairs.

"Do you mind having to live in the attic of your own house?" Bett asked as she offered Alice a steadying hand.

"Mind? Living on top of it is a lot better than living in the middle of it ever was. I don't think I was meant for the ground floor," Alice confessed, her spinning head pressed against Bett's enormous bosom until they reached the top stair.

17

"You all right now? Can you manage?"

"Sleep like a baby. Always have."

Alice began to have infantile dreams about those breasts, though a-
wake and sober she found them comically alarming rather than erotic,
eye-level as she was with them. Alice liked Bett and was glad, though she
didn't hold with women taking over everything, that Bett delivered the
mail. Bett had not only yellow hair but yellow eyebrows, a sunny sort
of face for carrying the burden of bills as well as the promise of love letters and surprise legacies. And everyone was able to see at a glance that
this postie was a woman.

Angel was probably Bett's girl, though Alice couldn't tell for sure.
Sometimes Alice imagined four-way orgies going on downstairs, but it
could as easily be a karate lesson. It was obvious that none of them was
interested in men.

"We don't hate men because we don't need them," said Trudy, the
one who memorized slogans; who, once she could fix a car, couldn't imagine what other use men were ever put to.

Hating men, for this crew, would be like hating astronauts, too remote an exercise to be meaningful. Alice knew lots of men, was more
comfortable with them than with women at the beer parlor or in the
employees' lounge at Safeway, where she worked. As a group, she needed them far more than she needed women. Working among them and
drinking among them had always been her self-esteem.

"Aren't you ashamed to sit home on a Saturday night?" Alice asked.

"We don't drink; the bars aren't our scene."

Alice certainly couldn't imagine them at her beer parlor, looking
young enough to be jail bait and dressed so badly men who had taken
the time to shave and change into good clothes couldn't help taking of-
fense. Even Alice, with her close-cropped hair, put on a nice blouse over
good slacks, even sometimes a skirt, and she didn't forget her lipstick.

"Do you buy all your clothes at the Sally Ann?" Alice asked, studying one remarkably holey and faded tank top Jill was wearing.

"Somebody gave me this one," Jill admitted irritably. "Why should
you mind? You're the only one of any sex who has a haircut like that."

"Don't you like it?" Alice asked.

"It's sort of male chauvinist," Trudy put in, "as if you wanted to
come on very heavy."

"I don't come on," Alice said. "I broke the switch."

At the beer parlor someone might have said, "Then I'll screw you in,"
or something else amiable, but this Trudy was full of sudden sympathy
and instruction about coming to terms with your own body, as if she
were about to invent sex, not for Alice, just for instance.

"Do you know how old I am?"

"We're not ageists here," Jill said.

"I'm old enough to be your grandmother."

"Not if you're still working at Safeway, you're not. My grandma's got the old-age pension."

"When I was young, we had some respect for old people."

"Everybody should respect everybody," Angel said.

"I have every respect for you," Alice said with dignity. "Even about sex."

"You know what you should do, Alice?" Angel asked. "It's not too late ... is come out."

"Come out?" Alice demanded. "Of where? This is my house after all. You're just renting the main floor. Come out? To whom? Everyone I know is dead!"

Harriet, rest her goddamned soul. Alice mostly pretended that she never spoke Harriet's name. In fact, she almost always waited to do it until she had drunk that amount which would let her forget what she had said so that she could say it over and over again. "Killed herself in my bathtub. Is that any way to win an argument? Is it?"

"What argument?" Trudy would ask.

"This bathtub?" Jill tried to confirm.

"How?" Angel wanted to know.

Later, on her unsteady way upstairs, Alice would resent most Bett's asking, "Were you in love with Harriet?"

"In love?" Alice demanded. "Christ! I lived with her for thirty years."

Never in those thirty years had Alice ever spoken as openly to Harriet as she was expected to speak with these females. Never in the last twenty years had Alice and Harriet so much as touched, though they slept in the same bed. At first Alice had come home drunk and pleading. Then she came home drunk and mean, sometimes threatening rape, sometimes in a jeering moral rage.

"What have you got to be guilty about? You never so much as soil your hand. I'm the one that should be crawling off to church, for Christ's sake!"

Sometimes that kind of abuse would weaken Harriet's resolve and she would submit, whimpering like a child anticipating a beating, weeping like a lost soul when it was over.

Finally Alice simply came home drunk and slept in a drunken stupor. She learned from the beer parlor how many men did the same thing.

"Scruples," one man explained. "They've got scruples."

"Scruples, shit! On Friday night I go home with the dollars and say, 'You want this? You put out for it.' "

"So what are you doing down here? It's Friday, isn't it?"

"Yeh, well, we split ... "

Harriet had her own money. She was a legal secretary. Alice remem-

bered the first time she ever saw Harriet in the beer parlor wearing a
prim gray suit, looking obviously out of place. Some cousin had brought
her and left her for unrelated pleasures. After they'd talked a while, Alice suggested a walk along the beach. It was summer; there was still light
in the sky.

Years later, Harriet would say, "You took advantage. I'd been jilted."

Sometimes, when Alice was very drunk, she could remember how ap-
pealing the young Harriet had been, how willingly she had been coaxed
from kisses to petting of her shapely little breasts, protesting with no
more than, "You're as bad as a boy, Al, you really are." "Do you like
it?" "Well, I'm not supposed to say so, am I?" Alice also remembered
the indrawn breath of surprise when she first laid her finger on that wet
pulse, the moment of wonder and triumph before the first crying, "Oh,
it must be terrible what we're doing! We're going to burn in hell!"

Harriet could frighten Alice then with her guilt and terror. Once Alice promised that they'd never again, as Harriet called it, "go all the
way," if they could still kiss, touch. Guiltily, oh so guiltily, weeks later,
when Alice thought Harriet had gone to sleep, very gently she pressed
open Harriet's thighs and touched that forbidden center. Harriet sighed
in sleeping pleasure. Three or four times a week for several years Alice
waited for the breathing signal that meant Harriet was no longer officially aware of what was happening. Alice could mount her, suck at her
breasts, stroke and enter her, bring her to wet coming, and hold her until she breathed in natural sleeping. Then Alice would go to the bathroom and masturbate to the simple fantasy of Harriet making love to her.

It wasn't Harriet who finally quit on it. It was Alice, shaking her and
shouting, "You goddamned hypocrite! You think as long as you take
pleasure and never give it, you'll escape. But you won't. You'll be in hell
long before I will, you goddamned *woman!*"

"We're looking for role models," Angel said. "Anybody who lived
with anybody for thirty years ... "

"I don't know what you're talking about," Alice said soberly on her
way to work, but late that night she was willing enough. "Thirty years
is longer than reality, you know that? A lifetime guarantee on a watch
is only twenty. Nothing should last longer than that. Harriet should have
killed herself ten years earlier, rest her goddamned soul. I always told
her she'd get to hell long before I did."

"What was Harriet like?" Bett asked on the way upstairs.

"Like? I don't know. I thought she was pretty. She never thought so."

"It must be lonely for you now."

"I've never had so much company in all my damned life."

To be alone in the attic was a luxury Alice could hardly believe. It
had been her resigned expectation that Harriet, whose soul had obviously not been at rest, would move up the stairs with her. She had not. If

she haunted the tenants as she had haunted Alice, they didn't say so. The first time Trudy and Jill took a bath together probably exorcised the ghost from that room, and Harriet obviously wouldn't have any more taste for the vegetarian fare in the dining room than Alice did. As for what probably went on in the various beds, one night of that could finally have sent Harriet to hell where she belonged.

Alice understood, as she never had before, why suicide was an unforgivable sin. Harriet was simply out of the range of forgiveness, as she hadn't been for all her other sins from hoarding garbage to having what she called a platonic relationship with that little tart of a switchboard operator in her office.

"If you knew anything about Plato . . . " Alice had bellowed, knowing only that.

Killing herself was the ultimate conversation stopper, the final saying, "No backs."

"The trouble with ghosts," Alice confided to Bett, "is that they're only good for replays. You can't break any new ground."

Bett leaned down and kissed Alice good night.

"Better watch out for me," Alice said, but only after Bett had gone downstairs. "I'm a holy terror."

That night Harriet came to her in a dream, not blood-filled as all the others had been, but full of light. "I can still forgive you," she said.

"For what?" Alice cried, waking. "What did I ever do but love you, tell me that!"

That was the kind of talk she heard at the beer parlor from her male companions, all of whom had wives and girl friends who spent their time inventing sins and then forgiving them.

"My wife is so good at forgiving, she's even forgiven me for not being the Shah of Iran, how do you like that?"

"I like it. It has dignity. My old lady forgives my beard for growing in the middle of the night."

They had also all lived for years with threats of suicide.

"She's going to kill herself if I don't eat her apricot sponge, if I don't cut the lawn, if I don't kiss her mother's ass. I tell her it's okay with me as long as she figures out a cheap way of doing it."

Alice was never drunk enough or off her guard enough until she got home, to say, "Harriet did. She killed herself in my bathtub." Nobody at the beer parlor or at work knew that Harriet was dead.

"I didn't ever tell them she was alive," she said to Bett. "So what's the point in saying she's dead?"

"Why do you drink with those people?" Bett asked. "They can't be your real friends."

"How can you say a thing like that?"

"They don't know who you are."

"Do you?" Alice demanded. "What has a woman bleeding to death in my bathtub got to do with who I am?"

Bett was pressing Alice's drunken head against her breast.

That night Alice fell asleep with a cigarette in her hand. When she woke the rug was on fire. She let out a bellow of terror and began to try to stamp out the flames with her bare feet.

Jill was the first one to reach her, half drag, half carry her out of the room. Trudy and Bett went in with buckets of water while Angel phoned the fire department.

"Don't let the firemen in," Alice moaned, sitting on Harriet's old chair in their old living room. "They'll wreck the place."

The fire was out by the time the truck arrived. After the men had checked the room and praised presence of mind and quick action for saving the house, the fire chief said, "Just the same, one of these nights she's going to do it. This is the third time we know of."

Jill, with the intention of confronting Alice with that fact, was distracted with discovering that Alice's feet were badly burned.

The pain killers gave Alice hallucinations: the floor of her hospital room on fire, her nurse's hair on fire, the tent of blankets at the foot of her bed burning, and Harriet was shouting at her, "We're going to burn in hell."

"Please," Alice begged. "I'd rather have the pain."

In pain, she made too much noise, swore, demanded whiskey, threatened to set herself on fire again and be done with it, until she was held down and given another shot.

Her coworkers from Safeway sent her flowers, but no one she worked with came to see her. No one she drank with knew what had happened. From the house, only Bett came at the end of work, still dressed in her uniform.

"Get me out of here," Alice begged. "Can't you get me out of here?"

In the night, with fire crackling all around her, Alice knew she was in hell, and there was no escape, Bett with her sunny face and great breasts the cruelest hallucination of all.

Even on the day when Bett came to take her home, Alice was half-convinced Bett was only a devilish trick to deliver her to greater torment, but Alice also knew she was still half-crazy with drugs or pain. There the house still stood, and Bett carried her up the stairs into an attic so clean and fresh she hardly recognized it. Alice began to believe in delivery.

"This bell by your bed," Bett explained, "all you need to do is ring it, and Angel will come."

Alice laughed until her coughing stopped her.

"It's a sort of miracle you're still alive," Trudy said when she and Jill came home from work and up to see her.

"I'm indestructible," Alice said, a great world-weariness in her voice.

"This place was a rat's nest," Jill complained. "You can't have thrown out a paper since we moved in—or an empty yogurt carton. Is that all you eat?"

"I eat out," Alice said, "for whatever business of yours it is. And nobody asked you to clean up after me."

"It scared us pretty badly," Trudy said. "We all came close to being killed."

"Sometimes you remind me a little of Harriet," Alice said with slow malice. "That's a friend of mine who killed herself."

"We know who Harriet is," Jill said. "Al, if we can't talk about this, we're all going to have to move out."

"Move out? What for?"

"Because we don't want to be burned to death in our sleep."

"You've got to promise us that you won't drink when you're smoking or smoke when you're drinking," Trudy said.

"This is my house. I'm the landlady. You're the tenants," Alice announced."

"We realize that. There's nothing we can do unless you'll be reasonable."

Bett came into the room with a dinner tray.

"Get out, all of you!" Alice shouted. "And take that muck with you!"

Jill and Trudy were twins in obedience. Bett didn't budge.

"I got you out because I promised we'd feed you."

"What you eat is swill!"

"Look, Angel even cooked you some hamburger."

"You can't make conditions for me in my own house."

"I know that; so do the others. Al, I don't want to leave. I don't want to leave you. I love you. I want you to do it for yourself."

"Don't say that to me unless I'm drunk. I can't handle it."

"Yes, you can. You don't have to drink."

"What in hell else am I supposed to do to pass the time?" Alice demanded.

"Read, watch t.v., make friends, make love."

"Don't taunt me!" Alice cried into the tray of food on her lap.

"I'm not taunting," Bett said. "I want to help."

Until Alice could walk well enough to get out of the house on her own, there was no question of drinking. She kept nothing in the house, having always used drink as an excuse to escape Harriet. There was nothing to steal from her tenants. She was too proud to ask even Bett to bring her a bottle. The few cigarettes she'd brought home with her from the hospital would have to be her comfort. She found herself opening a window every time she had one and emptying and washing the ashtray when she was through.

"You're turning me into a sneak!" she shouted at Bett.

"It all looks nice and tidy to me," Bett said. "Trudy says you're so male-identified that you can't take care of yourself. I'm going to tell her she's wrong."

Alice threw a clean ashtray at her, and she ducked and laughed. "You're getting better, you really are."

Alice returned to the beer parlor before she returned to work. She wasn't walking well, but she was walking. She had been missed. When she told about stamping out the fire with her own bare feet, she was assured of more free beer than she could drink in an evening even when she was in practice. How good it tasted and how companionable these friends who never asked questions and therefore didn't analyze the answers, who made connection with yarns and jokes. Alice had hung onto a couple of the best hospital stories and told them before she was drunk enough to lose her way or the punch line. She only laughed enough to cough at other people's jokes, which, as the evening wore on, were less well told and not as funny. Drink did not anesthetize the pain in Alice's healing feet, and that made her critical. Getting a tit caught in a wringer wasn't funny; it hurt.

"And here's one for those tenants of yours, Al, hey? How can you stem the tide of women's liberation? Put your finger in the dyke!"

It was an ugly face shoved into her own. Alice suddenly realized why a man must be forgiven his beard growing in the night, forgiven over and over again, too, for not being the prince of a fellow you wished he were. Alice didn't forgive. She laughed until she was near to spitting blood, finished her beer and her cigarette, and went out to find her car. As on so many other nights, even a few minutes after she got home, she couldn't remember the drive, but she knew she'd done it quietly and well.

"Come on," Bett said. "Those feet hurt. I'm going to carry you up."

Drunk in the arms of the sunny Amazon, Alice said, "Do you know how to stem the tide of women's liberation? Do you?"

"Does anyone want to?" Bett asked, making her careful, slow way up the stairs.

"Sure. Lots of people. You put your finger ... "

"In the dyke, yeah, I know."

"Don't you think that's funny?"

"No."

"I don't either," Alice agreed.

Bett carried Alice over to her bed, which had been turned down, probably by Angel.

"Now, I want you to hand over the rest of your cigarettes," Bett said.

"I'll leave them for you in the hall."

"Take them," Alice said.

"All right," Bett agreed and reached into Alice's blouse where she kept a pack tucked into her bra when she didn't have a pocket.

Alice half bit, half kissed the hand, then pressed herself up against those marvelous breasts, a hand on each, and felt the nipples, under the thin cloth of Bett's shirt, harden. Bett had the cigarettes, but she did not move away. Instead, with her free hand, she unbuttoned her shirt and gave Alice her dream.

As in a dream, Alice's vision floated above the scene, and she saw her own close-cropped head, hardly bigger than a baby's, her aging, liver-spotted face, her denture-deformed mouth, sucking like an obscene incubus at a young magnificence of breast which belonged to Angel. Then she saw Bett's face, serene with pity. Alice pulled herself away and spat.

"You pity me! What do you know about it? What could you know? Harriet, rest her goddamned soul, lived in *mortal sin* with me. She *killed herself* for me. It's not to *pity!* Get out! Get out, all of you right now because I'm going to burn this house down when I damned well please."

"All right," Bett said.

"It's my hell. I earned it."

"All right," Bett said, her face as bright as a never-to-come morning.

Alice didn't begin to cry until Bett had left the room, tears as hot with pain and loss as fire, that burned and burned and burned.

Charlotte DeClue
IJAJEE'S STORY

Blue Cloud Quarterly, Vol. 27, No. 4—1981
Brother Benet Tvedten, Editor

When you are traveling
and find yourself alone,
it is not wise
to think of yourself as ignorant.
Because when you travel alone
you have no one to depend on
but yourself.
And would you trust someone
you thought to be ignorant?

Just say, "I do not understand."
These things that you do not
understand...
put them into a bag
and carry them over your shoulder.
As time goes on,
the bag will get empty.

James Hazard
WHISKEY IN WHITING, INDIANA

The North American Review, March 1983
Robley Wilson Jr., Editor

Watching them drink shots was best.
That fierce color as if it were burned
into the glass—the shot glass itself
so specialized, small and hefty the way
a bullet is. Shots made them talk tough
and say fighters' names. Mickey Walker,
Willie Pep, Beau Jack, Stanley Ketchel,
and Tony Zale. They talked cuts and
knockdowns and recalled whole fights by the
round. I got excited. I'd be Tony Zale, eye
brows obliterated, and told them so. "Jesus
Christ, no!" They'd cock their heads
at the glass, the bartender would pour
another shot. "Jesus, not you, Jimmie."
They did that. Get a dream up, then tell you
it was no good. Like how proud they talked
about the mill, how tough and dirty they got
and then made you promise to do homework
so as not to be stuck like them. They said
don't drink whiskey too. In the bathroom
when nobody was home I'd be famous
in front of the mirror with a shot glass
of Pepsi, watching myself throw one back.
This was after my title fight which I won
after taking awful punishment just like
Tony Zale from Gary. I'd use my mother's
mascara and lipstick—to make
black eyes and bloodied places on my face,
tuck cotton under to swell a lip. I'd study
their Jimmie in the mirror: everything
they loved and warned me not to be.
Sock down another shot, wince the way they did,
and watch myself defy them by loving
what they loved, by fighting my way into
their dreams of themselves and out of
their dream for me.

Pentti Saarikoski
REVOLUTION

Toothpaste Press; *Poems 1958-1980* (1983), by Pentti Saarikoski
Allan Kornblum, Editor

1

crash
and the door flew
off its hinges
my hat too

too bad sir
you'll have to wait until fall
too bad the misses
have to leave their needlework
and milady her sewing machine

we can't have the banquet and ball
impossible
in this wind

such short-sighted doors sir
not to last one summer

2

what am I saying
what if there is no door?
soon we won't need one

they've stolen the horses sir
there they stand at the edge of the wood
a rider on each one
they have rifles sir

well I'm leaving said the housemaid
but I reassured her sir
only the gentlefolk will be killed
like you sir
but it was no use

better hurry now that you have no peace
to end this war with
a permanent autumn sir has been planted
for you
right here

leaves gone birds flown
now light the tree carries
everything ready for those who will come
to visit the past

3

mygod what are we going to do now
wailed milady
shut up no use bawling
snapped milord
and he was right

three bearded fellows stood in the doorway
no monkey business they said

that took care of milady but the whole era
was hung by its feet from the chandelier
and shot through the navel

4

winter now
air cold
ground hard
the rabbit goes hungry
in the wood
no food
soon snow
many feet deep

and what'll poor bunny do then?
don't you think we should fix that door
at last
comrade sir?

—translated from the Finnish by Anselm Hollo

photograph by Cristian; *The Chilean Spring* (1980)
Latin American Literary Review Press; Yvette E. Miller, Editor

Fernando Alegria
from THE CHILEAN SPRING

Latin American Literary Review Press (1980)
Yvette E. Miller, Editor

It seemed to me we had all lost our way: a young father, a crazy young woman, two children as shepherds or two stars in a world without lambs—only wolves—missing a sky; but also that childless father who buries his head between his shoulders and sees his reflection in the desert and in the sudden whirlwind of sand swaddling the tail of an airplane. Where are we coming from, if not from the same mystery out there, that great loneliness leaning like a bird on our metal wings and that same towering melancholy of mountains lowering like a screen in the Atacama sunset?

Did the man and woman in flight ever find the right road? They drink with good cheer and talk without listening, cross over mountains without recognizing each other, busy with the years that go by and others on their way, searching heedlessly for (lacking the will or the desire to find) themselves: a man and a woman thrown into a bottomless postal sack, parcels with no name or address or postage, stirring life about with a finger in a glass full of ice.

Maybe we'll find out the answer when we get there. But I've been there many times and the trip and the arrival are always the same: a gloomy wait, anxiety before the confrontation, a sad defeat. All I can see are faces reflected in dark glasses, scenes on an old porch lit with yellow bulbs, second-hand people I knew and loved who forgot me. I can't even find enemies who could help me figure what's been done and what's left to do. A simple indifference surrounds me and I slip inside it as if I'd ceased to exist.

Naturally I have the right to start over again, and, in what little night we have left, improvise some kind of peace with myself, perhaps even an arrangement—a kind of gentleman's agreement—with some God. Ah! if I could only go from supply to demand! Starting all over again is a matter of knowing who You are when I talk to You, and that there is no need for words, since You and I walk down the street maintaining a discreet distance, and that it's enough to nod agreement frowning slightly, or pursing the lips, to know our destiny, Yours and mine. As for Luz Maria and the children, something else awaits them.

To start all over again is to know for certain if this plane will make it, whether it will land on the chalk circle assigned to it, and if it can stay there; if the runway, the building, the people stretching out their arms on the roof, can be trusted or if it's all a trick; if the customs agents really see me and if their stamp is a secret signal to the police expecting me outside.

I ought to write first about my father, who never bothers me; in fact, he allows me to make my peace with something which may have nothing to do with him. Whatever was keeping us apart has been overcome. There are no doubts or suspicions between us. We are united by a certain calm consciousness of what we won't ever be, neither he nor I. It's possible my case is not completely clear to him. If my father were keeping this journal, he would leave a lot of empty pages, or he would fill it with pious reflections about the present and the future of the country. He would prefer to ignore the decisive turn of my twenty-seven years, overlooking the question he once posed to himself, or the answer he hides like a shameful address in his wallet. I don't know the answer with any certainty either, but thinking there is an answer already justifies my coming back home and my aspirations.

My father welcomed us with open arms, with that joy he prefers to swallow, which stiffens his back and makes him say, Fine, you arrived in good shape, how is your mother? The years have not been kind to him, as people say when they feel their own age in the gathering wrinkles they see in front of them. My father looks older, but even shorter than I am. His blue eyes are the same as Marcelo's and mine: they remind me of the photographs of me wearing my first suit with long pants, the one handed down from Marcelo years after he was photographed in the same pose. The height, the eyes and the pants give the three of us a family resemblance.

I know he's quite happy, although, really, I don't follow his activities that closely. I can't see him in detail or in perspective; I feel him carefully guarding his isolation. He's very much there, but reserved, like the neighbor we call on who asks us, What can I do for you?—without opening his door. The children will get on his nerves later, but now they amaze and flatter him. Flatter him? I'm using that word without caring if it's the most precise. It seems to fit somehow, because he probably thinks they continue the line but don't best him. They're on their way to where he's arrived, and just like him they'll have to wait a long time before they know they didn't arrive anywhere: that is, to achieve a modest displeasure and enough discretion not to despair and avoid unduly upsetting other people.

I don't know or ask if we're causing any inconvenience. I'm unaware if there's another apartment where he can get away from it all (I'm sure there is); another woman or other people I've never met who can take the place of my mother and us and who will never trust us an inch, hidden decently in a dining room or a kitchen or a bedroom, watching in silence. We're no family. Neither they nor we. Rather, we are families known for their lack of kinship. My brother and I were never born. As children we walked down dead-end streets, to schools with big patios and glassed-in galleries, chilly classrooms and portable altars. As we grew up we had long hair, we began to photograph the world, and followed our mother, isolated, distant, sitting pensively behind her typewriter.

The old folks fall apart; I mean, they slowly begin to separate, without it being too noticeable. They smile, converse, though not much; they suddenly draw a blank on what's being said. They eat at the same table; sometimes they're seen together on the streets. People observing them think they are living in a placid period of final waiting. But no. If one looks closely one will note that they each go down a separate road, drifting apart. They no longer sleep together. If we question them, the reasons they give us are vague. That one can't get to sleep and the other has rheumatism, that they wake up and pester each other, that one wants to sleep on the second floor and stairways are painful to the other. Smoke rings. First there were two beds, now there are two bedrooms, soon two houses. The marriage begins to look like a limited partnership. The partners know each other so well. They communicate by means of gestures. Not even gestures. They look or they don't look at each other and they've already said it all.

When did these folks first sleep in different beds? When in separate rooms? Neither Marcelo nor I could say. One day they were together, the next separate. Affectionate in the manner of casual friends on a trip. Suddenly, a sharp voice, a cutting phrase, a violent gesture that stops midway. They can't tolerate each other. In love, they despise or pity one another. A holding pattern begins. And then what will happen? Domestic tragedy, threats, last words? No. Neither of them has the character for that. They are withdrawn, ferocious and nearly implacable, but timid. They don't forgive anything. They might not reproach or curse each other. But, they don't forget. The insults keep bouncing around inside. But why did they get together in the first place. What attracted them? It seems impossible. It was always difficult for us to imagine that at some distant time our parents were sweethearts. Mother is larger than Father. Reach and weight. In total volume. She is tall and stiff and rather stacked. As her neck is a bit short, her head looks small and round. Her blue eyes glance with a kind of wounded confidence; they would like to smile but become hard and end up observing with distance and severity. She wears gray. Tailored suits. She has a bit of the nurse or the Lutheran lady down-at-the-heels. A daughter of Germans from the south of Chile. Blond tresses, log cabins, immaculate cleanliness, Teutonic discipline. It's somewhat eccentric to be so passionate, sentimental and romantic in a country of crazy Andalusians, not to say gypsies and Araucanians. She had a religious crisis when we started high school. She began reading her Bible out loud and drawing her own morals, which she would then pass on as ultimate truths to her maid. My father closed the door. Classified as a Protestant, she should preach and sing in other houses or in the street. By way of contrast, the old man returned to Mass, took communion, prayed as one possessed in the month of December. It was obvious to my brother and me that we weren't dealing here with a religious war but with something very personal, private. Divorces are not made of biblical interpretations. I imagine my mother was rebelling. I don't know exactly against what. Anything was possible. At night she read Selma Lagerlof, whom I always thought of as a great armoire with a mirror open on snowy plains. The duel between the two of them must have taken place in the bedroom, behind closed doors. She agitated, her face congested, her eyes flashing, without saying a word. He speaking rapidly to himself. She arranging papers, putting away her typewriter, keeping office hours. He, sarcastic, incredulous, impatient.

We were already in college when Marcelo told me one day that we were going abroad with her. No one spoke of separation. A "field trip." That's it. These boys need another environment, she said. My father remained silent. Neither for nor against. There was a moment when he seemed offended. "Your mother," he murmured, "has recipes for living, as if life were an apple pie." He sounded resentful. Though she was strict, he too could get his way. Mother followed a certain order, perhaps naive; Father ruled by force, without reasons.

The three of us emigrated to the State of Virginia. We were incredulous, apprehensive. My mother had the air of a pioneer. The old man stayed tight-assed. He gave us a short farewell hug. I think his hands were trembling.

Afterwards (in fact there is no clearly defined afterwards), my father stopped being either a hero or a villain and disappeared on a crowded stage. We went away feeling sure one day comes after another, that one night and another night together form a single thread. The abrupt change in languages disoriented us, the colleges had no records or systems, the apartments were smaller and the kitchens were harder to work in. We began to fade away, first our faces, then the lines in our palms; but there were things which distinguished us from each other and yet they too vanished, and I think my mother began to get us confused. Marcelo and I have the same beards; our hair unites us. Marcelo says it reveals my innocence. I say the same of him, but our smiles contradict us.

I returned to Chile for three reasons: my young wife; second, madness is contagious; third, suicide is also very contagious.

But children are another matter. They have heard the noises adults make and they know how we throw ourselves onto the floor, how we bite each other's legs and how we sing off-key in bed. Then, when we

decide to tear ourselves to bits in the streets and there are gun butts
whacking faces and boots trouncing the belly of the young professor
buried alive and hands lopped off a great guitarist, we go out and ask the
young people if they still adhere to the Christian doctrine and the Com-
mandments; we accuse them of their lack of charity and respect for in-
stitutions, and they respond with sexual wisdom by closing the door on
our fingers.

Later, in October, I would see a group of exiles trying to leave. The
plane was full of children. The flight for some unexplained reason
couldn't take off. The plane spent the night on the runway and the exiles and their children began to stink and get thirsty and approve suicide
resolutions.

A boy began to sing and his parents tried to quiet him. But he went
ahead and raised his voice, and his song was revolutionary; it insulted the
Armed Forces. When he came to the part where the poor would eat
bread and the rich would eat shit, after going through several "sons-of-
bitches," the soldiers arrested him and his parents, put them in a jeep
and, without magic, made them disappear.

Neither his father nor his mother scolded him because the child had
finally learned his lesson and was showing that you sing when it's hopeless, and the song is accompanied by blows, by blood and unconscious-
ness, if you have to sing among brothers.

But then, in July, back home for the first time in years, with no
chance to write, I thought about what my father calls roots. In reality I
was reaching for branches: I would go in and out of stores, stare at the
movie ads and newsstands, sit on park benches, get off and on buses,
surprised by a city I didn't know anymore, which I couldn't begin to
measure in hours or years. Santiago, crowned with snow, was living from
shock to shock. Small armed groups would hold up markets, shoot at
soldiers or *Carabineros*, blow up gas mains at night and high voltage towers, telephone installations. The truckers had been on strike for months.
Food was disappearing. In front of the markets the lines never moved.
From the outskirts people walked downtown and walked back home.
The city traced and retraced its steps, divided by implacable hatred. Dem-
onstrations and counter-demonstrations. Schoolchildren barricaded
themselves behind their desks, workers locked and chained themselves
in the factories, businessmen hid in automobiles to sell rotten meat they
carted up from the South in suitcases.

The city was like a wheel that begins to stop in a vacuum, losing
speed, turning ever more slowly, impelled by invisible gears, and though
we know it will stop, it turns one more time, and then again, until movement becomes imperceptible.

During the winter it wasn't as noticeable. People abandon the streets and the squares, they lock themselves up and stare out through the windows of the tall office buildings, pressing their faces to the steamed glass, and they let time pass knowing that something is about to happen —but not yet, wait for the coup. Perhaps it won't even be a coup but a small and precise push to make this gray, icy, humid winter pass and September burst forth in light and buds and flush the mountains with pink again. Suddenly Santiago becomes a vast mall where faceless people move about, a theatre setting whose doors and windows are half open, but as no one enters or exits we cannot tell whether the action has ended or is about to begin.

The lines stretch out, tired, silent. A block of indifferent men and women trying to reach the newsstand where cigarettes are sold, a thick line, disordered, more like a throng that turns one corner and then another, as if the ends tried to meet and swallow each other. Old men and women bundled up, steaming, complaining, inquiring without protesting, imagining, because they can't see them, the steel doors of the Pension Fund, and knowing they will never reach them because there will always be a clerk closing them with chains, repeating: not this month, not yet, the government and the cost of living and inflation, and the planning of Minister Vuscovic plus the U.S. embargo, not to mention the foreign debt and the Paris Club, not this month, they are preparing new forms and there is going to be a bonus, but you forgot the stamps, don't you see, not at this counter ladies and gentlemen, it's not in this building either, can't you understand? Go to the Treasury building, take all your papers, ask for your payment authorization, for your tax receipts, your tax roll number, the permit and the decree, and then ask in the cashier's office, but don't pay until they give you a number, and it's not my fault that people crowd and push, in this country no one dies of hunger, you voted for the Popular Unity so you'll have to put up with it, and don't hold onto the railings because the policeman will smash your fingers, and I am telling you again the doors are already closed, so you'll have to come back tomorrow, what stupid people, why don't you complain to the Comrade President?

But the line continues to stretch, swelling, curling, and now it's not a line, it's an assembly of women who clamor and push and crash against a metallic curtain, and they raise their empty baskets and shopping bags and they'd like to beat someone up, there is no flour or oil or bread, that's a lie, I'm telling you, I've been standing in line all night long and I know, even if you do tell me I won't believe you, because they were unloading last night and this morning early, that might be so but I don't see why you say it, there's nothing inside, the grocer is hiding, yesterday he fired into the air, he has a fortune hidden. The line loses shape, the women wrapped in their shawls push too much, this is not politics, you call starving kids politics? There's no milk or sugar, call the cops, someone should come and open that damned hoarder's door. And then the line will form again into a double line, coiling, without pushing, and in minutes it will curl around the corner, but minus bags and baskets, it's gas containers now and I'm telling you we've run out, there isn't going to be any so don't send your children because all they do is bother me, who said tomorrow? The company is in Monjitas, not here, take the shady side of the street, and I'm telling you not to bug me DON'T BUG ME, they'll knock the fence down, officer, shit what stupid people, there isn't any, can't you understand? The line continues to grow, a thick boa, hissing, slowly unfolding, dense, cold, nauseating, toward one hospital and then another, and then in front of the Emergency Entrance, it crosses bridges and strangles trains and buses, a line of coal and cement, of copper and oil, a thick snake, green, black, silver, red, winding through the market and the shops, from one side of the city to the other, through docks and offices, warehouses and storerooms, a line of empty ships, a line of asphalt and stone. Chile is one huge line. Hey, look at it on the map, a blue and white and brown line. It has always been a line, but not like the one that strangles us now, this dirty, bedraggled muffler that hangs from the neck to the ground and gets caught in the legs. There is nothing. Tell me what's left. Santiago. The buildings downtown are closed, the shops are only half-open, the banks and the insurance companies rusting, the jails open even on Sundays, the butcher shops are full of hooks stained with dry blood, and on the counters stacks of bones. But people don't die, they wait, neither advancing nor retreating, reading alarming headlines in the newspapers.

Down Providencia comes a long line of women shouting and beating pots and pans, down Teatinos Street groups of teenagers, in sweaters, their faces covered with handkerchiefs, wearing helmets and carrying sticks and chains, march at a quick pace, compact, dragging their feet, marking time:

> *Allende, son of a bitch,*
> *He's going to fall in a ditch...*

On the road to San Antonio striking truckers hide in the bushes counting their buckshot and setting their nail traps; commandos who will blow up the pipelines and the high voltage towers take position and aim; a freedom march arrives from Arica screaming; another line of trucks searches for its final resting place in the hills over Valparaiso; in the bay, under cover of fog, a gringo fleet levels its guns; on the docks a wet and faded sign says *The PU is screwed, be safe with UNITAS*; acrobatic pilots appear in the sky drawing a white line, but that white line started in Panama, sir, and goes all the way down to Magallanes; the planes write Djakarta in the sky and the letters last only a moment and then dissipate in the mountain gusts.

Finally all the lines are laminated together to form one huge tail that wriggles through cities and ports, parks and deserts, like a living labyrinth without beginning or end. Chileans wait for the coup to be done with, so they can enjoy spring again, and the coup is an empty truck that comes from the South and comes from the North, halting, grinding uphill, until it almost stalls, and finally stops at dawn, douses its headlights and draws out its small shining muzzles.

Seeing the shops shut, the downtown deserted, the small markets and corner stores at half mast and selling under the counter, listening to the easy-going relatives complaining too, desperate now because there is truly nothing available, while lucky people from uptown travel by car to the scene of the crime and pull into a circle around the taxi drivers and truckers who distribute meat, oil and enough whiskey to bathe in, at the blackest price in the history of Chile, it was obvious the circle was about to close.

One would mull over strange ideas, though one more than others: If the country is falling apart, is routed, why the inactivity of the Popular Unity government? No one works, or almost no one, neither the coupon clippers who walk through the streets with a smile a mile wide, nor the government employees, the doctors, lawyers or store managers. They stay home reading the newspapers or keeping a close watch on their TVs. The Workers' Federation says NO to civil war. The workers take over the factories, the industrial belts are tightening with a secret knot that frightens the pot-beating women. Why doesn't Allende defend himself? Why doesn't he take the offensive? The coup is coming? The coup is coming. What can we do?

During a family gathering I witnessed a curious debate among young people who felt responsible for the coming debacle; and each one, in his own sense of defeat, offered a way out which, in my opinion, leads to the same abyss. The young girl who works in a beauty parlor says: Power to the people, attack, strike before they do! You ask me how, what do you mean how, with the industrial belts, of course. But the dentist answers: We are not ready for a confrontation, it would be a massacre. Read *El Siglo*, comrade. The beautician argues that the people are armed. The student of architecture timidly refers to the "comrade soldiers and the comrade *Carabineros*." Dentist: You've seen what happened to the sailors who conspired with Altamirano—they were jailed and tortured. Read *Punto Final*, then. You spend your time reading and don't know what's going on in the streets. I'm talking about the skirmish between the workers of SUMAR and an Air Force contingent. They fought with small arms; the factory whistles blew and units from the industrial belts and the squatter settlements appeared. The Air Force men retreated. A victory for the people? Nobody took it that way. It was an exploratory mission by the Air Force to test the enemy, to gauge the degree of resistance and analyze the unknown factors. How do the soldiers of 1973 react to the working class? That's what I'm talking about, the comrade draftees. The comrade what? Let me finish. The draftee who hails from the countryside, the barrios and the outlying provinces, who's been listening for some time to the workers, the students and the activists defending Allende, and for whom certain words like "expropriation," "nationalization," "intervention" and "inflation" mean a lot, who has seen the marches and listened to thousands shout *Allende, Allende, the people all defend you!*, who knows there are lines for everything and food baskets for the poor: what does he say, how will he react? I'm not the only one who speaks of the people's resistance, that nightly shuffle of sandals through the shantytowns and that clink of weapons appearing and disappearing. What do the soldiers think of the middle-level purges? And of the generals who are falling by the wayside? What will the soldiers do at the moment of truth? Look, the Air Force took their puppies down to SUMAR to pinion the workers. They retreated, but I don't think there was any sudden panic among the officers. My question, then, is how long can the workers resist? The dentist steadies his glasses. Has anyone asked himself if this general rehearsal is an exact indication of the proportions of the confrontation? I think that Allende realized months ago the shape the conflict will take; it won't be between the forces of the extreme Right and the extreme Left, with the armed forces divided in the middle. No, things are much more serious. We've lost our chance. To arm the people these days is to send them to a collective suicide. And what do you suggest? I'm not suggesting anything, but we can discuss the reasons for the indecision, especially after the rally in June when political conscience reached a height of radicalization and the slogan *Power to the People* was strong. Allende, with 600,000 people marching the 4th of September and swearing to defend him, knows what he's doing, but it's possible that his policy is also suicidal. I'm judging it according to what he has stood for, what he has managed to do and what he has not done. The beautician tells him: Comrade, let's discuss the second element behind the growing sabotage against the popular government. I'm willing to accept that we are living in a strange sort of nightmare, in which we are both victims and accomplices: victims because the coup will be against us and I doubt we can defend ourselves; accomplices because we want to run and yet we don't run, and we want to shout and our tongue is tied, so we let the whole structure collapse on top of us and the monster strangle us. Just like in nightmares.

Supreme architect: Let's suppose a partisan observer had directed and programmed the events that were to occur between 1972 and 1973 so that Allende could be overthrown. Let us suppose that such an observer could have had alternatives, say: on the one hand a plan for a violent attack, a super-abundance of military power to produce a mortal coup, a *coup de grace*, and on the other hand, the possibility of a gradual weakening, an economic offensive, key strikes, hoarding and black marketeering, sabotage, the complete saturation of the national psychology with panic and discouragement, an old-fashioned coup, a relatively peaceful transition back to the old order of things. Common sense tells us that the second option would have been chosen. But, in these things the sense which dominates is not exactly common: someone decides to adopt the second plan, which is carried out to the next to the last act, and then, at the decisive moment, it's abandoned and the plotters fling themselves back into the first plan of attack.

While I listen to these speakers I think of the hardships they bear. Although they eat, they have to spend, naturally, more than usual, more each time. The black market gets dirtier and dirtier. The newspapers read by the dentist and the beautician and the architect and his wife inform them that the international credit agencies have clammed up for Allende, while they ply the Armed Forces with a glut of sweets, that Anaconda has started a pirate war against Chilean copper shipments, that the government would never be able to obtain spare parts for the truckers because the U.S. refuses to send them. Other speakers, from Ahumada Street and Huerfanos Street, for example, comment on hoarders' cellars, sealed and secret as bank vaults, on the superfreezers that look like frozen zoos, on the supersonic flight of dollars and the delicate pirouettes and falls of the shrinking and expanding Chilean currency.

El Mercurio released its editorials like heavy bales: Allende has led the country to chaos and to the edge of civil war. Chile? Full of foreign extremists who plot a Cuba-style dictatorship. The country is sinking, we must save it. Allende must resign. Let the military come. Or, better yet, let the military come and Allende leave.

Meanwhile the Fatherland and Liberty Movement doesn't need any speakers: its members are planting bombs, even in the cemetery. 250 incidents in one month. Radio and TV towers fall, water mains explode. When there is no one left to shoot they begin to shoot each other. One of their leaders, nicknamed Houdini, appears-disappears-appears in an airplane between San Carlos, the sea and Mendoza. He comes and goes, skimming the roof of the central police station, landing on top of the Supreme Court and taking off again.

It's been raining but now it's clearing. I'm going out to look for roots. They're in a low gray sky, close by the benches of Plaza Brasil, wrapped in thin blue smoke, moist, woven into dry fig trees and knotty cherries, abandoned patios, tin roofs and brick-and-lime walls, sticking the red plaque of the Heart of Jesus to the dull streetlights that have suddenly lent me a yellowish pallor among the men and women dressed in mourning who pass by in slow motion. The smell of wet wood joins me momentarily to this bench: it must've been summer then and boys and girls spinning through the plaza like figures on a silent carrousel, the slight perspiration of my girl friend soothes me. I let myself go in a long, dizzy embrace; the hooting of a factory siren comes from so far away; a circular ballet of miniature couples, silent, entwined in childhood kisses; my girl friend is wearing gloves because her skin is irritated by an infection; I love you, my darling, she says; the words are incongruous because she stole them from a bolero; old men leave the movie theaters shuffling their feet; the sky smells of dry grass and mint, but on her it looks like honey, and I fondly remember her green skirt, her white blouse; I kiss her neck and I touch her gloves and breasts; and now the plaza shimmers again in semi-darkness, cars go by splashing water and mud; I breathe deeply the rain, the sky, a bit of smoke along the ground. It's my open city.

I get on my motorcycle and go up San Diego Street, Avenida Matta, Gran Avenida, studying everything—the half-opened windows, marked doors, signs of something or someone I've been looking for—feeling the union of the night, the streets and the loneliness, in some man or woman who refused to touch me, who didn't let me get close, but whose smell I still carry in my body, and I would like to conquer our emptiness, the root that keeps us crying together, but there are only corners and blocks, missing relatives, unnamed and unnumbered bus stops, the nearby breathing of those of us falling in the city before we reach our terminal.

I come to wage war.
To wage war on the fields
of Castille.
Tired
of mounting.
Horse, my
horse: rest a while.
Now is the time to
make love under the
linden trees
lit up by March.
(I go away dreaming.
I come from a dream.)

Angel Gonzalez, who
wrote these lines, has
looked on me from a dis-
tance, his white beard and
wild hair, and in his eyes
I saw a weariness that has
not yet begun; but there
he is, bloody and breath
less, like this wound in
me today; I come from
waging a war, but I've
run out of time.

Afterwards I examine two snapshots of Luz Maria: In one she is running through the rooms of our house in Virginia and the boys are right behind her: they are running away from me because she told them I was about to stab them. In the other she stands on a shaky balcony on the seventeenth floor about to jump, wearing only a green transparent night-gown, her arms outstretched, the sky full of clouds, and down below heavy oaks; the night and the cries of birds have passed. In one snapshot I stand by Luz Maria, and it's true I deliberately began to fade out of the picture.

Luz Maria was the girl friend I never talked to: I made her up out of familiar things I saw at dusk in Forestal Park and Plaza Nunoa, things which I put together at night lying next to an open window, breathing silently like the trees, dreaming, sliding her across my chest, until I couldn't stand it any longer and I slid her across my belly with the palm of my hand, a whirling palm tree wet with fresh-smelling dew, an explosion of light on a red blinking stem, alive, on fire, and soon faint. Standing like a warrior on the corner of Purisima Street, a few steps from her door, I would whisper to my brother, waiting for the apparition which never appeared. It was enough to know she was inside, sensing or suspecting our nightly visits. What did she do in that house? I will never know. I was in love with myself and it hurt. But during the Month of Mary I would go to Vinita Church to catch her scent along with the lemon blossoms and the candle smoke, praying with the choir insistently, stumbling along, almost screaming with satisfaction near the end because our knees would hurt so much.

I never discussed my religious faith with anyone, especially the nocturnal crises from which I always returned wet and repentant. Or the guilt, because it wasn't rational. My whole life moved like a thermometer: from the chest to the belly to the underbelly. I wrote a poem entitled "The Fountain of Youth" to explain why the member always goes to the sacrifice, while the other two things swing outside and must be bells; the one is a cyclops and the others are blind men's guides. It didn't sound convincing so I tore it up. Instead I remember writing a notebook full of love poems in the style of Becquer and giving it to Luz Maria, who received it nervously, stuffed it in her school bag and never mentioned it again.

I've said religion was never discussed. It blended, I see now, with a tendency to efface myself; that is, to think of myself as a cosmic being, an adolescent who could fit into any shape or person, who should be received without question, accepted and loved for himself, made up of incomplete but active traits, not altogether under control. I was conscious of my head but not of the rest of my body (my cock was independent); I noticed that my nose grew suddenly when a girl told me so. The arguments about the existence of God which Father Ladron de Guevara sent up like smoke rings into the air with his deep voice, resonant and bland, didn't touch me. St. Thomas' proof and his metaphor of first causes would get mixed up with the image of the clock and its creator, to which several listeners in the classroom would object that, even if God were everywhere, he was not and did not want to be a maker of clocks or watches.

That the world had a beginning is not important to me. In fact, it annoys me. As far as God is concerned, the world shouldn't have a beginning. In the afternoon classes Father Alvarez repeated the proofs of God's existence, but then my stomach would growl and my throat would fill up with saliva. I didn't listen to Alvarez, tall and skinny, strangled by an enormous Adam's apple, hiding his vast hands like oars under his black robe, then taking them out to make gestures. The Dominican habit seduced me at a tender age and I told everyone my desire to enter the priesthood. No one paid any attention. I wanted to suffer, for people to say: There goes brother Cristian; he sleeps under the stairs, reeking in rags like Saint Alexis, wearing the remains of Housse Partie around his neck. Or to be stupid and sweet like Francesco, or a martial preacher like Father Melero, who after he was a captain in the artillery became a priest in Recoleta. I was never attracted to Saint Augustine or any of the other brilliant sinners—they scared me; not even to the Christians in the arena—I could never quite tell them from the lions. Nero attracted me because I was afraid of him; I found him wise and elegant. I was terrified of my parents' friends and relatives, whose self-confidence I considered a symptom of cynicism. Their houses set my teeth on edge; so did their conversations and their children, their taunts, their insolent and obscene laughter. My saints were long-suffering, complex, gentle suicides, who climbed on the cross shaking their heads baffled by the ferocity of their fellow men. I made my teachers nervous. My parents never said anything around me. I awakened sympathy in women and also wished to awaken it in men, who said I was too intelligent. To some I was a boy-man. To most, a wise monkey.

If faith was not a routine, nor understood, and if it was inconsistent but strong, where did it originate? Possibly in the indifference or ignorance of my father, or in the domestic way my mother managed to be completely wrong—thinking (my God!) her natural sanctity preserved her from the pitfalls of the world and the depths of hell. Such tricks of the devil only left me with the whiff of brimstone, not its taste or fire or the dream of redemption. To me faith meant sinning, since sinning was the only thing that gave any meaning to my prayers, confessions and communions. I didn't understand it that way, naturally, but that's the way I lived my faith, from church to church, from altar to altar, searching for cool, mysterious shadows, soft noises, rosaries, chords, solitudes, direct dialogue with the images and the paintings, defiant acts—praying in the streets, kneeling suddenly in the park, believing in the flight of the Image of the Virgin and in the miraculous pieces of Fray Andrecito's habit, knowing I was predestined. I was never sacrilegious or blasphemous. I always sinned through sex and repented and was forgiven. From the very beginning I kept up direct, secret communication with the Virgin and Jesus. My religion was and is the Mother and Son.

I have to insist on these things and make them clear, because they essentially explain my disagreement with the Father.

I really don't know why the Mother separated from the Father.

On the morning of the 11th of September I awoke with a start. In that first brief moment I didn't know if it was the presence of someone or a noise. I thought of the door. I had put the chain on, and the latch bolted both locks. The noise wasn't coming from the hall or the kitchen, it was coming from the whole floor. Lying on my back, leaning up on my elbows, I stared at the shutters. The apartment was rocking like a glass cage. In the half light I saw the lamp was also moving. I got up. My father was still asleep with his door closed. I turned on all the lights and walked unsteadily down the hall to the living room. The roaring noise stopped. But I heard noises outside and steps on the terrace upstairs. I lit a cigarette and stared out at the shadows running down Alameda. I noticed some movements on the roof of the house next door. I went back to the bedroom and turned off the light, closed the door and stood next to the window, feeling guilty, looking out that way from our 12th floor, unseen by anyone. But the figure on that roof fascinated me. Someone, a young man, was smoothly, delicately, sliding open a slab on the roof. He stuck his head through the hole, then without looking backwards, without even thinking that someone like me might be spying on him, he stretched out his right arm and started firing, in a sort of absurd way because he had a small-bore revolver in his hand that went off without even an echo, just a sharp report, like a firecracker, lost in the city dawn. I could see his dark hair and his striped shirt. He fired for a while towards the Alameda and then, with the same care and precision, he climbed into his hole, moved the slab and closed the roof. I didn't see his face, neither that morning nor the following night, nor all the other nights when he fired from there until they killed him.

I went back to the living room and picked up the phone. It wasn't even six yet. I had a mission to fulfill, and with my camera I would have to go to Tomas Moro, Allende's house. Marcelo was supposed to pick me up at eight. Although I had to call Luz Maria, I didn't exactly know what I was going to say. I could talk about the tremor or the planes, about the small helicopter that buzzed over the roofs of the San Borja Towers, where my father's apartment was, or I could confess that knowing the danger and feeling trapped I had changed my plans and was going to ask Father Juan to put me up at the monastery. I dialed Luz Maria's number, let it ring twice, hung up and dialed again.

"I was just thinking about you," she said.

"And the children?" I asked.

"They're still asleep."

"Did you see the planes?"

"They were skimming over the roofs. Then they came back in a few minutes."

"Now that we can go back to sleep the lions in the zoo are raising hell," I told her. "They must be scared."

I thought to myself they should throw the lioness in with them and imagined them jumping around gnawing each other among the eucalyptus, rolling in the gutter and coming out all muddy, dragging the lioness by the nape, like cats, and writhing till they passed out on the horse and donkey carcasses all over the floor.

I continued: "The sun is coming up in the park; I can see light through the blinds. The dogs are making a racket down there too. And a guy in the house next door began shooting."

"Who is shooting?"

"I don't know, someone down there. Nearby."

"And the dogs?"

"You know the ones, the woolly bitch looks like a schoolgirl lying on the grass, gazing towards the river, maybe she hears the lions too. There are about seven dogs from the slums of Bellavista, dripping wet, with their tongues hanging out. The horny bastards. I can't tell if that's foam coming out of their mouths, I hope it's steam, I can't see that far."

"Do you want me to come over?" she asked.

"Not now. I'll call you in a little while. I want to talk to Marcelo."

Later, drinking black coffee, I thought, looking through the twisted slats of the Venetian blind, I might have invented the park, but not the noises or the lions and dogs. Luz Maria wouldn't hesitate to come, leave the children, take a bus. She would be tangled up over and over again in this sheet I use to cover and uncover her with each time as if it were the first time. Luz Maria, a small white statue with soft down and tanned belly, a bun on the nape of her neck and a sad mouth, and I, easing my beard between her round breasts, searching for some meaning in her long legs, breathing in the smoke of felled trees and the cool mist of the southern-most islands she brings from the South, deciphering the way of that routine never completely learned. I know that today, at this hour, facing the dawning park, seeing the smoke that rises from the ferns and the dusty silver acacias, by the yellow paths, close to the river's wall, she will be here, and it will be like the first time.

The phone rang again.

"Do you want to meet me at Baquedano?" Luz Maria asked.

"Now? It's not even six o'clock yet, and I have to go to Tomas Moro. Well, just five minutes, a cup of coffee."

I dressed and went out hugging the wall, my coat collar turned up and hands in my pockets. Nobody on the streets. I thought that night I

would have to speak to my father and give him my gun. Later. A little
traffic on the other side of the park, a few taxis, no buses. I was surprised to see just a couple of cops at the American Consulate. I was used to
the huge green cages, the plastic shields, the riot squad trucks filling
with water. Plaza Baquedano was deserted. I looked out at it from my
corner, next to Bustamante Street. The old lady in the newspaper stand
poked her nose in her cup of coffee. Luz Maria didn't take off her raincoat. She lit a cigarette. I kissed her hands. There was another couple
close to us, the woman doubled up over the table, the man whispering
in her ear. When Luz Maria began to drink her espresso I saw her hands
were trembling: "Last night, after supper, the same old argument began.
I stated my position. They told me it was like listening to a cassette of
El Siglo. My poor mama sounds like an old fossil but she chokes on the
words."

"What are you going to do with the children?" I asked.

"They'll stay with her."

"I'll have to go away, if only for a few days. Besides, the old man
won't want to move."

"What happened?" she asked.

"I don't exactly know what happened."

Luz Maria looked at the clock, said something else about the children, something I don't remember, and I kept thinking what it would be
like if we could live as the rest of the world, without having to explain
anything. But Luz Maria was tying the belt of her raincoat and I was
pleased that she looked distant again, worried about something besides
me, willing to help me but also ready to leave.

Later on that morning of the 11th, I went to La Moneda in Allende's
famous blue Fiat. A unique mission: to photograph certain details of
something that, once consummated, would reach epic proportions. The
country is being saved. NO TO CIVIL WAR. How? Who can save the
country from an armed struggle? These questions don't work out.
Things don't follow anymore. Politics is a game of cards. Cut and shuf-
fled daily. The card game of professional politicians. Outside, in the
streets, another game is taking shape. And it has nothing to do with
cards. It's possible that the people—disdained and forgotten when they
don't try to march—will say suddenly: YES TO CIVIL WAR. Because
they feel in front of them a road that opens abruptly. No one thinks of
alternatives, then, or consequences. But, where are the arms? This battle
which begins in familiar surroundings and extremely loudly will not be
maneuvered from outside.

Allende rides with his chauffeur, his bodyguards and his political advisor. They speak as if in asides, without really feeling the words. Keeping my mouth shut, I move my camera, aiming and shooting. I think of
Marcelo who would like to be in my place, and of Luz Maria. If she saw
me, she might come to admire me.

The president was saying to his political advisor: "I could write it to-night or, better yet, dictate. I could give you the gist right now."

He becomes thoughtful, though something may have caught his eye on the last corner we passed. The street is empty. Traffic will start up on Providencia. It's possible, perfectly possible they will try something. One or two trucks would be enough. Put the second one at that tight curve on Eleodoro Yanez, just before Providencia. That's how I'd do it. But what good would it do now? They've got all the aces.

Allende keeps speaking with the same voice he had yesterday and for the last few months, in that paternal tone he's picked up, wise but tired. It's a counterpoint to the right-wing stridency. He's the man who has nothing to lose . . . 10 million people yell fire, trampling and crushing each other in one narrow doorway, he tells them to be calm. Can't you see that the people, all the people, are with me? Stand in lines, be calm, there is no need to be apprehensive, and please, no empty sacrifices or useless heroic gestures. But he said the other day at Tomas Moro that the alternatives are simple: he will complete the people's mandate, fin-ish his term and go home; or he will die assassinated.

What is he thinking now? He looks out the window and seems serene. Crossed hands, fingers intertwined, freckled skin with red hair. Rigid, a cold stare behind thick glasses. Fearless? Irresponsible? Not at all. He's going to his office to fulfill his duty.

"The final version of the speech," Allende says, "was drafted last night. We will go on the air at twelve or a little after. But not in the af-ternoon. Make sure we can go on nationwide before two."

"The meeting at the Technical University is off, right?"

"No. We should be able to settle this thing soon enough. If every-thing's under control by 10 we go to the University."

The advisor tries to say something but is interrupted.

"Yes, comrade, I understand perfectly, but I don't agree. We'll give an alert but let's not stir things up and provoke another crisis."

And the military people purged recently? And the stacked deck held by the generals? What's up? Do you know? Don't you?

He continues to stare at the houses, trees, streets, that disappear as we pass by. I know that Allende knows. I think I understand why he's calm. He looks at the time. It's been ten minutes since we left Tomas Moro. One can't speak now of forebodings. If we know anything it's be-cause the facts are spread out on the table, face up. No intuitions. For me it's the last day; I don't exactly know what will happen. Today, as I write this, I think of him and of myself. Chileans will finally understand what pathetic dreams their myths were made of. Not Allende. He never saw the myths around him, only men and women instead of shadows crowding about him. He has struggled and made sacrifices for them, flar-ing in anger when he looked underneath a uniform and found nothing, reprimanding the youth who won't talk with him but would waylay him arrogantly with a bomb in hand. Patrician, white-haired, virile, suddenly pugnacious and hot-headed, he is trying to make a revolution. And this with Chileans who don't want a civil war, but rather a kind of peace that combines considerate oligarchs, long-suffering workers, a middle class that will somehow make ends meet, and the armed forces, whom everyone respects because they can overthrow governments, any government they please. Allende expects to last three more years . . .

We're past the dangerous corner. I don't know which car we are in the formation: the last or the middle? Allende wants the radio. Any station. Music. Another. The same. Put on some news, he says. The driver searches and searches. The funny thing is the music sounds all the same. They are playing marches, and at first I don't recognize them, but soon I do. They are German marches, I tell him. I remember a war movie, says the driver. Why, asks the President, what movie? Haven't you seen it? These are marches from a Nazi film. Another station, comrade, put on the news. But now the stations are falling silent, falling off the dial. Allende notices it. A silence remains that fills with static, and then another sound, distant, near, distant again. A formation of planes flies over us, out of the leaden sky and into the clouds over the sea. Allende looks at them and says nothing. They disappear. They've probably looked on us as a curious group of wheels and blue roofs romping down the Alameda. Maybe they didn't even see us. I think for them we no longer count.

I would like to say goodbye to Allende but I realize this would be completely absurd. No one is thinking of goodbyes except me.

"Listen," he says, "find Olivares and tell him we are ready to go on the air."

The Fiats stop suddenly. Doors open and close noisily. I can hear the hollow sound of weapons being readied. Near our Fiat is a swarm of bodyguards. I see muzzles and triggers everywhere. The palace guard rigidly comes to attention. Allende gets out, salutes, enters La Moneda rapidly. He has an automatic rifle in his hand. One bodyguard walks on his right, slightly ahead of him, his finger on the trigger, observing everything, moving steadily but gracefully. Something of Kung Fu in his actions, but also a down-to-earth grace, cool and fast, opening, closing, turning, advancing a few steps and imperceptibly retreating.

Stunned, I remain. I would have liked to shake his hand. I wouldn't have known what to say, whether to warn him or cheer him up. The flag blazes over La Moneda. I want to tell him he is a good man, that he doesn't deserve this fate, that he isn't getting out of a '73 Fiat, but really he's stepping out of the 19th century, from the old Republic. It's just a conspiracy, an insurrection, secret agents everywhere, truckers with dollars, cunning and devious enemies who know how to strike and then hide. Nothing more. To say nothing else to him, but to see in his eyes one more time, the last, the sadness of a brave and wounded man, and to let him see the same sadness in mine. Nothing else. But he is already inside and lost in the Winter Garden. I see his back. He's forgotten me.

—translated from the Spanish by Stephen Fredman

Naomi Shihab Nye
NOBODY'S NEWSPAPER

Pig In A Pamphlet, No. 5—1983
Harry Calhoun, Editor

> "The outraged Costa Ricans mooed like cows
> outside the Santamaria Museum, claiming the
> bones of their hero Santamaria were really
> those of cows, horses, and pigs."
> —*The San Antonio Express-News*

Nobody's newspaper tells what the Costa Ricans did
when they finished mooing. Did they move home in herds,
or stand silently all night waiting for the morning
to open like a giant barn?

The measurable world gleams in the oily eye
of the printing press. It has your death date
in its teeth. It can't sleep
while you are sleeping.
A million yards wait for the thud in damp grass.

I dreamed we were taking back our names,
the newspapers emptied like a cup.
Because the stories end without ending
and the world laps them up,
because the bone of opinion is a shaky bone,
neither cow, horse, nor pig,
the headlines were blank that day.
Now we had to make our own news.

Never forgetting that a great man is dead,
just forgetting what they said about him.
Then go on living. With marrow,
identifiable, recognizable, and true.
Nobody's newspaper does what you can do.

Anna Kiss
EMPEROR BUTTERFLY

New Rivers Press; *Turmoil In Hungary* (1982; ed. by Nicholas Kolumban)
C.W. Truesdale, Editor

We made the corn-stalk violins wail and strode the fields
with the wind; we often sat down tongue-tied and peered
into tulips. At times, with a walking stick, we made
everything ring because nothing wanted to make a sound.

We had life to shield us from defeats: in the evening the
women washed their children's feet and put apples in their
hands. We warmed ourselves in one bed, just like swallows
and young spiders, listened to easy conversations and
watched the beams where the emperor butterfly passes the
winter. We saw the dead; a cradle swayed. The crab apples
froze. Old folks planted seeds at the end of winter in a
flower pot, filled with soil. They placed the pot on the
round stove. And we waited.

When they took away the men, the women became sad.
And the fields. Alien soldiers came, hunting for more alien
soldiers; they screamed for their mothers in their sleep.

When the horse carcasses were buried and they
partitioned the land, we still knew nothing about the
outside world. But about people, everything.

—translated from the Magyar by Nicholas Kolumban

photograph by Peter Korniss; *Turmoil In Hungary* (1982; ed. by N. Kolumban)
New Rivers Press; C.W. Truesdale, Editor

51

Hattie Gossett
ON THE QUESTION OF FANS/
THE SLAVE QUARTERS ARE NEVER AIR CONDITIONED

Conditions, No. 8—1982
Dorothy Allison et al, Editors

when i went to cuba in 1973 going there was still a mortal sin against
    imperialism that couldnt be stamped on your usa passport so
    you had to go to mexico or canada or europe first where there
    was a cuban embassy that could issue you a visa and an airport
    that would service cubano airlines.
also you usually had to be sponsored by some male dominated white leftist
    revolutionary organization and you had to go in a delegation
    composed largely of them unless you went as part of a delegation
    of male dominated black leftist revolutionaries who got there
    by hijacking an airplane.
the delegation i traveled with was of the former persuasion since i didnt
    have enough nerve to be hijacking no airplane and we found
    ourselves staying in mexico city a little longer than we had
    planned due to bureaucratic circumstances far far beyond our
    control.
while we were waiting we had meetings.
in between trips via the muy clean and pleasant subway to the visa office the
    pyramids the visa office the anthropological museum and back to
    the visa office again we had meetings and spanish classes (i learned
    donde esta el bano) and meetings.
well it was summer and even mexico city with its way way way high up above
    sea level altitude which caused me to fall right out in a cold
    faint in mid sentence within hours of getting off the plane was
    warm so i was using my 5&10 cents store imitation chinese
    foldup paper fan a lot during the meetings cuz of course the
    group wasnt staying in an air conditioned hotel.
my fan wasnt even nothing exotic like marabu or peacock feathers or
    delicately wrought filigree of ivory or teakwood.
well to my surprise the foldup paper fan bothered the white male leftists.
i really wasnt ready.
i really wasnt ready for the severe criticism i received about my dangerous
    bourgeoise female tendencies viz a viz the fan (they never touched
    on any of the things about me that could have stood some criticism)
the white boys told me fans are symbolic of the worst aspects of privileged
    womanhood; think they said of the french and italian baroque court
    ladies or the greek and roman demi mondains and how they all

sipped wines and ate roasted meats and sugary tidbits and fanned
themselves at the expense of the sweat and blood of the masses
the white boys continued while sweating profusely themselves and
trying in vain to shake up a little breeze with their damp limp
handkerchiefs thus unwittingly giving gross evidence of the lack
of understanding of the true historical conditions surrounding
the development of the masses and especially the wimmin masses.
think i pleaded of the wimmin slaves (unwaged and waged) laboring in un air
conditioned cane cotton corn and tobacco fields and un air
conditioned factories offices bedrooms laundries and kitchens
when they were able to snatch a moment or 2 away from
baroque incorporated or ms demi for themselves in a corner
somewhere.
what do you think they were doing?
fanning themselves of course.
fanning themselves and each other while sipping cool water tasting morsels of
food exchanging dreams thoughts plans and schemes.
fanning themselves.
fanning gnats ticks flys mosquitos and wasps away.
fanning up freedom struggles.
fanning honey fanning.
only the slaves were the wrong class and color to have their fans qualify
for most museum displays.
well the white male leftists didnt wanna hear about my greatgreat
grandmamas and aunties and neighborhood ladies doing no
fanning.
talk about cultural imperialism!
counterrevolutionary bourgeoise female tendencies was their considered
unwavering judgement.
well time passed and eventually we got to cuba around 2 oclock one morning.

my strongest first impression is of cuban women easily and familiarly handling
large guns at that hour as part of the regular civil guard
duties.
then i remember checking into the hotel nacional in havana near the ocean
and taking a predawn stroll along the malecon looking at the
waves and loving the caresses of the tropical breeze.
then going to sleep and waking up and going out in a minibus on 2½ weeks
worth of visits to factories schools hospitals museums movies
radio stations housing developments beaches and nightclubs and
meeting cuban wimmin who were seriously struggling against all
kinds of contradictions and gasp! fanning themselves.
cuz you know there was very little air conditioning so people sweated and
fanned a lot.

and the cubanas had these bad paper fans with all kinds of color reproductions
of revolutionary people and scenarios on them.
well you know i enjoyed myself in cuba dont you.
i fanned right along with the cuban wimmin and felt right at home.
and everytime i saw a cuban woman with a fan i would ask the white male
leftists if she was a counterrevolutionary bourgeoise female
like me.

Jack Anderson
THE INVENTION OF NEW JERSEY

Release Press; *Selected Poems* (1983), by Jack Anderson
Larry Zirlin et al, Editors

Place a custard stand in a garden
or in place of a custard stand
   place a tumbled-down custard stand
in place of a tumbled-down custard stand
   place miniature golf in a garden
     and an advertisement for miniature golf
      shaped for no apparent reason
      like an old Dutch windmill
in place of a swamp
   place a swamp

         or a pizzeria called the Tower of Pizza
         sporting a scale model
           of the Tower of Pisa
         or a water tower resembling
         a roll-on deodorant
         or a Dixie Cup factory
           with a giant metal Dixie Cup on the roof

In place of wolverines, rabbits, or melons
   place a vulcanizing plant
in place of a deer
   place an iron deer
   at a lawn furniture store
   selling iron deer
     Negro jockeys
     Bavarian gnomes
     and imitation grottoes
     with electric Infants of Prague
in place of phosphorescence
   of marshy ground at night
     place smears of rubbish fires
in place of brown water with minnows
   place brown water

         gigantic landlords
         in the doorways of apartment houses

which look like auto showrooms
auto showrooms which look like diners
diners which look like motels
motels which look like plastic chair covers
plastic chair covers which look like
plastic table covers which look like plastic bags

the mad scientist of Secaucus
invents a plastic cover
to cover the lawn
with millions of perforations
for the grass to poke through

In place of the straight lines of grasses
place the straight lines of gantries
in place of lights in the window
place lighted refineries
in place of a river
place the road like a slim pair of pants
set to dry beside a neon frankfurter
in place of New Jersey
place a plastic New Jersey

on weekends a guy has nothing to do
except drive around in a convertible
counting the shoe stores
and thinking of screwing
his date beside him
a faintly bilious look
perpetually on her face

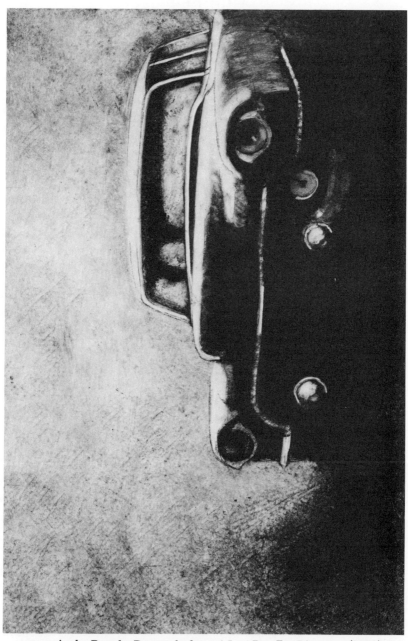

monoprint by Douglas Dusseault, from *A Last Day For Dinosaurs* (1983)
Appolyon Press; Douglas Dusseault, Editor

Pat Therese Francis
THUNDER

Primavera, Nos. 6 & 7—1981
Karen Peterson, Ruth Young et al, Editors

I used to meet him at
the bowling alley.
He was fourteen, laughed too loud,
and was hellbent for victory
over the pins, stand-up clowns
with big hips and sunken chests.

I never bowled, preferring the
vinyl closeness of the ladies' room
with its pink-framed mirrors
and sweaty princess seats.
I could stay in there for hours
with four or five friends
teasing our hair tall as women,
chewing Teaberry gum and
wondering if our lips
looked like ripe figs
after we greased them
with tubes of shared lipstick.

Feeling my way back,
it all tastes like smoke now,
rings of Teaberry-tobacco breath
sent up one blowing winter day
behind the bowling alley, where I
got warm inside the boy's mouth,
where, still in earshot
of the thundering black balls,
I wrapped my tongue around his
and licked the edges
of the coming storm.

photo by John Rosenthal; *Carolina Quarterly*, Vol. 32, No. 3—1980
Emily Stockard, Marc Manganaro, Editors

Steve Kowit
LURID CONFESSIONS

Carpenter Press; *Lurid Confessions* (1983), by Steve Kowit
Bob Fox, Editor

One fine morning they move in for the pinch
& snap on the cuffs—just like that.
Turns out they've known all about you for years,
have a file the length of a paddy-wagon
with everything—tapes, prints, film ...
the whole shmear. Don't ask me how but
they've managed to plug a mike into one of your molars
& know every felonious move & transgression
back to the very beginning, with ektachromes
of your least indiscretion & peccadillo.
Needless to say, you are thrilled,
tho sitting there in the docket
you bogart it, tough as an old tooth—
your jaw set, your sleeves rolled
& three days of stubble ... Only,
when they play it back it looks different:
a life common & loathsome as gum stuck to a chair.
Tedious hours of you picking your nose,
scratching, eating, clipping your toenails ...
Alone, you look stupid; in public, your rapier
wit is slimy & limp as an old bandaid.
They have thousands of pictures of people around you
stifling yawns. As for sex—a bit
of pathetic groping among the unlovely & luckless:
a dance with everyone making steamy love in the dark
& you alone in a corner eating a pretzel.
You leap to your feet protesting
that's not how it was, they have it all wrong.
But nobody hears you. The bailiff
is snoring, the judge is cleaning his teeth,
the jurors are all wearing glasses with eyes painted open.
The flies have folded their wings & stopped buzzing.
In the end, after huge doses of coffee,
the jury is polled. One after another
they manage to rise to their feet
like narcoleptics in August, sealing your fate:
Innocent ... innocent ... innocent ... Right down the line.
You are carried out screaming.

Mary Gray Hughes
THE STUTTERING PRIEST

Puckerbrush Review, Vol. V, No. 2–1983
Constance Hunting, Editor

He stuttered even before he became a priest. Episcopalian, of course. No one in his family had ever been Catholic. But the hand of the Lord, he said to anyone who listened, not only beckoned but plain shoved him deep into the faith and right on through, if late, into the cloth of his people's persuasion. Yet not acceptance and the years of study in the seminary, nor admission to the diaconate, nor ordination to the priesthood itself, not even his first appointment to a parish softened the explosions in his speech.

And who in the congregation could not believe at his final, desperately achieved, "P . . . P . . . P . . . P . . . PEACE be with you"?

"You have a great future," Dr. Stone told him afterwards. Dr. Stone was the Rector.

"You think so?" he asked. He was a large man and his whole body was alive with eagerness. His intense, glasses-caged blue eyes searched quickly over every angle of the Rector's face. "Really?" he said. "You mean that? You are en . . . en . . . en . . . en . . . en . . . ."

'Needling,' was he trying to say? Dr. Stone was already shaking his head to deny it.

"Helpful," he burst out.

Dr. Stone blinked.

The congregation stood in line to meet him as they filed out of the imitation medieval church. Few called him Father Masterson, or Father Toby, yet. But most of them shook his hand, pumping it up and down and up and down, when they met him and several held him by the elbow, too, cushioning him protectively, even though they probably had to look up at him when they told him how much they had enjoyed his sermon.

"First one I ever heard like it," a silver-haired man said. Dr. Stone quickly introduced them for the silver-haired man was Mr. Haimer who sat on the vestry.

"Glad to have you, and your lovely wife too, of course, with us, my boy," Mr. Haimer said, although the new priest was no boy. "Josh Stone here," Mr. Haimer said, "has probably told you I don't care for the new prayers and services. Too feeble, all those modern words instead of what we're used to. A sizeable number of us in the congregation don't like them. What do you say?"

"We absolutely must examine them openly and with thorough study," he said. "Nothing is more important. C...C...C...C...."

He gave up and swallowed hard to give himself a better chance. The whole subject of Biblical translations and the new forms of prayer service fascinated him. In the seminary he had argued for the continual need to have the most accurate translations new scholarship could provide and for new services that would give church members greater closeness and clarity.

He had finished swallowing and tried again, "C...C...C...C...."

Mr. Haimer was growing restless and burst in, "Yes, I see you take it seriously. Maybe I am too quick in some of my judgments. Mrs. Haimer says so. I admit I like being quick and a bit of a joker, too, even in business. But if you have good arguments, I'll listen to what you say. I've heard of your record in business. You were going to be made a partner of your CPA firm. That's impressive. Only you went into the ministry instead. We're lucky to have you aboard this old ship. Did Josh Stone show you around? We've got our own mini-gym in the church. Some of us think it equals the Y. Now a man your size can't be too careful. You'd have to exercise. What's your sport?"

"W...e...i...g...h...t...s," the new priest said.

"What?"

"I l...l...lift weights," he said, and as he said it, in the midst of the line of people waiting beneath the peaked stained glass windows, he bent, raised an imaginary weight from knee high to a chest rest, paused, then with a triumphant grunt and shove hoisted it straight up above his head, full stretch, his hands made into fists to hold it.

"You're a joker, too, hey?" Mr. Haimer approved. "Terrific. A man your size could really lift them. Only, we don't have any, do we, Josh? No, we don't. Maybe we could borrow some from another gym, but so far we haven't had to do that. We've had all our own equipment here."

"It's no p...p...issue," the new priest said. "Absolutely no issue at all. I have my own."

"You do? That's well prepared. See here," and he took the new priest's arm, "you are a solid addition. The Bishop wrote us that and now that I've seen you, I believe it. I may not like all these new goings on, but you're worth listening to. We're lucky to have you."

After the rest of the congregation had been introduced to him and the members finally trooped out of the vast, empty building, the two clergymen swung the heavy Gothic-style doors shut to lock them, and as they did Dr. Stone said to him, "You've no idea how convincing you are."

Yet possibly he did. He volunteered so often and found so many unexpected ways to be made use of. He moved the heavy furniture each Wednesday for the women's prayer session because earlier in the day the members of the exercise and dance classes would have lined the walls with the couches. He sat on Tuesday afternoons for an hour with those waiting for family counselling and he stayed on afterwards when there were any teen-agers. He set up a new system of accounting to record fund raising for maintenance of the organ. He even helped the repairman mend the old antique clock in the tower because he was not afraid of heights. He was all over the church. Outside it, too, he found parishioners who had needs for him.

He was magnetic in the hospitals.

"D...D...D...D..." "Don't be afraid, even of death," he meant to say to the heart attack patient. But fear had faded already from the old man's face as he reached out, ignoring the dangling IV, to take the new priest's hand.

"Don't try so hard," the sick man said to him with concern. "Relax. That's the secret. I've learned that here. It's the secret of life. I won't even talk much. And think good thoughts, that's an answere, too. I think good thoughts. Why I was saved by this attack. Do you know I might have died if I'd gone on living the way I was?"

He urged the priest to sit, sit, even on the bed beside him and when the new priest did the bed shifted beneath his weight.

"We all do too much," the man in the bed said. "You, too. I can see that. You've been so kind to my wife. She told me you'd offered to help her do our accounts. And she told me you talked to her an hour Saturday. But you mustn't do too much. And don't you worry about me. I'll see to it I don't overdo at a single thing. Matter of fact, I think I better rest now."

And before the new priest could discuss anything with him he had settled deeply into his pillows and asked in a careful voice for prayers. The new priest stood to read them.

"Nice prayer book," the other said in almost a whisper. It was a leather bound gift to the priest from his firm when he had left to go to the seminary. He opened the book to the prayers for the sick and began to read and as he did he could not help but see between the words he read, the ill man lying, eyes closed, hands clasped upon his chest, the IV dangling from his arm and a special rapture on his face at every word mangled by a stutter.

Then there was Mrs. Haimer. She called him into the church one Friday when she was cleaning. She was not only Mr. Haimer's wife, she was one of the leading members of the League of Martha's Handmaidens. Once they had cleaned altar cloths, but since finances had required they washed and cleaned the church itself, and, recruiting men into their fold, did all the work of maintenance themselves and claimed they had all come to care more for the church by doing so. She, Mrs. Haimer, had her hair wrapped in a tight bright colored cloth for cleaning when she called to him.

"I want to tell you something," she said, and beckoned so he had to follow her deep inside the church to one of the little alcoves where her cleaning materials were. She kept looking about to be sure there was no one else to hear her.

"Something I've never told a soul," she said, and she stepped close to him. "You know those stories of weeping statues in countries like Mexico and Italy, places where they believe those things? You know those?" She looked again to see no one was near and then she said, "Well, I, when I wash the statues in these alcoves," she said, "I weep."

"Oh, Mrs. Haimer," he said to her, "Mrs. Haimer, my good friend, you really should consider the strong likelihood that in these circumstances maybe it's the d...d...d..." 'Detergent,' he was trying to say, 'detergent,' for its strong smell was tingling in his nose, but he could not say the word. He swallowed and swallowed again and tried, "the d... the d...d...maybe it's the d...the d...d...d...the d...d..."

Alarm was rising in her face. What on earth did she think he was going to say? The Devil? Not the Devil? Fear had transfixed her. He swung his head hard, like a golf club, breaking free of the spasm of the sound and burst out... "LOVE."

He was as surprised as she.

"I knew you would understand," she said. "I knew I could tell you. I could tell you anything."

And it seemed she might want to take his hand so he put both of his behind him and held them there.

"Your coming here has meant so much," she said. She was still standing close to him. "My husband says so all the time. It isn't just the vestry's duties that bring him to church now, you know. He doesn't mind the new services when you are there and you give the sermon. He keeps telling all sorts of people to come."

It was true. More and more people were coming those Sundays it was certain he would preach. Extra chairs had to be put in the little side chapel even at early communion if it were known he would deliver the brief homily. And at the main service, when he was to give the sermon, the center pews in the large nave were becoming so crowded members of the congregation sitting there had to press close against one another in their increasing numbers, waiting for him to go, large and unstumbling, up the high twisting pulpit stairs to preach and often gasp and stammer out his words above their heads. Some Sundays he could not even begin but clung to the pulpit's rim while his head jerked back and down, back and down, like a dog working helplessly on a stuck bone. Those were the Sundays he stuttered most and were the Sundays the dispersing congregation shook his hand the longest and with the greatest fervor as they told him how much they liked the service and how much the sermon meant.

It had not been that way in business. In business he had deliberately assumed a brisk, stern manner and worked hard to make up for the weakness in his speech, and he had been successful. His clients and the partners in the firm and even the secretaries simply waited until he could go on and finish what it was necessary for him to say so the accounting could be done. They read no special meanings into the spasms between some of his sounds. That had begun the second year he tried to enter the seminary.

The first time he had been told no. But he would not give up, or waver. He had gone to the seminary a second time and that was when they asked openly about his stuttering. He told them he had never spoken differently and had been taken finally to Mayo's when he was an adolescent. When all their tests were finished the doctors met with him and his parents and explained in some detail about his case and finally at the end they said, "There are no cures for some defects."

It had been a hard thing for him to say. The sound "d" often caused him trouble and it took him many efforts to say it to the interviewing committee but they waited until he finished and when he did they agreed to let him enter.

In the seminary itself the stuttering made no difference. Not until his final interview. Then the Bishop and the Commission on Ministry kept him for a long time, not, as with many others, to discuss his wife, for she was liked although they had no children, but to discuss his stuttering. They asked him repeatedly and in many different ways if he knew and understood all its problems and, again, if he were sure, really sure, he knew what he was doing. None of his answers gave them satisfaction until unexpectedly he stood and vehemently said that all right, all right, but by G...G...by G...by G...G...G...but G...DID, HE DID, yes. Know. What he was doing. The Bishop and the Commission changed then. It was as if they had what it was they had wanted, and he could not forget that it was after he had stuttered hard they decided he should be ordained.

Since then he was uncertain how to write his sermons. If he typed them, double-spaced and with wide margins and no notes added in his own handwriting, and if he practiced their delivery, he almost did not stutter. If instead he used an outline of essential points written on loose cards and chose the key words carefully—for he could tell, who better than he? the words that might make him stumble—then in the rush of preaching freely and with this seeming spontaneity he would strangle on a sound and once that started it would continue the rest of the way through.

When he began giving sermons in the seminary he found he liked best using the cards with an outline of a few words. He liked the closeness to the listeners the freer speech gave him even if he did stutter more. In the seminary he had been better in the more spontaneous sermons and here in the parish he kept a pile of clean new cards in his desk drawer. When he had finished reading and thinking about his sermon and had it typed, then he would copy on cards the texts to be read out in full and following that an outline of key words and phrases he would need to give his sermon. Only now when he wrote those few words down he would hear always in his head his own voice stuttering, though in his thoughts, as in his private prayers, he never, really, stuttered.

But he did know what he was doing, he told himself. Just as he had told the Bishop and the members of the Commission. All that was different now, all that had changed, the only difference now was . . . was that . . . was . . . .

He put his pen down on his desk beside the little pile of cards. He had been scheduled to give six consecutive sermons on the Church's new services and prayers and the new translation of the Bible they were using. All six sermons were to be followed by discussions at the social hour afterwards. It had been his idea to give one sermon but the number had been stretched to six by Mr. Haimer, who said there was clearly so much the new priest had to say. Dr. Stone agreed, though it was unusual, but too many of the departing faithful, as Mr. Haimer called them, had been leaving. Mrs. Haimer told all the Handmaidens to come to every service and to bring members of their families and their friends, too. Already, Mrs. Haimer said, more than usual were coming when he preached and look how many of them were staying for the discussions. Why if it went on this way, she said, why there was no telling where it would end.

She told him that after he gave the third of the six sermons he was to deliver. All he had to do now was give three more.

He did not pick up his pen. "A lesser man," Dr. Stone had said to him, "might mind the crowds you draw. I think it's fair to call them crowds, don't you, Toby, since so many are not regular church-goers? But I'm glad for you. They must have warned you in the seminary of the risks inherent for you in your stuttering. I'm sure they must have. All I can say is you certainly do manage well."

And this morning, as he came into the church, Mr. Haimer told him several of the parishioners who had been going to leave were returning. Even some of those going to a church in Cloverdale, which celebrated with the old service, were coming back. "They're like me," Mr. Haimer said, beaming at him. "I told them you can persuade anyone of anything."

The work for the sermons had all been done. The next one to be given was already typed and lay on his desk so the crux of it could be taken out and written on the cards. It had not taken him long to do the work because he had been studying the subject for years. He had studied Greek and his first Aramaic the year they would let him into the seminary. Once in the seminary he had written papers on different translations and the history of the church's endless effort to understand the Bible's meanings more accurately and present the message in terms closer to the people. It had taken him years, years of hard work and of study, to learn what he knew and the same was so of his teachers before him, and all of that, that pile of folders with his notes and papers and the lists of books that he had read, that mattered. That mattered as much as the other, as much as anything. It did, it m...m...m...m... he flung at himself in his thoughts where he never, truly, stuttered, until finally and at least he finished...MATTERED.

He was beginning to sweat. Because the room that he used as an office was hot. It was an oddly shaped room. It was a misshapen tongue of space cut out by ten-foot high partitions from the empty area of the huge, supposedly medieval building. All of the partitioned rooms were hot for under the new economizing restrictions the air-conditioning was used only in the nave and on the hottest Sundays. The new priest wiped his palms thoroughly across his black trousers. But he did not pick up his pen.

"I don't think you know what you mean to us," Mrs. Haimer had said to him. "Do you remember that evening we were so loud in our prayer group you overheard us? Charlotte was being silly and she asked did we think it was all right to pray for a superb figure, and Elsa said it just depended on how over-weight you were. We were all laughing and then there you were. I bet you don't even remember. We were so taken aback, ashamed, like little girls. Only you said, good friends, you mustn't have any qualms in the least or be at all uneasy for there's always much love for a clown (but it was 'c...c...c...c...c...CLOWN,' that he had said) and Elsa, who was visiting us, you made her feel so good. She even comes back sometimes. You see, you do us all good."

Must he, he wondered, go unknowingly only, then, into the country of good? Could he do no good except when unselfconscious and unaware? That which he had not asked for—so many coming and with such strange fervor—it did not help him to have been given. Could he not take a part of it only, a little bit, fewer in numbers perhaps and with a lesser faith?

He got up. He was enormous above the small church desk. "We've no money nowadays for repairs so you be careful you don't break it," Dr. Stone had said. "We'll be expecting better financial circumstances with you joining us, and not just from your accounting skills."

He moved away from his desk and walked around the oddly shaped space of his room. Why did so many come? No matter how he spoke he stuttered, some. Those fresher, open sermons, the ones with room for freer and more spontaneous preaching, they had always been the best ones he had given. "Oh, that last was terrific," Mr. Haimer had said to him on Sunday. "The best yet. There's real excitement in the old church now. Don't mind what Dr. Stone said. I couldn't help but overhear him telling you in the changing room that we all know how ambitious you are. He's bothered because you announced an extension of your discussion time into the social hour. He's something of a prima donna, that's all. He's been putting that 'PhD, Princeton' after his name on every piece of paper that comes out of the church and he must have got that degree decades ago. It's understandable he should say what he did to you. Anyone would recognize it for what it is. Pay no attention to it, it's only human."

He set his head against the thin partition wall. Why did so many come? What more than what he had studied and learned to tell them were they getting? And why so many?

He was sweating so the skin of his forehead felt attached to the partition. He put his hands as well against the wall at a level a few inches below his head. "Don't give a second thought to Josh Stone," Mr. Haimer had continued on Sunday. "You just think about all those people you've got staying late. You've got them right where you want them."

He pressed the palms of his hands flat against the partition's surface. The surface was perfectly smooth. "You have a great future," Dr. Stone had said, the first Sunday. So this was his future, this was his faith's fate —that playful, silly, happy phrase he and his wife and their friends and all those from his office had used at the firm's farewell party for him. This was his f...f...f...faith's f...f...f...f...Stop. S...s...s... stop it. STOP. This was it, then. This was. This.

If he pushed hard on the partition he could topple it over. If he pushed with all the strength of his shoulders it would crash flat onto the floor. Where? On the floor of the kindergarten through third grade church school room which was also the choir's Sunday changing room and was the room beyond his. Beyond that was the library, secretary's office, and room used on Sundays for the nursery. Beyond the exercise, dance, and women's prayer room. Then Dr. Stone's office. And beyond, the large and empty church.

He pulled away from the wall. He turned around and went back to his desk and sat down at it. He took his pen and one of the cards and wrote across the top to be read out in full:

"Translation it is that openeth the window, to let in the light; that breaketh the shell, that we may eat the kernel."

Preface to the King James Bible, 1611

Beneath he also wrote in full:

I am no clear window to the light. I am simply what I am. You must always remember that, for your sakes, and for mine. You must remember that I am in every way a stuttering priest.

James Bertolino
FROG VOICES

Beloit Poetry Journal, Spring 1983
Marion K. Stocking, Editor

for Philip McCracken

The swamp is silent.

Dawn's slow voltage
reaches wild
currant, & each twig,
each slim living rheostat
feeds light to the blossoms.

Then one by one open the gold
& green flecked eyes of the frogs.

Over the distant Bering Sea,
over resting
bowhead whales & sea birds at roost,
a missile punctures the brilliance
of morning sky.

Shivering ponds of swamp water
harbor a grim reflection
as the projectile descends its chilling arc.

Suddenly the frogs begin.
Their voices rise,
feathery trebles, croaks and trills
all weaving a shield
of sound.

When the missile explodes

the blinding egg of fire is enclosed
by singing, then is repelled
into cold space
beyond the range
of song.

Robin Morgan
PHOBIPHILIA

13th Moon, Vol. 5, Nos. 1 & 2–1980
Marilyn Hacker, Editor

Do you smell smoke?
If you don't, it's not
because a tenement isn't burning—
down the street, in Teheran, Derry, Beirut, or Phnom Penh.

Did you just hear a scream?
If you didn't, it's not
because a woman wasn't raped
since I asked if you smelled smoke.

Did you notice anything funny
about the three men across the street
watching as you came in?
If you didn't, there's nothing
to laugh about.

Three out of four agor-
aphobiacs
seem to be women. Agoraphobia
means, simply, fear of
leaving one's home (or sometimes
one's room) and also means fear
of open or public places—
like the street or supermarket or movie theater,
playground or newsstand or subway or bar.
Three out of four.

This is the most common phobia,
they say, among women. It's the one I
don't share, used as I am
to leaving my clearest messages in open
or public places, such as poems
like last desperate biophide notes.
More and more what I fear
is the coming or being home, safe
where the silence, not walls, may close in,
or the heights be eroded or

71

the floors themselves under one's feet burst
into flame.

Those other phobias—such as anxiety at
certain elements (water or fire), or alarm
at particular animals (dogs, cats, strange men),
or terror at heights, depths, enclosed places—
these are more common, especially to women,
than agoraphobia, which means consequently
we have no hard
statistical data on them.
They are more integrated through daily living,
better clenched, sweatily, in the palm. They
need not paralyze the phobic, they are less drastic
and so less reported. Many claustrophobiacs,
for instance, are in the closet.

But less drastic? Myself, as I grow
older, I smell smoke more often. I've become
a quite keen smeller of smoke these days.
In the middle of the night I rise
to check the gas jets, the fireplace, the boiler.
I keep flashing out of the corner
of my mind on flames
beside the bed *too late oh now too late*
or dancing along the beams *the ceiling's*
caving oh my god or puffing like cumulus
kumquat-colored clouds along the wings
of the planes that I, like a doomed Dutchwoman, fly
—always barring the
barring the
like a wall of red roar, a wind-
tunnel oven barring
the door.

Reincarniacs among you will assume
this is because I was burned at the stake—not once
but perhaps again and again until embers
still glow in my skull's milkglass globe, or crackle
each knuckle or flicker each cell from red to white
bloodheat or smoulder discreet at the marrow
to mirror internally what my charred bones
can no longer feel. Believe what you will.
I am done with simplifications.

Analysands among you will sift
for the burnt child in my past who
honestly never was there. Believe
what you will. I am done with neat formulae.

Pragmatists among you might just note
that I live in a hundred-year-old tinderbox
near a slum where junkies and bums patrol
deserted buildings, looking for places to light
inside campfires, keep warm. Or
that a firehouse clangs regularly, one block
away. Or that the flue in the fireplace
is almost as temperamental as the runaway
oven or recalcitrant wiring or
cunningly antique gas heaters who hiccup
and belch as if they constituted
a tragic Greek chorus comprised of W.C. Fieldses.
The wretched of the hearth indeed.

A pragmatist just might discern
the dishes still ticking, the clocks
to be laundered, the statues of goddesses
melting before such banked heat as the heart's
wild denial of all my mere mortal humanity:
an arson so simple we have no statistical
data on its daily practice.

A pragmatist just might be getting somewhere
by inquiring as to the reasons, objective,
for why I haunt the dark
rooms, touching lightly the gas jets, sniffing
the ashes, disbelieving assurances no matter
how patronizing, watching the cats (my reality checks).

As for flying, it used to delight me.
I've done it too much. And I'm done for.
It's bound to end badly
unless I can learn not to care.

What I care for increasingly, though,
is my phobia wisdom: getting to know
all my phobias, getting to hope they like me.

They are practical, radical groundings

of abstract and liberal paranoid theory.
They are my practice. They are
rehearsals—not, as is thought, spokes
to be touched, or cracks in the sidewalk
which must be avoided.
They hone my technique.
They accustom my waking.
They array my going forth like a bride.

Are your palms getting sweaty?
Did you just hear a scream?
Do you smell someone burning?

photograph by Sachiko Tamura Hamada; *Primavera*, Vols. 6/7—1981
Karen Peterson, Ruth Young et al, Editors

Wendell Berry
THE FEAR OF LOVE

North Point Press; *A Part* (1980), by Wendell Berry
Jack Shoemaker, Editor

I come to the fear of love
as I have often come,
to what must be desired
and to what must be done.

Only love can quiet the fear
of love, and only love can save
from diminishment the love
that we must lose to have.

We stand as in an open field,
blossom, leaf, and stem,
rooted and shaken in our day
heads nodding in the wind.

EXCEPT

Now that you have gone
and I am alone and quiet,
my contentment would be
complete, if I did not wish
you were here so I could say,
"How good it is, Tanya,
to be alone and quiet."

Thomas R. Smith
TWO POEMS ON THE FEAR OF LOVE

Yarrow, Vol. 2, No. 2–1982
Harry Humes, Editor

1. Answered

The aging woman helps her mother up from the table.
They speculate calmly about frost that may come tonight.
All afternoon winds bruise the lake,
lifting up waves, throwing them down.
Men row to shore and lash their boats to the dock
with a joyful brutality, jerking the ropes taut.

2. In Fear of Love

Your hair, your arms, these gifts of earth—
your table is ready, your basket is laden with sun.
I wake slowly to the scent of bergamot from your rare tents
    pitched on sand.
What if I'm not yet human enough to love you?
I move under cover, even in my own house,
even in the birch woods of these pages,
afraid of the toad under the trapdoor,
the lantern hanging in the window.

Charles Bukowski
FUNNY MAN

The Midatlantic Review, No. 11–1979
Billy Collins et al, Editors

Mr. Geomethel liked to hold Saturday afternoon parties
at his house, we always got invitations, and I think
it was my 3rd or 4th wife, she always wanted to go,
and she'd keep at it until it was more miserable to
be with her than to be there, so she won, we went up
to Echo Park, parking above on the hill, looking down
at the small grey house, people standing in the yard
were as dull as last week's race results, she got
excited seeing them, I suppose I kept her too much
away from that sort of thing, she was a country girl,
honest and healthy and full of fondness for the masses.
I liked to eat candy bars in bed with her and she had
the most marvelous cross-eyes, we went down the path
and here were people in the sun and Mr. Geomethel and
the grey boards of the house and chuck holes in the
ground and everybody holding to some odd impulse, some
mystic reason. when you looked into their irises you
could see the back walls of their heads where suspicious
flicks of downcast mould were imbedded. my country girl
liked people, not only Mr. Geomethel but Chuck and Randy
and Lila and Creasefoot, and the dog wagging. she, my
3rd or 4th wife, she went from this person to that,
from this group to that finding intense and interesting
things. I drank what I could of the very bad wine,
vomited secretly behind bushes as she finally vanished,
wanting me to search for her but I puked, drank more,
waited, said yes or no to a few questions passed to me
through the air, then she appeared again to tell me that
Mr. Geomethel had taken her to his bedroom to show her his
paintings, and she was surprised, she said, they were *very*
good.
every man, I answered her, probably has some kind of decency
if you look long enough. Mr. G's decency, I continued, was
probably his *very* good paintings.
she seemed angry at that, showed me her heel and walked up
to 2 young men leaning up against a slivered fence. they
seemed happy to see her.

I went inside to the kitchen, opened a cupboard and found
an almost full pint of vodka. I poured a ¾ vodka and a
¼ water. I found a Pall Mall upon the sink and lit it.

and I knew that my 3rd or 4th marriage was over: out of
my jealousy and envy and all the horrible things. "you
lack self-confidence," she told me. I knew that and I was
very glad that she knew that. I had a bit more of my drink
then went into the yard and when she sneaked a look at me
she knew that I had passed over to the other side and that
I would not come back because of all those horrible things,
and I felt wonderful like a mallard rising with the hunters
too drunk in their boats to blast me down for their dogs.
still, she walked over and tried me:
well, I suppose you want to *go* now, just when things are
livening up?
I'd like to go, I said, but this is as good as any. I
can stay.
for me? she asked.
for us, I said. and finally I was no longer bored.
and when Mr. Geomethel came up and asked me how it was
going I told him that I liked his party.
and he said, why, I thought you were a *recluse*?
I am, I told him.

now my wife no. 4 or 5, she doesn't like parties but, of
course, there are other problems.
I still get these regular invitations to Mr. Geomethel's
parties.
I basket them neither in hatred nor in joy
and wife no. 3 or 4 phones sometimes
weeps
says that what she misses is my humor, it's such a rare
thing. and I wonder about that because I never remember
her laughing
except with other people
like at Mr. Geomethel's parties.

79

Lynda Barry; *Big Ideas* (1983), by Lynda Barry; The Real Comet Press
Catherine Hillenbrand, Editor

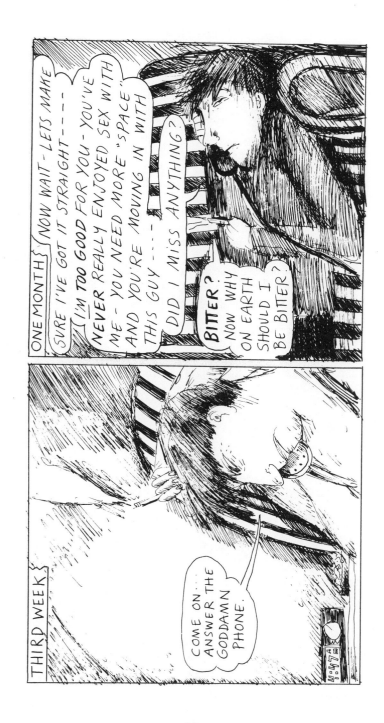

81

Carol Flint
A TROIS

New CollAge, Vol. 10, No. 3 (chapbook issue)—1980
A. McA. Miller, Editor

We three, being thoroughly post-
Modern and having hung long enough
Over and on-the-rocks, each wonders if

The other two are willing. Someone must
Have mentioned risk. The blend of Perls and
Tonic has just a whiff of the transcendental cork

To tip the balance. Choosing how to rock
The boat becomes the game. Deciding which one
To sit with in the booth, and who

To face is taking a chance; a diagonal to
Cut across these table tops of sanity.

But soft, at least as soft as ennui, we move

To let the ice cubes melt, certain we can swallow
Them when they lose their edges. Symmetry is dead;
And we both—that is we all—have read the New

Age journals. The fate of dyads allows
Us such freedoms. And the maybes lead
Into an infinite white where there is no How
To Proceed. Who leads and who follows
Should get lost in the dance; for what's in a step?
                                            But, god,
Something common is cutting in now.

Michael Tarachow
WALKING IN THE MIDST OF OTHERS

Pentagram Press; *The Turning Point* (1981), by Michael Tarachow
Michael Tarachow, Editor

distance
is one trick of the mind
to ignore

we are connected
with strong and good friends
no matter the miles we move in
spirit through the various woods
and ways of their lives

moving among others
we perchance appear no different
but we are

in such strict resolve to hold
to this measure each alone
we bring ourselves together

Joe Smith
ULRIKE MEINHOF

O. Ars, No. 1 ("Coherence" issue)—1981
Don Wellman, Irene Turner et al, Editors

The day Ulrike Meinhof died the sun sparkled like a gold tooth in a gypsy's mouth. After weeks of cold and overcast the sun returned from the Mediterranean with Vivaldi's sky in a blue suitcase. Old people led dachshunds on leashes across the patch of tender grass marked off for dogs. It was far and away the warmest day of the year so far. Mothers scolded infants undressing themselves in sandboxes, men with a day off played chess in shirt-sleeves.

White flames of spring crouched in buds on the chestnut trees. The only person wearing a coat was the wintry old man squeezing shambles of an accordion for pennies in perpetual shadow the day Ulrike Meinhof was found hanging in her cell.

This Ulrike Meinhof, the Germans used to say, it must be that Andreas Baader the anarchist seduced her. Why else would an attractive young woman with a career in journalism, a regular column, good salary and pension benefits, why else would she want to leave home and throw bombs and kidnap politicians? A newspaper in Hamburg or Bremen. No, not Bremen. A regular column. A promising future and that gangster Baader is still at large!

A chance wind blew a scrap of the latest news towards the bench where the foreigner sat or he might not have known the day Ulrike Meinhof hung herself. He played sometimes with children in the park on the swings or carousels, with little Hans in his lederhosen, Greta, mocking Dieter, and little Leni whom he found one icy sunrise bawling in a snowstorm.

Crystals glittered in her carefully braided hair, tears shone on her cheeks. She wanted to die. But why? he asked, kneeling beside her on the sidewalk. Because I have to go to school, she wept. Let me die.

In far-off China along a mild coast frail shoots of snow-peas were reaching out for things to clutch, a branch, a stake, a string. Her fingers curled around his hand that way. Sure as the heavens fell in white flurries

84

to the earth, she was tugged along a path she never made. Her mother demanded, her father insisted, society commanded, her sisters helped with the homework. It was a rebuke to the whole intricate and awesome system if Leni refused to sit with her classmates and learn about the world from someone approved by the proper authorities, certified and safe. If she failed to attend, something was seriously wrong with her.

She heard her father's strap in all the voices of her elders. The foreigner watched her go, bent beneath her satchel, a small cry in a deaf country trudging through the bitter snow. And the sudden shout of green was wasted on her the morning far and away the warmest of the year so far the day Ulrike Meinhof died.

Randee Russell
POWER STORIES

Carolina Wren Press; *Bombs* (1982), by Randee Russell
Judy Hogan, Editor

"Being cared for like a precious thing will not make you weak," she said. "It will make you powerful."

This was said to me at a party by a stranger who'd been eavesdropping on a frightening conversation I was having with my friend.

The words came from my elbow and when I turned to see who'd said them there was a tiny, pretty, older woman, around 50. Later I learned that she was the daughter of a celebrated Belgian artist who had outwitted the Nazis to save his family. So she'd had some dealings with power. But when I met her I was struck by her delicacy—she did not look powerful at all.

I had been telling my friend about waking up from a bad dream two nights after my husband and I left each other—lying there in the dark so tense that the blood in my cells felt still, like the blood in steaks under cellophane on a butcher's counter.

And my friend was saying, "But why didn't you call me?"

"If anyone had touched me or spoken to me," I said, "I would have blown apart like a dropped egg. I have to learn to face this thing alone."

"Oh no, Humpty Dumpty," said my friend, laughing, hugging, patting my back. "I could take care of you."

Which was about to start me crying when the stranger, whom I had not noticed at my elbow, said:

"Being cared for like a precious thing will not make you weak. It will make you powerful."

"Elise," said my friend, taking the stranger's hands which were delicate like a blown glass ballerina. As I said, she did not look powerful.

And of course I was angry that she had been listening and embarrassed for being close to tears, so I wanted to get away.

But my friend happened to mention that I am a writer and Elise liked that. She kept holding my hand long after we had finished shaking hands. Smiling, asking questions in her French-laced accent, so that by the time she let go, I did not want to leave anymore. I was enchanted.

And the three of us talked late into the night. And Elise told these stories about vulnerability and power—"The kind of power," she said, "that David had over Goliath. It wasn't from God," she said, "It was from something he got from his people, from his tribe and his family— that intense, enfolding love that puts you in touch with your own inner invincibility so you choose the right weapon instinctively."

These stories were told to illustrate her beliefs. And though I am a-
ware that people often give out personal parables to make a point, still
some people's stories stay with you and these *have* stayed with me—and
helped.

1—Being Cared For Like A Precious Thing

When the Nazis invaded Belgium, the name of Elise's father was high
on their list, not only because he was a Jew, but because he was an articulate, thoughtful man and they considered that more dangerous than
anything.

But when the SS men came to their village, they stopped first at the
local tavern. She says this was common practice among SS ranks—that
officials encouraged drinking at every level. And that her father always
said it was to mute the last voice of humanity crying inside them against
the things they were ordered to do.

So when the Nazis came, the tavern owner's boy ran six miles of back
roads to warn them.

She remembers the family was just sitting down to lunch when he
ran panting across the lawn, his face rosy, his breath steamy. And that
even before he spoke, her father began to move.

There had been lots of talk about Nazis before then, the kind of talk
children hear through walls when parents sit up with friends late into
the night. Talk heard not in words but in tones and rhythms. That for
months before this day the tones and rhythms had been sad and scared.
And when the tavern owner's boy ran across the lawn, she immediately
knew it had to do with all that.

But now her parents did not seem frightened.

She remembers her father collecting canvases from his studio and the
walls of the house. All the canvases, those from friends and students,
those that weren't finished. Bringing them out onto the lawn.

She remembers her mother instructing the children "Take your warmest coat, one change of underwear, one book, something small you
would not want to leave behind." And how her mother whistled a Bach
minuet as she packed the lunch they'd been about to eat into a wicker
basket.

Then Edgar Godin packed his family in the deep backseat of his open
car. Elise and her sister and her mother, packed like crystal with feather
pillows underneath them and the canvases tied over them—over her, her
favorites of all she loved best about the home they were leaving: small
deer nosing raspberries the color of stained glass windows, mandarin
ducks in their neighbor's barnyard pond, puffed up woodpeckers on a
tree with too much snow.

Years later she would see her father cry when a friend told him of
the French border, of pleading with cocky kid soldiers, glimpsing freedom through barbed wire.

But she had never seen him funnier than he was that night as he took them easily *into* Germany, wearing silly driving goggles and a lime green ascot, sipping cognac and explaining in flamboyant gestures to the sleepy guards that he was curator of Musee Belle Arts in Antwerp and that Herr Bijeau, an influential sympathizer of the Nazi cause, had ordered these paintings to Bonn for safe keeping.

Twenty miles into Germany, they feigned death, doused the car with gasoline, lit it and pushed it from the bridge. She remembers how fiercely the canvases caught, how they sizzled as they sank beneath the water. Then her family disappeared into the thick fog of the German forest where they remained secretly and excitingly alive, sleeping in shelters abandoned by hunters gone to war. And there was wild food—berries and nuts and fiddle-head ferns in spring.

She remembers snaring small deer with her father. How the first time she helped him butcher one he bent down and ruffled her hair in exactly the same way he had always done when she would sit all afternoon and watch him paint. She remembers how this day he got a little blood on her, just as he had sometimes gotten paint on her before—that it all seemed the same.

2—*Will Make You Powerful*

But in the dead of winter, the deer were scarce and there was little else.

It turned out though that Elise and her sister could go into the small town markets and buy food and no one would notice. The German countryside was full of shy, poor children. The people in the stalls would look at them coldly, expecting them to beg. And then when they didn't, when they actually had a little money, the people would sell to them cheerfully, generously, never questioning where the money came from, where the children came from. She said you could see relief in their eyes, not to have to say "no" to another hungry child.

So they were safe in the towns. But walking back there were Nazi patrols, suspicious of everything. You would hear their powerful cars in the distance, the half-growl, half-purr of those engines. You had to listen carefully so you could run into the forest and hide.

And she was listening carefully—only there had been a snow which muffled the sound so she never heard it 'til it was suddenly there like a ship bearing down on a swimmer—the big black car with the gunner platform on back. She remembers the brilliant, snow-reflected sun flashing off the driver's black glasses, the gunner relaxed against the rail behind the machine gun—its bird-like tripod legs, his legs fat inside gray leather britches.

In the corner of her eye she saw that her sister had lunged to the side, lay badly hidden, half behind a snowbank. Her sister with four rabbits, and where do these ragged children get money for four rabbits? And why does one of them hide? And why do you speak with an accent, child? And where do you come from, children? You are not German children!

Elise says she will never understand why she did what she did next. She did not decide to do it. She cannot imagine how she got her legs to move.

But suddenly she found herself skipping out into the path of the gunner car. Skipping, giggling, holding out her hands the way children do when they dance into streets to greet parades of soldiers coming home.

And the driver swerving crazily—this man who would have killed her, nearly killing himself to avoid killing her. An instinct.

She says the gunner shook his fist until the moment before the car rounded the next curve.

That before it disappeared, right before she vomited, he threw her a kiss.

photo by Kathleen Childers; *Sing Heavenly Muse!*, fiction issue—1983
Sue Ann Martinson, Editor

Thomas McGrath
REMEMBERING THE CHILDREN OF AUSCHWITZ

Thunder's Mouth Press; *Echoes Inside The Labyrinth* (1983), by Thomas McGrath
Neil Ortenberg, Editor

We know the story. The children
Are lost in the deep forest—
Though it is the same forest
In which we all are born.

But somehow it has changed:
A new kind of darkness,
Or something they never noticed,
Has colored the pines and the larches.

And now appears the Bird,
(Bird of a strange dreaming)
To lead them, as tales foretold,
Over the little streams

Into the garden of order
Where trees no longer menaced,
And a little house was protected
Inside its candy fences.

And all seemed perfectly proper:
The little house was covered
With barbwire and marzipan;
And the Witch was there; and the Oven.

Perhaps they never noticed—
After all that disorder
Of being lost—that they'd come
To the Place named in the stories.

Perhaps there was even peace—
A little—after disorder,
Before they awoke into
A dream of deeper horror.

And now the Bird will never
Take them across the river

(Though they knew how to walk on water).
They become part of the weather.

They have become the Ascensions.
When we lift up our eyes,
In any light, we see them:
Darkening all our skies.

Phillip McCaffrey
APPREHENSION

Lame Johnny Press; *Teaching The Door To Close* (1983), by Phillip McCaffrey
Linda Hasselstrom, Editor

An eight year old and the heifer
stand in clover, eye to eye,
negotiating: her patient cud
against his nervous arrow.

The mother look of the cow
gleams at him, steady, moist,
as big and dark as a target
aimed at this heart.

And he might have shot her with rubber
—except her chewing never stopped
and out of her lip a hairy stubble
twitched, like broken shafts.

Marge Piercy
SIX UNDERRATED PLEASURES

Open Places, No. 36–1983
Eleanor Bender, Editor

1. *Folding sheets*

They must be clean.
There ought to be two of you
to talk as you work, your
eyes and hands meeting.
They can be crisp, a little rough
and fragrant from the line;
or hot from the dryer
as from an oven. A silver
gray kitten with amber
eyes to dart among
the sheets and wrestle and leap out
helps. But mostly pleasure
lies in the clean linen
slapping into shape.
Whenever I fold a fitted sheet
making the moves that are like
closing doors, I feel my mother.
The smell of clean laundry is hers.

2. *Picking pole beans*

Gathering tomatoes has no art
to it. Their ripe redness shouts.
But the scarlet runner beans twine
high and jungly on their tripods.
You must reach in delicately,
pinch off the sizeable beans
but leave the babies to swell
into flavor. It is hide and seek,
standing knee deep in squash
plants running, while the bees
must be carefully disentangled

from your hair. Early you may see
the hummingbird, but best to wait
til the dew burns off.
Basket on your arm, your fingers
go swimming through the raspy leaves
to find the prey just their size.
Then comes the minor zest
of nipping the ends off with your nails
and snapping them in pieces,
their retorts like soft pistolry.
Then eat the littlest raw.

3. *Taking a hot bath*

Surely nobody has ever decided
to go on a diet while in a tub.
The body is beautiful stretched
out there under water wavering.

It suggests a long island of pleasure
whole seascapes of calm sensual
response, the nerves as gentle fronds
of waterweed swaying in warm currents.

Then if ever we must love ourselves
in the amniotic fluid floating
a ship at anchor in a perfect
protected bloodwarm tropical bay.

The water enters us and the minor
pains depart like supplanted guests,
the aches, the strains, the chills.
Muscles open like hungry clams.

Born again from my bath like a hot
sweet tempered, sweet smelling baby
I am ready to seize sleep like a milky breast
or start climbing my day hand over hand.

4. *Sleeping with cats*

I am at once source
and sink of heat: giver
and taker. I am a vast
soft mountain of slow breathing.
The smells I exude soothe them:
the lingering odor of sex,
of soap, even of perfume,
its afteraroma sunk into skin
mingling with sweat and the traces
of food and drink.

They are curled into flowers
of fur, they are coiled
like hot seashells of flesh
in my armpit, around my head
like a dark sighing halo.
They are plastered to my side
a poultice fixing sore muscles
better than a heating pad.
They snuggle up to my sex
purring. They embrace my feet.

Some cats I place like a pillow.
In the morning they rest where
I arranged them, still sleeping.
Some cats start at my head
and end between my legs
like a textbook lover. Some
slip out to prowl the livingroom
patrolling, restive, then
leap back to fight about
hegemony over my knees.

Every one of them cares
passionately where they sleep
and with whom.
Sleeping together is a euphemism
for people but tantamount
to marriage for cats.
Mammals together we snuggle

and snore through the cold nights
while the stars swing round
the pole and the great horned
owl hunts for flesh like ours.

5. *Planting bulbs*

No task could be easier:
just dig the narrow hole,
drop in the handful of bone
meal and place the bulb
like a swollen brown garlic
clove full of hidden resources.

Their skin is the paper
of brown bags. The smooth
pale flesh peeks through.
Three times its height
is its depth, a parable
against hard straining.

The art is imagining
the spring landscape poking
through chrysanthemum, falling
leaves, withered brown lushness
of summer. The lines drawn
now, the colors mixed

will pop out of the soil
after the snow sinks from sight
into it. The circles,
the casual grace of tossed handsful,
the soldierly rows will stand,
the colors sing sweet or sour.

When the first sharp ears
poke out, you are again
more audience than actor,
as if someone said, close
your eyes and draw a picture.
Now open them and look.

6. *Canning*

We pour a mild drink each,
turn on the record player,
Beethoven perhaps or Vivaldi,
opera sometimes, and then together
in the steamy kitchen we put up
tomatoes, peaches, grapes, pears.

Each fruit has a different
ritual, popping the grapes
out of the skins like little
eyeballs. Slipping the fuzz
from the peaches and seeing
the blush painted on the flesh beneath.

It is part game: what shall
we magic wand this into?
Peach conserve, chutney, jam,
brandied peaches. Tomatoes
turn juice, sauce hot or mild
or spicy, canned, ketchup.

Vinegars, brandies, treats
for the winter: pleasure
deferred. Canning is thrift
itself in sensual form,
surplus made beautiful, light
and heat caught in a jar.

I find my mother sometimes
issuing from the steam, aproned,
red faced, her hair up in a net.
Since her death we meet usually
in garden or kitchen. Ghosts
come reliably to savors, I learn.

In the garden your ashes,
in the kitchen your knowledge.
Little enough we can save
from the furnace of the sun
while the bones grow brittle as paper
and the hair itself turns ashen.

But what we can put by, we do
with gaiety and invention
while the music laps round us
like dancing light, but Mother,
this pleasure is only deferred.
We eat it all before it spoils.

Jeff Tagami
NOW IT IS BROCCOLI

Greenfield Review Press; *Breaking Silence* (Asian American poets)—1983
Joseph Bruchac, Editor

My mother who loses a piece
of herself each day
is bowing before the conveyor belt
as a river of broccoli
rolls by under the fluorescent.
All night
at the canneries of J.J. Crosetti
she trims the yellow and bunches the green.
Trims and bunches.
Until the colors blend
and she is lost
before this river of one color
that is neither green nor yellow
and unable to hold it back
lets it slip past her.
She remembers, once, in another shed
slicing off part of her index finger.
It wasn't the pain
or horror she remembered
but how the day was hot
and the shade of the corrugated
tin roof bore down cool
on the back of her neck
and the metal click
of the spinning rollers
echoed in her ears
long after the crates had passed.
It wasn't the kindness
of the floor lady turning off the machine
that she wanted to remember—
the floor lady who would just as soon
bark at her like a dog.
It wasn't the concern
of the forklift driver who searched
between the chopped heads of cabbage
thinking the finger could be sewn back.
No, it was the face

she longed for, that serene
face she lost years ago.
A face the young woman
across from her now owned
who did not once look up from her work
who smiled
as if remembering a silly joke
or the slight tremble
of her boyfriend's lips
as he kissed her goodnight.
Now she keeps the finger in the freezer
in an envelope with a plastic window.
Because it is still a part of her
she cannot let go, like her man
who pickled her miscarriage
in a bottle of alcohol could not let go.
For two years
he kept it beside the bed.
Each night he held it up to the lamp
stroking the glass clear of his choked breath
as if to contemplate a son without future.
Finally, as if that bottle
could no longer contain his grief
he buried it beneath the porch steps
near the mint.
Now it is broccoli
and my mother must be careful
though she has given up forty years
to the passing of vegetables
though she knows the knife
and the fat clumsy fingers
that betray each other
though she knows
broccoli is only a river
through which we carve our simple life.
Her raised knife wavers in the air
while the colors go on playing tricks
with her eyes, and the nail
of her clipped finger
slowly turns black
behind the box of frozen peas
and ice cubes.

photo by Barbara Cech; *Dacotah Territory*, No. 16 (hotels & cafes)—1979
Mark Vinz, Editor

William Kloefkorn
ON THE ROAD

Dacotah Territory, No. 16 (hotel & cafe issue)—1979
Mark Vinz, Editor

for Michelle

Supper at Marlo's Cafe
in Watertown, South Dakota:
two strips of bacon
on a hamburger patty
rife with cheese,
all welded snug as rivets
to an unburned bun.

For two bits the jukebox
will do its best
to keep your mind
off your French fries:
O dropkick me, Jesus,
through the goalposts of life!

A hundred miles, more or less,
to Aberdeen,
where from an unscreened window
near the top of the Ward Hotel
the points of a deserted Spur Lounge
look like the Seven Heavenly Sisters
dressed fit to kill.

In front of the OK Tire Store
a trucker pullchains his air horn
until all of the geese
this side of the Badlands
take up the song.

Inside Room 500 the radiator
does a small unobtrusive dance,
melting the last of the snow on Channel 3.

The bedsheets smell of starch.

There is nothing any longer left to do
or undo.

So I think of my family,
of my wife,
of the four children, one by one,
of the first grandchild,
now 3.5 days old,
out of the hospital and at home now,
and at the edge of sleep

I see her guileless breath usurp the cracks
of her white small-slatted crib,
shaping then its charge
to outfox the keyhole:

on then beyond the melodic heft
of Marlo's Cafe
in Watertown, South Dakota,
to the Ward Hotel in Aberdeen,
to Room 500,
to the bed where nearer now to the edge of sleep
I welcome it to breathe it in
to breathe it out again,
and on and on.

O Michelle!
O infant far from everything but home!
On our long descent to sleep
we are all of us one family, after all,
and all alone.

Leonard Nathan
JUST LOOKING, THANK YOU

Cincinnati Poetry Review, No. 10—1983
Dallas Wiebe, Editor

And when suddenly it hit me
that I would never get taller
or wiser or learn Greek
or interpret birds for humans
or humans for humans, never
get the first prize or be kissed
for courage, never be more
than the third (if that) person
to be contacted in case
of an emergency or love,
only a guilty bystander
who didn't get the facts straight
and who envied the truly good
and the lucky,
      I was not sad,
merely a little relieved,
feeling the spirit warmly
dissolve in my flesh like soap
in bathwater, and the food
placed before me then,
even the mashed potatoes,
became intensely personal,
and the stars over my head
unimportant except
as somehow necessary
to the local situation,
and the wars abroad something
to measure indifference by,
and you, the same as always—
turned sidewise with your own
occult obsession, and I felt
like a man in a hiding place
from the wind, or like a shadow
of a rock in a weary land,
secure in the dry lull
or depression between cause
and effect, for whom eating

mashed potatoes was OK,
and OK also allowing
the birds to mean nothing,
the humans to mean whatever
they mean, or so I believe
I believe—and just looking,
thank you, just looking.

James Grabill
ARS POETICA

Bluefish, Vol. 1, No. 1—1983
Anselm Purlatore, Editor

The source unfolding bodily rhythm, impulse, local current
and grain, dreamtime sightings beneath workings,
the feel of a pattern, its content a species,
                              pacing,
passion and calculus of stalks, burrowings and thermal
makeup, infrared history, dock labor, how this developed,
that we developed, how grace comes in, that vision
transcends power, observes it, feels for it, sees around
it, to the planet holding it,
                    the webbings and links,
white shadows, crossings, sweltering magnetic extrapolation
edge that appears and disappears all over habits and speech
with northern lights, knowledge of an unknown working,
the wide moment, long afternoons, short weeks, lost hours,
the source unfolding
                    a future where buildings float,
angry drivers surrounded by red specks, blue light
back in night warehouses, the Blue Pearl that Muktananda
meditated on, became, observed, held bodily, working,
the blank of metals, smack of hammer, smack of needle,
smack on flesh curve, fields of Bach plants, fields
of the incline,
                to murky soundings from far off,
that are here in arcings, tiny curled hairs on the cloth,
the slippery tonguing, throbbing of the pod before opening,
mysterious centralia,
                    jays in the air, crows in each feathery
atom, herons of the crow breath, earthen breathing banks
of root brine with wiry fish in troughs of the sky passing
over knowing ledges, for the latent emissary, the poem
rising out of the earth and standing up into someone,
fathers who give another birth, mother who gives an earlier
bearing, birth where it is summer
                    and we dwell, the cows
in each stone, moth in the shade of a short pencil,
the crushed possum where cars have been, concrete
with its ear to the core, flash of Brazilia at night

driving into Portland,
                    what lets us have the space,
that silver coins overcome their need, that the lines
of force in an interval near the conveyor belt
are syllables in the word Dakota, how the bending trees
bend not in space but time, and we continue
through one another.

Bill Nelson, from *A Man In Stir* (1983), by Theodore Enslin
Pentagram Press; Michael Tarachow, Editor

Linda Gregg
GNOSTICS ON TRIAL

Graywolf Press; *Too Bright To See* (1981), by Linda Gregg
Scott Walker, Editor

Let us make the test. Say God wants you
to be unhappy. That there is no good.
That there are horrors in store for us
if we do manage to move toward Him.
Say you keep Art in its place, not too high.
And that everything, even eternity, is measurable.
Look at the photographs of the dead,
both natural (one by one) and unnatural
in masses. All tangled. You know about that.
And can put Beauty in its place. Not too high,
and passing. Make love our search for unhappiness,
which is His plan to help us.
Disregard that afternoon breeze from the Aegean
on a body almost asleep in the shuttered room.
Ignore melons, and talking with friends.
Try to keep from rejoicing. Try
to keep from happiness. Just try.

Ronald Koertge
THE THING IS TO NOT LET GO OF THE VINE
—*Johnny Weissmuller*

The Wormwood Review, No. 92—1983
Marvin Malone, Editor

Of course he is right, otherwise he would
not be Tarzan King of the Jungle, but Tarzan
King of the Emergency Ward.

But he is not right all the time. Like
the vine, his advice has an end. For him
it might be when Simba and Tantor grow immune
to yodels and he has to face the evil white
men alone. When Jane is old, her little
bark skirts no longer fetching. Or when
he is just tired, the trees seem taller
than before and every vine a python.

So there comes a time at the edge of some
sinister veldt when the thing to do is not
hold on but let go at the peak and fly
into the arms of the Ape Mother at whose
dark and leathery breast we rest content
at last knowing what it is we have been
all this time hurrying through the forest
toward.

drawing by Donna Dennis; *Oink!*, No. 17—1983
Paul Hoover & Maxine Chernoff, Editors

Les Standiford
GUERIN AND THE PRESIDENTIAL REVUE

Pawn Review, Vol. III, Nos. 1 & 2–1978
Tom Zigal, Editor

Age-aching Guerin, his doorman's blue and gold uniform gone slack at every seam, stared blankly at the letter in his hand while the elevator buzzed and buzzed at his ear. Someone on eight wanted to come down, but he didn't hear a thing. The letter was short, a few lines typed on stationery from a law firm with more partners than words in the message. "New owners," Guerin mumbled. "Mandatory retirement." The buzzer rang and rang again, a wasp caught in a bottle.

He cast his veined eyes out from the elevator cage to the calm lobby where no one ever sat. No one, that is, except an occasional wino or hoodlum. And Guerin had spent twenty-nine and 11/12ths years making sure there were very few such interlopers in the lobby of the Andrew Jackson. *His* building had maintained its reputation, even if the neighborhood had gone to pot. With his thin, darting body, his wild bush of white hair, his oddly formal speech, he had become a fixture. He was a doorman's doorman and had been since he could remember. He had prevailed implacably through six sets of lobby furniture and two major remodelings. He carried twice the seniority of the largest of the lobby plants. Yet suddenly, it was as if he had come down with the wilt or the black leaf fungus—he was on the way out.

A moving van pulled up across the street and Chauncey, doorman at the Van Buren there, saluted the truck smartly. Chauncey was, like Guerin, one of the few true doormen left in the neighborhood. He understood the importance of form. Standing at least six feet in his trim and lintless uniform with its bright buttons, he exuded style as well. He was what you looked for in a doorman, if you were looking for a doorman. Guerin smiled thinly at the letter in his hand. While unwelcome, the message was not a total surprise. He ignored the buzzer, which had become one unending whine, undulating waves of rage that pushed down an unknown finger on eight.

Guerin knew that the van would be carrying away, not dropping off. No one moved to the neighborhood these days. The Marshall, four doors down, was operating at 42% occupancy. The Garfield, at the corner, held 51%. The Harding, once the showplace of the area with its enormous lobby chandeliers and birdseye maple paneling, had become a Job Corps training center. The Taft, a massive building with the first heated swimming pool in the city, had been converted to public housing by the planning board. Fuentes, who had been retired as the Taft's doorman at the time of the conversion, confided to Guerin that the deal had been arranged. A member of the planning board owned a secret interest in the building and realized a handsome profit on the decaying property. "And now they dump egg shells and baby shit in the swimming pool," Fuentes had told him, for he maintained his tiny apartment in the basement of the building. "It is like murder. Her heart is broken."

Guerin had nodded in sympathy then, and he nodded again now as he thought of the embittered Fuentes. Not a great doorman, for he had been at it only ten years. But the man understood the key thing about buildings. Understood they had lives of their own, with feelings, varying moods, that they required care, yes, but most importantly, appreciation. Indeed, Fuentes recognized the spirit of the massive buildings, and it was a pity he had lived to see the Taft reduced to a shambles. Guerin avoided the park where he knew Fuentes would be found, slumped alone on a bench, cursing fate and the planning board alternately. He did not enjoy Fuentes's diatribes, for they had kindled a fear in himself. And now the fear had come to roost, he thought, as the buzzer whined at his ear.

"Hey man. Your buzzer ringin' right off the wall." The voice broke into Guerin's reverie, and he looked up quickly to find the urchin he had chased off the gold brocade couch a dozen times in the last week. The boy had poked his Afroed head through one of the swinging doors that flanked the main entrance, a grand revolving fan of a doorway where the child usually played. Or tried to.

"Please to remove your filthy hands from the glass," Guerin told him.

"Ain't you gonna answer that buzzer? What you get paid for if not?" The boy had stepped inside and Guerin could see the imprints of his hand on the doorway behind him. He would have chased him out and gone at once to wipe the glass clear, but now he was aware of the buzzer, which sounded as if it might burn out in a shower of sparks.

"No fooling around down here," he wagged his finger at the boy. "If anything is missing, I know who to come after."

"Hey man, I won't be messin' with none of the place. I just come in to be sure you on the stick, that's all." The boy hooked his thumbs in the beltless loops of his ragged jeans. He sported a t-shirt several sizes too large, emblazoned "Visit Virginia Beach" in faded red letters.

Not a bad idea, Guerin thought, as he pulled the door closed. He gave the boy one last frown, then punched the button for eight. The buzzing stopped and a calm settled into the cubicle of elevator. The tiny room glided smoothly up its shaft with an easy hum, and Guerin felt a momentary content. He was a mote traveling in the artery of the building, a permanent antibody in its blood, content to cruise forever if he could. And then he remembered the letter. News that he had anticipated in his worried moments, to be sure, but the letter made it so final, so abrupt, somehow.

The car stopped at eight, on an even keel with the floor of the hallway. It had not always been so easy. Not until they had installed the automatic system some years before. Up to that time, it had been a challenge to stop the box precisely even with the floor. It was also a mark of your true doorman, Guerin thought, an opportunity to display one's craft. Of course, there were the inevitable misses that even he was occasionally party to, followed by the embarrassing corrections and the exasperated sighs of the passengers anxious to step off or on, but by and large it was a chance to show your stuff. Now, you pushed a button and scratched your ear or your ass, if you wanted. A perfect stop, every time.

Mrs. Hereford was standing before the opened elevator doors, her face gone blood-red, her massive cheeks quivering with rage. "I...I...I..." she was saying.

"Good morning, Mrs. H.," Guerin said, his doorman's demeanor clicking on. "Your dress so becomes you, I thought it was someone else. From the television, I think." Guerin bowed as he spoke, ushering her into the elevator with a flourish of his braided cap.

Spittle trickled down the woman's chin, but she had already calmed. "You don't say so," she said, dabbing at her face with a lace trimmed hankie. "You don't mean it." She sighed involuntarily as she leaned her bulk against the back of the compartment.

Guerin punched the button marked for one, and turned to smile and nod at her, "Indeed. A perfect vision you are this morning."

The woman blushed a huge wave of a blush, and dropped her face into her fist. Guerin watched the dimples winking in her quivering arms. She was actually giggling now, and he knew she had already forgotten her wait. Mrs. Hereford was only sixty-four, but fading fast into senility. The demands of her massive body had surely starved her brain, he reasoned. Her husband had been dead for twenty years, a diving suicide from this very building. Shattered the front awning and sprayed the sidewalk for a hundred feet with every part of himself, Guerin recalled. He did not understand how she could stay there. Even he got queasy thinking about it.

The elevator settled with a pneumatic hiss, and Mrs. Hereford lumbered out, toward the swinging door to the left of the main entryway. She was far too large for the revolving door, a lesson learned in another painful episode. The fire department had been called to remove her, and Guerin had been hard pressed to keep photographers away from the scene. Thank God she'd been caught on the lobby side, he thought, for he had been able to exercise his authority to keep the reporters outside. One scandal was surely enough for any person.

When Mrs. Hereford was a step or two from the doorway, she saw him. The boy lounged in one of the massive arm chairs, blowing imaginary smoke rings from an invisible cigar which he tapped as he spoke. "Bring my car round to the front, Hey-soos. And tell the mad-damn that we ready."

"Oh my!" Mrs. Hereford said, beginning to wave her hankie at her throat. "Oh my goodness!!" She turned to Guerin, jabbing her free hand at the boy who did not acknowledge her presence.

"I think we be going to the club right now, Hey-soos," he said. "And then maybe we'll take in the polo game." His face beamed as he closed his eyes and tapped his ghostly ashes onto the champagne carpet.

"He's on the furniture," Mrs. Hereford gasped.

"Do not worry," Guerin told her as he hurried from the elevator.

"We got to be makin' it right away, Hey-soos," said the boy, who came suddenly alive and scurried toward the revolving door at Guerin's approach.

"I don't know how much longer I can put up with this," Mrs. Hereford said as the empty door snapped around and around before them. Guerin stood beside her, watching the boy dodge the traffic in the street outside.

"When Stanley was alive..." she began, and Guerin knew that the familiar story was on its way. She would tell him about her husband, a trader in commodities, who had predicted the invasion of the blacks and browns into the neighborhood. His scenario did not end there, however. He likened the United States to the Roman Empire, which he maintained had finally been toppled by the licentious influence of the dark princes of Northern Africa. Shortly before his death, Guerin had seen him outside the building distributing leaflets which quoted Shakespeare, St. Augustine, and Benjamin Franklin in support of his terrible fears. "... And he was right!" she concluded, sweeping her hand in the direction of the departing boy. "He just didn't have the heart to see it come true." She sniffled into her hankie and moved toward the door.

"Heart," Guerin repeated.

"My poor Stanley," Mrs. Hereford said.

As the huge woman pushed her way outside, Chauncey spun through the revolving door at her side. Mrs. Hereford glared at Chauncey, especially at his ebony skin.

"What's the matter with the wrinkle?" Chauncey asked as they watched the woman waddle toward the corner.

"Mrs. Hereford is grieving this morning her departed husband." Guerin was now wiping the handprints from the swinging door.

"What I got to do with her husband?"

"I couldn't say." Guerin phrased his answer so that it would not stand as a lie, technically. He liked Chauncey and did not like to see him upset. A doorman with trouble on his mind tended to forget little things, those *touches* which made all the difference.

"Well, we losing the Carters this morning," he told Guerin, lifting his cap from his greying, close-cropped head. "That's the sixth this month, and nobody moved in to take up the slack."

"The sixth," Guerin said, shaking his head sadly. He felt the crinkle of the letter at his breast pocket.

"Yeah. And I'll be missing old Mr. Carter, too. He used to slip me all those skin books when he was finished, that old sucker."

Guerin nodded. He thought of the Baxters, fifth floor, who dressed in black lingerie and carried on with whips and chains. Mr. Baxter's heart had given out in the middle of such a session one night and Guerin, of course, had been the first one called. He had plenty of time to inspect the bedroom of the Baxters, which looked to him like a torture chamber from a late night movie. Mr. Baxter was eighty-seven at the time of his death. His wife was twenty.

She stood by the bed, wearing only a garter belt, a glisten of perspiration still fresh on her swelling breasts. "What'm I gonna do bout this old fart," she drawled, her lips pouting. Guerin turned from her evenly tanned body to stare at Mr. Baxter's purple face. She had been a waitress at a coffee shop when Mr. Baxter bought her. *Bought* her. "Ten thousand in a special account. It's mine after six months," she whined to Guerin. "But he's sposed to be around to sign for it and now what?"

She brushed at a lock of bleached hair pressed to her damp forehead. Her lower lip quivered beneath her phosphorescent lipstick and her eyes pinched as if she would burst into tears at any minute. Just as well, Guerin had thought, a show of grief was the least anyone deserved.

"What's going to happen, Mr. G.? Where all the people going, anyways?" It was Chauncey speaking, wiping his brow as he stared at the movers who swarmed about the Mayflower van like ants.

"They are moving to the hills, I think," Guerin answered. The memory of Mr. Baxter's strangled face would not leave him. "But as to what will happen, I couldn't tell you." As he spoke he fingered the heavy stationery at his breast.

"Well, you got that social security if nothin' else, huh?"

But Guerin shook his head slowly, and Chauncey stepped back to look at him skeptically. "What you saying? Everybody has the social security!"

"No. No social security. I have none. I am paid by cash and no taxes." Even as he spoke, he remembered his youthful pleasure in the arrangement. Then, more cash meant more cash, period.

Meanwhile, Chauncey was shaking his head in disbelief. "Hoo-eeeee! You done messed up, then, Mr. G. You mean they giving you no kind of a pension plan?"

"No pension plan," Guerin said, and then he produced the letter for Chauncey to inspect.

Chauncey read the letter twice, tracing the text with his finger the second time, and then looked up at Guerin with narrowed eyes. "There was a man over to see me about a job last week. You might want to go see him."

"What job is that?" Guerin felt a hollow ring in his voice.

"It's standing outside one of those joints on the North Beach, hustlin'."

Chauncey dropped his eyes as he spoke, and Guerin turned away, feeling grey weather moving in.

*   *   *   *   *

The movers had slammed the doors on the van and Chauncey was standing near the curb, sending them off with a smart salute. The long blue tails of his double-breasted coat flapped in the breeze that usually came in the afternoon. Mrs. Hereford had returned from her daily trip to the grocery bearing another large sack of cat food. She kept a number of animals, "To quiet my memories," in her words. She also paid Guerin a little extra to carry the soiled litter to the basement and to keep news of the cats' presence from the owners. Guerin nodded as she passed and she smiled in return. "I'll take myself up, if you don't mind," she told him, and Guerin stepped back to his post inside the door. He was philosophic about the cats. If they made her feel better, why shouldn't he help her hide?

Everyone does the best he can, Guerin mused, most of the time, at least. And it had been his business to be there when there was a little slip, a breakdown in the functioning. It was part of being a doorman, he nodded, as he watched his counterpart across the street.

Chauncey spun deftly on his toes as the truck turned a corner, and walked with precise steps back into the Van Buren. Take care of what's left, Guerin thought. He fingered the brass buttons on his own coat absently, trying to imagine himself stationed outside a North Beach clip joint....

....where a thin, white haired man with watery blue eyes lifts a wrinkled hand at a passerby in a business suit. "Come in please, sir. We have the most wonderful women on the strip," comes the croaking voice.

The man in the business suit stops and turns, and it is Mr. Baxter, his face a ruin, as purple as it had been in death, his eyes bulging, his tongue a swollen beacon at his open mouth. "I'm looking for pain," the creature says. "A show with pain. Beating. Hurting. Sick, filthy things. I want good entertainment."

"We have it inside, Mr. Baxter. Please! We have the shows with the most lovely ladies on the strip." The crumbling doorman bends with a flourish, indicating the entrance of the club with a cat o' nine tails, which he holds in his hand. Mr. Baxter hurries in then, his eyes protruding wildly, his face glazed with a thin film of sweat.

Others are passing by, and the tiny man with the bulbous, veined nose and weary eyes begins to shuffle his feet, does a wing and a buck, balances the whip handle on his nose. A small crowd gathers, faces peering at him with death's head madness.

"Please to come inside now," the old man implores them.

"We want the finale," a voice calls from the crowd.

"Where's the rest of the act?" a woman's voice echoes.

"I'll finish it," says a huge man with a shaved head as he steps forward. He pulls a thin dagger from his belt and plunges it deep into Guerin's chest. The fount of red sprays over the crowd.

"I think I'm going to come," says a voice.

"Mmmmmmmmmmmmmmmmmmmm—good," says another.

"Some goddamn great show, huh?" smiles the bulletheaded man, turning to the crowd for approval. Guerin has sunk to the filthy sidewalk, the feet are scurrying past him, bored already with this act. . . .

He opened his eyes, then, and indeed there was a sharp pain blooming at his chest. He drove his hand quickly inside his coat and clutched at his heart. The pain sprung up in his hand at that motion, and he immediately calmed. It was a toothpick, left from lunch in his shirt pocket.

"Hey man, you not lookin' one bit good." It was the child from the street, whizzing in circles before his eyes. The boy had run the revolving door into a furious spin and now clung to one of the push bars, his feet drawn up off the tile floor.

Guerin recovered his breath gradually, then stepped toward the spinning door. He was about to reach out, to slow it down, but stopped suddenly, realizing he could break his arm easily. There was nothing to do but wait for the thing to die by itself. The boy closed his eyes and hummed the noise of an engine as he went. Guerin stood waiting and cursing himself for greasing the bearings so thoroughly.

When the door finally slowed, the boy released his grip and opened his eyes as he staggered drunkenly across the lobby. Guerin snatched him immediately by the collar of his t-shirt and marched him back toward the door.

"You better not be hurtin' me," the boy yelped, his eyes still vague from the whirl.

"There is no hurting," Guerin replied, pushing the swinging door open with his free hand. He was about to pull the boy out after him, when he heard the voice, a firm command at his ear.

"You better unhand my boy, white man!"

Guerin froze, his hand unclasping from the boy's shirt obediently. Carefully, he turned to find the mouth that had spoken the husky threat, and when he did, his ancient heart banged at his ribs. She was lovely. Her eyes perfect oval pools, even if a bit pinched in anger now. A thin nose, thin upper lip, with pouting lower, a smooth curve of chin. All framed by a tightly curled, cropped Afro that gleamed in the play of the lobby lights. Guerin's fright slid rapidly into awe.

"Your child...I mean...that is, he could have hurt himself..."

"No way I'll hurt myself ridin' a rocket ship!" The boy stepped between them, thrusting his chin forward. His mother turned her frown his way.

"I told you not to be playing on that door again." She looked back to Guerin, who was tracing the curves of her blue knit dress. Not exactly a model's figure, he was thinking, for it was a bit full in the breast, but her hips were slim and her legs delightfully tapered. By the time he forced his eyes to meet hers, her face had softened.

"I'm sorry," she said. "I didn't mean for him to be messing around here."

Guerin bowed his most gracious doorman's bow. "As I say, I would want nothing to happen to this fine boy."

"No boy around here!" The child was glaring at Guerin.

"Hush!" His mother took his shoulder and turned to leave. "You're in enough trouble right now."

Guerin racked his brain for small talk, anything to keep her there. "You are new to the neighborhood, I suppose?"

"And we'll be leavin' soon as we can, too." It was the child peering around his mother's legs.

"That's all I want to hear from you," she said, pointing an ominous finger. Then she turned to Guerin with a hint of a smile. "I'm sorry. I don't want him to be talking like that, but..."

"It is a hard world," Guerin broke in, his palm raised. He wanted to be helpful, agreeable. To *keep* her somehow. Her face was Christmas, her voice tower bells rolling down green hillsides.

"We've just moved into the Taft. And I appreciate your concern for my son." Her speech was precise, but there was also that throaty resonance. She turned to go once again, but Guerin called after her in an eager voice.

"Perhaps you are an actress?"

She stopped and looked back over her shoulder, her smile bloomed fully now. It seemeed a familiar pose to Guerin, who was sure now that he had seen her somewhere. "Well," she said, ducking her head slightly. "I have done a commercial or two."

And then she was gone, her hips winking as she led her son across the lobby, the sidewalk, the wide street toward home. Guerin stared after them until they had turned the corner where the Taft stood. There had been no ring on her finger where he'd feared there would be, and he stood wondering if he might find a potion to turn him young again. The flurry she had stirred beneath his ribs was a gift from the heavens. Such excitement came only rarely for him these days, and during the long dry spells he worried that he had become bereft altogether. In his younger days, he had been no stranger to the company of women, even if his responsibilities had kept him from marrying. Somehow he had always felt that he would find his ultimate comfort with women. They carried about them an eternal sense of promise, of possibility no matter what, and for that, Guerin was grateful.

"A lovely woman," he sighed, tracing the smooth curves of her face in his mind's eye.

"You got that right, Mr. G." Startled, Guerin looked up to find Chauncey at his side, grinning and bouncing on his toes. His counterpart had obviously been watching from the lobby of the Van Buren. Doormen missed very little, Guerin nodded, at least, your *true* doorman.

"And who *was* that vision of delight, my man?"

Guerin shrugged, affecting unconcern. "It is the mother of the child I am chasing from the lobby of this building every day."

"Better you let him come around as much as he wants," Chauncey said, shaking his head. "Or better yet, send him on over to my place."

A taxi glided to a stop in front of the Van Buren even as Chauncey laughed. Still, the man had hustled from Guerin's lobby and was across the street before the passengers had alighted from the cab. The grey in Chauncey's hair was surely premature, Guerin thought, rueing his own age again. Chauncey too was unmarried.

"I want to stay a lover," he once told Guerin. "And if I got married, then I'd have to be a fighter."

Perhaps it was good advice. Guerin's own was a more practical reason, however, After the accident in the mine, he alone was responsible. His mother sat in her chair and stared out the window, unblinking as the seasons came and went, and Guerin was responsible. Who else? He had sensed, though his mother never spoke after the word had reached her, that she was waiting by the window for his father to burrow back up from the bowels of the earth that had swallowed him and that she did not want to miss his emergence.

Thus, there had been nothing for Guerin to do but put his books away and go to work for the many years that she watched and waited. First, there was the rent for the small house and their food, and then, after he left for better work in the city, a sum to be sent for the woman who cared for her. And finally, a large sum due the hospital where she lingered her final weeks. There had always been just enough for all that, even though he'd promised her they'd be rich someday. Ah well, he thought. Ah well. There were other problems now.

The loss of his job, most especially. He'd been at it so long, he wasn't sure what to do now. Yes, there were plenty of agencies. State agencies and federal Manpower Development agencies and city agencies and private agencies of all kinds, fee paid and not. Fuentes had told him all about them a few months back. Fuentes had also told him about the number of jobs open to those with his particular background.

"They say to me, 'No one often calls for a seventy year old man with ten years doorman's experience.' So I tell them, I do any kind of work. And they say, 'You have to have a speciality,' and they keep me down as a doorman on the little card, I know, for nobody ever call."

Fuentes would be sitting in the small park near the Taft right now, talking to the pigeons, Guerin knew. The birds evidently felt compassion, for they clustered about him in unusual intimacy. Often they perched on his very shoulders, as if he were a monument to something, a crumbling statue who sometimes sneezed. Fuentes had finally been given a parttime job by the city planning board as the Taft's "Maintenance Advisor." He was to keep a list of problems as they developed in the building and to call them to the attention of the board's office, which in turn would inform the crews of maintenance men and janitors who traveled from building to building in the vast network of public housing.

"But they never fix nothing," he told Guerin. "They come and drink vino in the hallways and piss in the corners and laugh if I point to them the bulbs that burn up or maybe a stair where it breaks."

Poor Fuentes, Guerin thought. And then with a start he realized. Was it not "Poor Guerin" as well? With his shoulders sagging he walked slowly, cautiously, outside to make sure that no winos or hoodlums lurked in the evening shadows. The air had turned murky and tasted faintly sulphurous. Still, he stayed long enough to be sure there were no immediate threats to his building. Then, satisfied, he returned, set the locks that secured the lobby from all but the tenants with keys, snapped on the floodlights that washed the recesses of the building's perimeter, and finally, descended to the small apartment that was his, at least for the time being, in the cool bowels of the Andrew Jackson.

In his dreams, Guerin jumped from the clutches of one monster into the ready jaws of the next. A battalion of lawyers in identical pinstriped suits chased him through the vacant canyons of the city's streets and onto a pier, where they tied huge bundles of documents printed in an undecipherable language to his legs and cast him into the suffocating water.

He woke, flailing at his sheets, soaked with a perspiration that he first mistook for the sea. Then, no sooner had he lapsed back into sleep than he found himself naked on the stage of a smoky nightclub lit with purple floodlights. His genitals, nothing special in any case, had shrunken there into a tiny withered knot, and the patrons, the same faces who had cheered his death in another vision, howled now in derisive laughter.

He was chained upright against a large pillar, defenseless as Mrs. Hereford advanced toward him, her enormous sagging breasts shuddering with every step. In the wings of the stage, Chauncey stood in his doorman's uniform, a coiled whip in his white-gloved hand, apologetic expression on his face. "You gotta take work where you find it," he called to Guerin, as Mrs. Hereford sank to her knees. The crowd howled with delight as she ripped her teeth deep into Guerin's flesh.

When he woke, Guerin drove his hand between his legs, fearful she had taken everything. He lay with his heart pounding, the sheets wrapped like snakes at his trembling calves. This would not do, he realized, more exhausted now than he'd been when he retired. He would have to make provisions for his future, or he would be swept away in the night, sucked without a trace into one of the dreams which he feared were not dreams at all.

*   *   *   *   *

That afternoon, after Guerin had polished the brass on all the doors, twice chased away the child—whose name, he volunteered, was Alfie—carried down Mrs. Hereford's formidable bag of cat litter, and read and reread the letter of termination until the folds had begun to crack. Chauncey appeared in front of the Andrew Jackson, along with a thick-lipped man wearing a fedora pulled low on the brow.

"This is Mr. Max," Chauncey told Guerin. "He and I been carrying on a little business, so when he stopped by, I said maybe he'd talk to you. I said maybe you were just the man he needs."

"Numbers," Guerin blurted, the word springing out with its own volition.

Mr. Max's flat eyes snapped alert, suddenly. Guerin touched his own lips, wondering why he had said what he'd said. Mr. Max's grey cheeks had taken on twin points of pink. "What'd he say?"

Chauncey held his hand between them. "It's okay, Mr. Max." Then he turned to Guerin. "Keep your voice *down*, my man. Mr. Max is come to do you a favor."

"Favor?"

"This is the man who needs somebody out on the street. In North Beach, remember? You were saying you'd like to find out about it..."

"I said I would not..."

"Hey! Hold up now!" Chauncey turned to Mr. Max whose eyes washed up and down the busy street. He seemed anxious to move. "Hold on just one minute here, Mr. Max. I'll talk to him in private."

"I gotta be getting along," Mr. Max said, although Guerin could not detect movement at the man's lips. It was as if a ventriloquist, hidden somewhere nearby, powered the speech.

"It'll just take a second," Chauncey said as he led Guerin aside.

When they were out of earshot, Chauncey took Guerin's arm in a tight grip and began to whisper furiously. "Now listen, goddamnit! This is some very good bread we're talkin' about. Mr. Max *needs* us."

"Us?" Guerin said, glancing at the swarthy man who bounced nervously on his toes near the curb.

"Damn right, us! Mr. Max just bought the place and needs some people he can depend on. My job is to keep an eye on the crowd inside. You just get them in there in the first place. It's easy."

"But I've had dreams," Guerin protested.

"Dreams?" Chauncey's voice rose, incredulous. "*Dreams?*"

"More than dreams. Omens. I saw myself there, *in* such a place. There was danger. Men who would . . ."

"Dreams?" Chauncey was shaking his head. "Mr. Max is going to triple your salary and you stand there telling me about some *dreams?*"

"Triple? Three times?" The memory of Mr. Baxter's face, which had swum up with the thought of the dreams, began to fade just as rapidly from Guerin's mind. He needed to make provisions, did he not?

"Just to start," Chauncey replied, laughing. And then he turned to tell Mr. Max they'd be there, as scheduled.

*   *   *   *   *

At eight the next evening, Chauncey clattered up to the front of the Andrew Jackson in a pickup he had borrowed from a friend who held the maintenance contract at the Harding. The bed was filled with clattering mop buckets and empty drums which had held various cleaning fluids and acids.

"Not exactly a Cadillac, is it?" Chauncey spoke as Guerin climbed stiffly inside. Guerin wore his only suit, a double-breasted model he'd owned for many years, dark grey with smudged pinstriping, and he looked doubtfully at the grimy seat before he finally settled. Chauncey sat on a towel, protecting his own light blue leisure suit with its ivory buttons and smart white piping at the pockets. The collar of a navy satin shirt lay smoothly upon the lapels of his jacket, and a dark tuft of hair curled at his open neck. The grey had disappeared from his temples, and Chauncey laughed at Guerin's stare.

"You don't have to be a Greek to use Grecian Formula," he grinned, tapping his brown cheek.

"It's quite a transformation," Guerin agreed, fingering the tiny knot of tie at his own throat. The contrast in their dress had only further depressed him. He was certain he was making a mistake.

"Well, you're not lookin' half bad your own bad self," Chauncey said, even as his eyes flicked from the ancient suit to the bright red tie.

Guerin had retrieved the thing from the discarded effects of Mr. Baxter soon after the man's death, but he had never worn it before this evening. Though it made him thicktongued himself each time he thought of its original owner, Guerin had had no choice. He could find no other tie in his room. Moreover, he had encountered great difficulty in fashioning a knot which did not seem to strangle him, and even now he worked uncomfortably at its tension.

"Did you lock up early, like I said?" Chauncey glanced at Guerin, guiding the truck out into the traffic with one hand draped easily over the wheel.

"Yes. As you suggested." Guerin felt a great sense of guilt descend on him as he spoke. He had never, never in his nearly thirty years, left his building early. He was certain that some one of the tenants would notice. Surely, someone might even complain to the new management.

"Well, don't be sitting there worrying about the new owners," Chauncey said. "You already been fired, so they can't fire you again."

Guerin pondered the wisdom of Chauncey's statement for a moment. "True, but there is always the matter of a good reference. Many employers will want to ..."

"Mr. Max don't ask for any reference but mine." Chauncey smiled as he cut off the debate, then whipped the pickup through a sudden opening to the right and drew it to a noisy halt in front of the Taft. Immediately, two sacks of water plummeted from an upper floor, exploding near the fender of the truck. A rotted cabbage thudded off the hood, followed by a jagged brick which crashed into the bed.

Chauncey thrust his head out the truck's window and craned his neck toward the building's dark roofline. "Mr. Max wouldn't like that shit!" he shouted, and the barrage ceased. He pulled his head back in, grinning. "I told you we be joining up on the right team, Mr. G."

Guerin nodded slightly. "And what reason has brought us to the Taft, to come back to the point?"

"Why, the vision, my man. We have come to pick up the vision." Chauncey was beaming as he spoke.

"Vision?"

"Yeah, the vision. That A-number-one delicious lady who was knocking at your door a few days back."

Guerin felt a sinking in his stomach. "Surely you haven't deceived a woman of ... of ... some quality into ..."

"You mean class, Mr. G. Class. That little lady has class. Mr. Max is always on the lookout for class. One look at her and he gave me the word. 'Sign it up,' he said. 'Find out what it takes and sign it up.' "

"But she seemed to be different in some way. It was as if she ..."

Again, Chauncey broke him off. "Listen here, Mr. G. Lola in there is twenty-nine years old despite what her face says today, and her old man gone off on a terminal nod. Which leaves her and that kid with nobody payin' the rent, and every day that goes by moving her on over the hill. Twenty-*nine*, Mr. G. In her game she's almost a wrinkle. We just doing her a favor, that's all." Chauncey paused to glare at him. "So now how about holdin' up on all this bleeding heart stuff, huh? Mr. Max is helping *every*body out."

They sat silent then, until she walked out, a vision indeed in the cool evening air. The glare from the lobby lights shadowed her face and cast a glow about her closely cropped hair. The dress she wore was silklike, and tight at the breast and hip. But when Guerin alit to hold the door for her he noticed the heavy makeup at her eyes and cheeks. The artificial lashes made her look sleepy, and a little sad as well. He wanted to dab at the makeup with his handkerchief, but instead he managed a smile.

"Let's get it on," she said in her husky voice as she climbed aboard.

"Right you most definitely are," Chauncey said, and he stomped the accelerator to the floor.

They had to circle the block near the club several times before Chauncey spotted an opening in a delivery zone. He propped the "Cleanup in Progress" sign in the window and they walked quickly along the busy sidewalk to the place which had been named, as Guerin read in cursive neon, *Diablo*.

It was flanked on the right by a deserted coffeehouse with an ancient advertisement for Peter, Paul and Mary still dangling in its grimy window. On the left side of the club was a brightly lit storefront with revealing magazine covers filling one window, and a welter of sexual devices strewn in the other. In one corner, Guerin could make out a mailed fist attached to a suit of armor clutching a large rubber cast of a penis. Protruding just behind the foreskin was a thin blade of razored steel which gleamed in the blinking red neon like the fin of a murderous shark.

Guerin felt his knees going weak. His breathing became labored and sweat broke out on his brow. The visor on the suit of armor was slowly lifting, and he could see the swollen features of Mr. Baxter glowing purple behind the mask's opening. The red tie closed into a knot at Guerin's throat. He closed his eyes and had begun to sink to the pavement when Chauncey caught his arm and pulled him roughly through the door of the club.

"This is your last shot, Mr. G." Chauncey's voice hissed in his ear. "This is incredible money for a guy in your position. Now quit jackin' around!"

Guerin nodded then, and mopped at his face with his sleeve. As his eyes adjusted to the dim light, he could make out the waitresses moving from table to table in diaphanous gowns trimmed in ostrich feathers.

Their breasts and thighs loomed like shallow reefs beneath the blue haze of their dress, and Guerin felt a lump rising in his throat. Their hair was wrought high on their heads and jewelry dripped from their ears and throats and wrists.

"Mr. Max runs a class operation," Chauncey whispered loudly to Lola, careful that Guerin should overhear. Lola nodded slowly, but Guerin was sure he saw her wince. At any rate, she would not meet Chauncey's eyes. On the small stage behind the bar, a thick green light bathed a woman who was inviting intercourse with an incredibly endowed dwarf. She had bent over backward at the end of a low bench, her eyes rolling toward the invisible ceiling as her hands beckoned to the leering figure before her. He was moving in like an eager sailor on his short bowed legs when Guerin turned away.

Mr. Max had arrived and was bent in close conversation with Chauncey. He looked up from time to time at Lola, who stared back with blank eyes of her own. "Younger," Guerin heard the man say once, though he could not see the lips move. And then, while he could not be certain, he thought he heard the word "Pigtails."

Chauncey all the while was nodding, nodding, nodding. And finally they turned together to stare at Guerin. Mr. Max shrugged and looked skeptically at Chauncey, who whispered quickly in the man's ear. Then, Chauncey beckoned and Guerin stepped up to them.

"Mr. Max wants for you to bring them inside," Chauncey told him. "He wants you to rap to the Johns on the street so they get curious. Once they come through that door, you don't worry. Right?"

"What am I to say? To make them curious?"

"Tell him I say to use his imagination," Mr. Max seemed to say, though Guerin saw no movement at his lips. The man's eyes roamed Lola's body. "Tell him I say to get them inside, I don't care what he tells."

Chauncey turned to Guerin. "Mr. Max says that a doorman of your class and experience will know what to do."

"And tell her how to dress," Mr. Max added liplessly, gesturing toward Lola. Behind them, the woman on the stage had begun to groan even though the dwarf was still a foot outside her.

Chauncey swallowed quickly and turned to Lola. "Mr. Max says, would you like to come to the dressing room now?" Lola shrugged and moved away after them. Guerin took one last look toward the writhing woman on the stage and struggled quickly outside.

As he stood uncertainly on the sidewalk, Guerin heard the muffled roar of the crowd rise in counterpoint to the wails and shrieks of the woman on the stage. He had not uttered a word to the passersby, but a number of men and even women had already entered, drawn by the noises which escaped the doorway. Across the busy street he could see another club with a crowd gathered at its front. "El Gato Mambo," blinked the neon script above the milling group. The pitchman, who stood above the crowd on a small platform, was wearing a turquoise cocktail gown, its neckline cut to the pit of his hairy stomach. The man had curled his medium-length hair, and snakelike bangs fell onto his flushed brow. He had rouged his cheeks heavily and there was a wide gash of bright lipstick at his twisting mouth.

"We got the young stuff inside," he called, his eyes rolling and his tongue tracing his bright lips. "Kiddies! Hey! The whole world wants a twelve year old!"

There were shouts of agreement from the crowd and he turned to pull a cord that dangled from the marquee. A curtain drew back from the window then, and the crowd pressed closer. Guerin saw a pair of identical twins smiling out from behind the glass. Their breasts were nothing more than boys' nipples, and at his distance he could see no hair at their thighs. The two had turned to embrace when the pitchman pulled the curtain closed again. A groan of disappointment rose from the crowd, and the hustler smiled a vicious smile, ushering hordes of them through the smoky entrance.

Guerin staggered back against the window of the deserted coffeehouse, then, and at the same time a voice asked wetly at his ear, "What you all got inside there, pops?"

Guerin was dazed. His breath was shallow and his sight seemed to be dimming. The chemical smell of the air was choking him. He looked for the face of the speaker, but the face was masked in shadows from the storefronts. Then, unbidden, the words tumbled from Guerin's lips.

"Beautiful women. Pain. Lovely bodies. Blood. Sharp teeth. Razors. Whips and knives." As Guerin listened in horror to his own litany, the shadowy figure made eager grunting noises deep in its throat as it hurried inside the club. Guerin reeled back toward the street, grasping a parking meter for support as his head whirled.

Traffic had jammed the street before him, taxis jockeying with the ornate El Dorados of the pimps for positions near the curb. A Rolls Royce painted electric green crawled slowly by, its windows blanked by silver one-way glass. A small camera rose from the car's top as Guerin watched, and its blank eye made slow revolutions of the scene around them. As the car drew abreast of him, Guerin saw something trailing from the closed rear door. He thought at first that someone had caught the hem of a gown there, but when he looked closer he saw that it was hair, wet and matted with some dark substance.

He opened his mouth to cry out then, but hesitated, looking around him. Cry out to whom, he thought. A drunk collapsed over the hood of a car nearby, mumbling incoherently. A man staggered toward him from the dark reaches of the block, his white face a beacon in the distance. As Guerin watched, the man leaned against a parking meter with one hand and worked at his lifted foot with the other. Finally, he raised his shoe and turned it upside down. A stream of blood poured out, spattering darkly on the pavement. The man cast a murderous glance Guerin's way, and Guerin kept his own face averted until the spectre had crossed back into the shadows.

"Dreams, eh?" He spoke derisively to his wrinkled hands. "Hah!" When he raised his head, the green Rolls had disappeared in the endless river of traffic. Strange that he had almost called for help, he thought, in this place or any place. In his thirty years at the Andrew Jackson he had learned, above all else, not to cause alarm. *He* was the one paid to take care of trouble and to keep the police away at any cost. Perhaps he *was* getting old. After all, he had learned well when to look the other way, and when to lend a hand lifting the mysterious bundle into the trunk of an idling limousine. He knew as well the gouge under the ear that would lift a drunk in speechless agony and the piercing gaze and nod that would chase the junkie without a scene. Nothing surprised him in his post at the Andrew Jackson. The crumbling of the neighborhood had only increased the call for his craft. "Oil on troubled waters," as Chauncey had put it. "We're the necessary men."

Surely, then, there was no reason to feel as troubled as he did in this place. It was simply the stuff of his old job writ large. He could learn to feel at home. Especially at three times the pay. At his age, he should be grateful. Chauncey was right. Mr. Max was a man to take one's ease from. He nodded, and the visage of Mr. Baxter swam into view, nodding his agreement as well.

"Slime. Curve of thigh. Beatings. Emerald eyes. Razor slashing." The words flew from his mouth then, and hurrying bodies lunged through the door of the club.

Across the street, the pitchman for El Gato Mambo raised his voice in competition. "We've got DEATH. Actual DEATH, ladies and gentlemen. Actual murder on film from Argentina. YOUNG death!" Several cars stopped immediately in the near lane of traffic, their occupants rushing through the door of the club. The pitchman smiled at Guerin then, calling across the clamor of the traffic and the gathering crowds. "Now top *that*, honey! Can you top *that*?"

Guerin nodded slowly, talking to himself now. Yes. Yes, we can top that. We *could* top that. Here, we could top it if we wanted. Just a word to Mr. Max. And as he thought of it, the hand fell sharply on his shoulder.

He spun, expecting at last a bulletheaded man with a thin stiletto poised. Ah well, he was ready. He expected it now, this end. So let it come. And when he opened his eyes, he found Chauncey.

"You doin' just fine, Mr. G. They been pouring in." Chauncey smiled and clapped his shoulder.

"So our employer, he is satisfied, eh?" Guerin knew his own face was slack, despite the pounding of his heart.

"Well, yeah, he's okay. I mean he's never really *happy*, you know? But he says you're doing okay."

Guerin nodded as Chauncey continued. "It's like he told me, he owes us something. And Mr. Max always pays a debt."

"Us?" Guerin looked closely at Chauncey.

"Well, sure. I mean, I been doing just fine with the numbers, you know, and when Mr. Max put you out of business there at the Jackson..."

"I think I do not understand," Guerin broke in, raising his palm to stop Chauncey, who turned left and right to make sure no one was near.

He leaned closer and whispered fiercely in Guerin's ear. "Well who did you think bought up your building, my man? Mr. Max needs to *diversify*."

"Diversify?" Guerin repeated as Chauncey moved away from his ear.

"Sure. Mr. Max and his partners. They been moving into some things you wouldn't believe. Apartments. Sporting goods. Things like that." Guerin stared at the man, wondering if he could trust the words. "And you know what's next?" Chauncey's voice dropped to a confidential whisper once again as Guerin shook his head. "Hospitals! There's your *big* money."

"Hospitals," Guerin repeated dumbly.

"No cost control. Plenty of cash flow. Junkie doctors. Nurses on the hustle. Medicare. Blue Cross." Chauncey's eyes were bright. "We joined the right team, Mr. G." Guerin nodded slightly and Chauncey started for the door, then paused. "Oh yeah. I wanted to tell you. Lola's goin' on here in a minute. You might want to catch a bit of it."

Guerin stared after the departing Chauncey until the door of the club had swung shut. So there it was, eh? Mr. Max, the new owner of the Andrew Jackson. And, so it seemed, the Van Buren. Perhaps he had also swung the deal for the Taft. And how many others? Ah well, Guerin thought. Ah well. What did it matter? If not Mr. Max, then surely someone else. But still, he was bothered. Three times the salary and he could not rid himself of the nagging feeling.

He had felt no strain looking the other way for Mr. Baxter or Mrs. Hereford or for any of the rest of them all these years. Never had it bothered him as it bothered him now. And he could not say why. He was a doorman's doorman, and he had simply switched doors, hadn't he?

The roar of the crowd rose inside and Guerin knew that she had appeared. They were applauding that freshness that he knew would be visible, even in the thick red or blue or green light they had cast upon her. *Especially* in that light. You could not fool such a crowd. They appreciated innocence.

"Smooth cheekbone. Shattered eyesocket. Fragrant hair. Icepick. Face acid." The words tumbled from his lips and the passersby turned sharply and rushed in. Guerin walked slowly to the curb to watch the traffic pass, his heart groaning with each step. He leaned against a pole there, the traffic and the crowd a dull roar in the distant background. The tie was a stranglehold at his throat. He knew he could not loosen it. He felt a kind of satisfaction as it tightened, in fact. Mr. Baxter's face loomed before him, smiling his tongue-swollen smile. Guerin nodded, waved a greeting to the man, wondered what they'd find to do together. He smiled as his breath grew ever shallower. Perhaps there *was* a retirement spa waiting somewhere for him. A garden of unearthly delights. A line from a shampoo commercial, wasn't it?

And then, as he sunk toward the center of that dream, he saw it from the last corner of his sight, the dart of familiar figure through the traffic. At first he thought that it was the dwarf from the club, but immediately he corrected himself.

"You lookin' like death warmed over," the boy called. "You have to be sneakin' up on your pillow to catch any rest!"

The boy was heading for the door of the Diablo, Guerin realized, and he pushed himself with a great effort from the pole. "You will not go inside," he croaked, his voice slowly returning.

"If I rode that nasty truck bed all the way down here, I can stand it in there," he answered, easily outdistancing Guerin's feeble pace to the entrance.

By the time Guerin arrived inside, the boy had disappeared in the milling crowd. He spotted Chauncey, however, who stood by a glowing cigarette machine, surveying the packed house with his lips pursed and his nead nodding, nodding, nodding with satisfaction. Guerin elbowed his way to the man and grabbed him by the arm.

"The boy," he said breathlessly. "The boy has come in here."

Chauncey looked down at him casually. "What boy is that?"

Gesturing frantically, Guerin drove his eyes past Chauncey to the stage where Lola, dressed up as a giant Raggedy Ann, knelt before the bulk of a huge man in a gladiator's costume.

"Her son! It is her son! The child from the lobby!"

Chauncey shrugged. "So?"

At that moment, the gladiator swung a gloved backhand at the woman, whose red pigtailed head snapped away toward the crowd. Blood and the white nuggets of teeth sprayed over those nearest the stage, and a howl of joy rose in the packed club. Chauncey lifted his arm to restrain Guerin.

"Don't get all worked up. It's just like in the movies. She keeps all that stuff hid in her mouth."

Guerin pulled furiously from Chauncey's grip and plunged into the crowd, but Chauncey only laughed. "Hey Mr. G.," he called. "Don't get hot. I'll talk to Mr. Max. Maybe we can work the kid into the act."

Guerin tried to shut his ears, tried also to forgive his friend. It was the place, surely. Meantime, Mr. Baxter's tie had tightened at his throat until he thought he could no longer breathe, and he struggled to loosen the knot that had turned to steel beneath his fingers. His hands had begun to sweat with his exertion, and as he looked down to guide his fumbling fingers, he crashed into a gowned waitress who carried an enormous tray of drinks. Straws, fruit, ice, and a wave of brownish liquid engulfed the nearby tables, and angry shouts winged Guerin's way.

Guerin mopped at the gown of the waitress, whose heavily made-up face glittered with the wreckage of the drinks. "Clumsy, fucking sonofabitch," she hissed in a razored voice.

"Please. I'm sorry. Have you seen a small boy?" Guerin pleaded, dabbing at her face with an ancient handkerchief he had drawn from the breast pocket of the suit.

"You get that across the street, dumbjohn." The girl brushed Guerin's hand away and bent to recover her tray.

"But I don't understand. I saw ..."

"You get the young stuff across the street. Boys or girls either one." She glared at him, her voice fallen from anger into boredom. She was pulling at the thin gown which had pressed itself to the plane of her perfect chest.

"No! Please. You don't understand. I do not want such a young boy as that. I am looking for a child who has run inside this very place." He paused, searching for the words. "Listen. I am the doorman for this club. The doorman!"

At last a glimmer of concern crossed the woman's face, and she nodded as she bent to check her gown. "Right. He didn't *pay*. I'll keep an eye out, okay?"

Guerin sighed and cast his eyes over the sea of faces. On the small stage the gladiator drove his knee into the face of Lola, whose pigtails flew high with the jerk of her head. The crowd roared its approval.

"Please," Guerin caught her arm. "If you see him, a small one, also black, and wearing a t-shirt ..."

"Right. I'll tell him he's gotta pay up or get out," she winked at Guerin then, and was gone in the crowd.

No help, Guerin thought. Was there *no* help? The air was even thicker now with smoke and his eyes began to burn and blur. A rough hand swept him aside, and his leg cracked sharply against the edge of a chair. "You think I got X-ray vision, grandpa?"

Guerin swung to find the complaining face, but could see only vague shadows. His lungs felt as if they would burst, and his leg throbbed.

The gladiator had jerked Lola upright by her slender arm and now pulled her head back by her own hair. A fat man wearing the discarded red wig jumped up and down before the stage, his mouth working frantically.

"Bones!" he was screaming. "Smash bones!"

And then, as the stage spotlight switched from blue to yellow and grew a bit in size, Guerin saw the boy, alone at a small table in the front row. A waitress was bending near him, placing one of the tiny clip-joint bottles of beer on the table top before him. As she turned to leave, the boy winked and patted her swelling hip through the thin gown.

A hand grasped Guerin's arm then, and he turned to see a bespectacled thin man in a tweed coat, carrying a note pad.

"I'm doing a paper," the man said in a high voice. "And I'm curious to know why you, a senior citizen, would frequent such an establishment as this?"

"I do not frequent," Guerin told him, shaking the insistent hand from his arm. "I have business just now."

"Well, yes, many of my respondents have made it very clear that they do not come often, but I..." The voice droned on, but Guerin had turned back toward the child, and began to wade through the tightly packed tables.

"Hurt! Oh, hurt! Hurthurthurt!" cried the fat man wearing the red wig. The gladiator smiled down at the crowd. The boy stared up at the spectacle on the stage, beer bottle poised in his hand.

"I heard you ask the waitress for a young man," the man in the tweed coat called after Guerin. He smiled shyly and lowered his voice when Guerin turned. "If you'd just spend a few minutes with me on these questions, then maybe you and I could go somewhere and..."

"HURT BAD!!" screamed the fat man.

And Guerin exploded.

"There is no more hurting!" Guerin commanded, first to the man in the tweed coat, and then in a shout that carried to the man in the red wig. "THERE IS NO MORE HURTING!!"

Surprised by Guerin's cry, the gladiator swung about, pulling Lola to face the table where the boy sat.

"Hey! That's my momma!" the boy cried, and the bottle crashed to the floor from his frozen hand. His eyes locked on the eyes of Lola, who struggled through her own shock onto her knees.

"Honey, it's just pretend," she cried, her mouth twisted. The boy bent forward.

"Pretend?" He was shaking his head, trying to clear it, as from a blow.

"Like the wrestlers. On television." Her eyes were pleading.

"Break something. Cut something!" The fat man had recovered from his surprise. The gladiator nodded and swung a heavy mace in a tight circle above his head.

"You see, I'm researching the effects of Watergate-related social disintegration on our mores." It was the man in the tweed coat, his hand stroking Guerin's thigh, where the collision with the table still pained him.

"You're not really hurtin'?" the boy asked, and Lola shook her head, smiling.

"And there's good money in it?" The boy's expression had begun to soften.

"ENOUGH, I SAY!" Guerin shouted, and he leaped onto the stage, snapping the tie with one enraged slash of his finger. The crowd applauded, suspecting some new twist in the act. The gladiator looked at Guerin with mild surprise, but shrugged and massaged his gloved fist, uncertain how to respond.

"Get him off!" The voice of Mr. Max cracked and echoed through the crowded room, and Guerin, the gladiator, and Lola looked quickly down at the figure of the owner who stood jabbing his thick finger toward them. Just behind him was Chauncey, who struggled forward, waving Guerin off the stage with frantic motions.

"He's not supposed to be there!" Mr. Max called to the gladiator, and for the first time, Guerin thought he could detect a twitch at the man's swollen lips.

"Too bad for you," the gladiator said with a smile, his eyes measuring Guerin's thin frame.

"You shouldn't have come up here," Lola said, her eyes worried.

"Look out for *your* poor ass!" the boy called.

"Crush things! Rip things!" the fat man called. "Throw parts out here!"

"I'd like to get a question in, if you don't mind," the tweed man was saying. He tried to climb onto the stage, but the gladiator caught him in the chest with a kick that split the microphones with its cracking.

"Mr. G., you gonna mess up a sweet deal." It was Chauncey, pleading as he struggled close to the stage.

"Enough hurting," Guerin said, to everyone. He spread his arms to the crowd and called it louder. "Enough hurting!" But the crowd roared its disapproval.

"Get him offa there!" Mr. Max shouted, and the gladiator finally sprung into action, making a wild rush at the thin, white haired man.

It was a frozen moment, as Guerin would describe it later. The man in the gladiator suit spun toward him, but there was plenty of time. There always had been. The scene's pace seemed to slow to that of an intricate replay for a sports highlight.

Chauncey turned his head, afraid to watch. Lola too averted her eyes. The boy looked on eagerly, however, ready for whatever happened next. Mr. Max also watched calmly, his orders given now. The man in the tweed coat twitched on his back beside an overturned table. The fat man jumped up and down, but slowly, as if there were a trampoline beneath him. He held his groin with both excited hands and squealed. Then, all the faces in the crowd pressed forward in a languid, uniform movement, as if a silent wind had pushed them so.

Even Mr. Baxter's face swam into focus then, above a front row table. He raised a glass and winked a vein-exploded eye at Guerin. Somewhere at the fringes of the crowd danced a small figure, Fuentes perhaps, waving a blue pennant emblazoned in white: "GO BROOKLYN DODGERS."

At a table in a quieter section Guerin saw that the Presidents had gathered, the bearded Garfield, bald and phlegmatic Van Buren, portly Taft, puzzled Harding, and of course, Jackson, with his white shock of hair and stiff collar. And Justice Marshall was there as well, though he had been given a table of his own, off to one side, and presumably at Jackson's request.

Guerin knew his mother had come in too, though he could not spot her as he looked, and his father was out there as well, though his coal-blackened face would be hidden in the dark shadows of the further reaches.

All of them were there, watching. Anxious to see how he would do. Appropriately so, Guerin thought, as the gladiator clomped his ponderous, threatening steps across the stage. A retirement party, though of strange complexion, to be sure. Or was it something else?

Thirty years with the company honored here tonight. The glorious past summoned up to view, to *meet*, the present at this momentous instant. The words rose in a cartoon bubble from Chauncey's plead-

ing face: "Don't fight it, Mr. G. We're all in the same pot, cookin'!"
The black man's arm swept slowly around the crowded room.

Yes indeed, Guerin thought, yes indeed. They had gathered, but primarily to be sure he could still do his part of the job. He could explain it to Chauncey another time. This was *his* moment, meanwhile. His eyes had fixed on the figure dancing at the fringe of the crowd, waving and thrusting with the pennant of the ancient team. Indeed, it was Fuentes, and the banner carried good advice. And with that, Guerin realized suddenly and with absolute certainty that he would always have his place, Mr. Max or no. That he had merely to insist upon it. And so he took the advice of the waving pennant and made a step aside, and the action resumed its normal pace.

The gladiator roared past Guerin with the haywire momentum of a careening truck. The retiring doorman extended the foot of his uninjured leg and caught the gladiator's ankle. At the same time he gave him a vigorous clap on the beefy back. One did not spend thirty years as a doorman and not know when to get out of the way.

Guerin smiled at the thought, as the gladiator exploded through the flimsy backdrop of the stage and crashed into what sounded like truckloads of stored trays and glassware dropped suddenly from the edge of an endless cliff. Though they were no longer visible, Guerin was certain that the Presidents and the Parents had heartily cheered.

He blinked his eyes, then, for the houselights had come on fully and the patrons were milling out, mumbling their disappointment. A man seated where the visage of Mr. Baxter had swum was pitched face down on the drink-puddled table. The man in tweed had disappeared, the pages of a shredded notebook littering the floor nearby. Mr. Max was also nowhere to be seen, though Guerin could sense his beady stare from some dark corner.

"I have to thank you, I think," Lola said as she took his arm. Her free hand traced her swelling lip, where the gladiator had misjudged a bit.

"We *all* be moving into the Taft, now!" Chauncey said, shaking his head.

"We lost out on some good bread for sure," the boy agreed. "But my man abso-*lute*-ly handled that wrestler dude."

Guerin looked up from the boy's bright face in embarrassment, then caught a last figure moving toward the door. For a moment he thought it could be Mr. Max, but it was in fact the pitchman from the El Gato Mambo, who raised his blond wig like a cap in salute.

"A fine show, honey!" he called as he left. "One of the best *I've* seen."

Guerin bowed then, thinking of it as a curtain call, and Lola and the boy delivered applause that was thin, but sweet in his ears. Indeed, the retirement letter still crackled in his breast pocket, and the sulphurous presence of Mr. Max loomed in the further shadows; but on the other hand, he had closed *this* show, and worry could wait for another day.

As he nodded to himself, the last cloud of smoke trailed through the door, a kind of ragged pennant against the chaos of the street out there; and close behind, Guerin urged their tiny group on.

Dorothy Allison
WHEN I DRINK I BECOME THE JOY OF FAGGOTS

Long Haul Press; *The Women Who Hate Me* (1983), by Dorothy Allison
Jan Clausen et al, Editors

When I drink I become
                the joy of faggots.
I try not to drink too often.
When I was younger I couldn't drink at all.

I have grown into this joy
this sense that the night is full of possibilities
conversation an art that can be perfected
with gesture and ease and a glass in the hand.

When I was young I said I would be a writer
    with no sense what it could mean
    how hard it would be.
My friends talked sympathetically
of another friend from Texas
who had driven to Florida in an antique car
who was known for how charmingly he could weep.

A Writer, a Poet, he would drink and talk to me
of how all the men at school wanted to fuck him
of his desire to leave them at the pavement edge
knowing they would remember and want always
his car,   his tears,   his ass,   his poems.

Sensitive,
everyone was sure he was sensitive.
He told me how when his roommate stood
silent over his bed,
he reached up, slapped him,
slapped him again.

"He wanted me, you know."
I knew.

His roommate used to talk of how he resisted it
the desire, the burn for a beautiful boy.
A scholar of greek and latin and buggery

138

when he drank he became foolish
his moustache hanging damp.

"I wanted him, you know."
I knew.

In the middle of the night I dream
old friends and lechery.
Since I do not drink, I burn.
Is this what everybody knew that I didn't?
how desire and denial roll in the glass?
how the fire, the fire consumes?

She had hands with fingers like tapers
lean legs, dark hair, a car.
Everywhere I saw that car
just the briefest flash of her
hair, legs, fingers and gone.
Sensitive,
God, she knew she was sensitive
and when I stood over her
she slapped me with the delight of a boy.

"I wanted her, you know."
They knew.

Their poems were published everywhere.
I made a small fire of mine on the beach.

There is a small fire in a glass of whiskey
a backfire that counters the fire inside
like the fire in the eyes of an angry woman
who suspects that inside her hides a faggot
standing silent over someone's bed
holding still for the blows the sensitive give.

photograph by Lynn Saville; *Manhattan Review*, Vol. 3, No. 1—1983
Philip Fried, Editor

Martin Espada
WAITING FOR THE COPS

Bilingual Review, Vol. VIII, Nos. 2 & 3—1981 ("Hispanics In The United States")
Gary D. Keller, Editor

In front
of the public housing project
someone, a big man,
was murdering a junkie.
A scream falsettoed
through Brooklyn's
blind street-vendor night
in two languages.

This junkie tried
to steal a car
under the one street light
that wasn't broken,
and now he was telling
the neighborhood
about the dizzy rush of death,
a crazy sidewalk mystic
predicting his own
assassination.

The buildings were priests
with nothing to say,
a squat and pious brick.
Windows awoke
in dim and yellow fear,
overlooking a one-act play.

Down below,
someone, a brown man,
walked out
and stopped the killing
of the junkie.

His wife called the cops.

Three men
wrestling, stiff-armed,

in the street,
voices broken bottles
slashing at the moment,
nerves protruding like wires
from a blasted fusebox,
waiting for the cops
to arrive
to start the killing
so that the cops could stop it.

Three clowns
playing to an empty
coliseum,
gravediggers
trying to avoid
the subject of death
and waiting for the cops.

Waiting for the cops.
Waiting at the welfare
and the free clinic
and the jail (can't make bail).

Waiting for the gypsy cab,
or the ambulance.

Waiting for the boss
and his punchclock lectures,
waiting for the landlord's
pipe-busted heat,
waiting for the caseworker's
ritual humiliation
and then the check.

Waiting for Jesus.

Waiting for work.
Waiting for the liquor store
to open,
or the pawnshop.

Waiting in fluorescent cubicles,
abandoned hallways,
chain-gang shuffle lines,

haunted bus stations,
weary laundromats,
prison visiting rooms,
all faintly smelling
of urination.

Waiting
waiting to wait
waiting not to wait
waiting tables
waiting for the sake
of waiting
hating the waiting.

"Call back if somebody
gets hurt, lady."

Waiting for the cops.

Frank Espada, f. *The Immigrant Iceboy's Bolero* (1982), by M. Espada
Ghost Pony Press; Ingrid Swanberg, Editor

Colleen McElroy
from MEMOIRS OF AMERICAN SPEECH

I. Reed Books; *Winters Without Snow* (1979), by Colleen McElroy
Ishmael Reed, Editor

you will learn to speak
just repeat after me
please
      thank you
           hello
your arms will move in 80° arcs
your tongue will click
without drooling
you will identify ships
in the harbor
   say it
         S.S. Ulysses
              Ticonderoga
   now
        slowly
you will know the meaning of color
   green grass
         good
true blue
         fine
black night
        red blood
stop
   it's not your turn
raise your hand only if you hear
the sound
pay attention
move your head with your hands
try this
   MyFathersaysbaNanaNanaoil
don't stammer
        speak slowly
follow me
     you will need this
inhale   exhale
       watch closely
          count this

one thousand bars in this block
one hundred whores
you must make decisions
you must cast a shadow
let's say it together
        the policeman is my friend
the city's too pretty for death
this is a circle
                this is a square
these blocks are all the same
speak clearly
                listen closely
once more
                after me
the baby is normal
                        normal

Judy Grahn
SPIDER WEBSTER'S DECLARATION:
HE IS SINGING THE END OF THE WORLD AGAIN

The Crossing Press; *The Queen Of Wands* (1982), by Judy Grahn
John Gill & Elaine Gill, Editors

He is singing the end
of the world again,
he has sung it before.

When he flattened Troy to the ground, seven times,
left Carthage salted like a fat old hog,
Africa, "conquered," he said, he announces,
he is singing the end of the world again,
millions burned in Europe, butchered in
Africa, millions blown to bits in China,
Russia and now in Central and South America,
thousands of tribes
and villages destroyed, the matrix
of whole peoples, cultures, languages, genetic
pools, ways of describing, gone, gone,
apparently, according to his song, whirled up into
his description of the past.

He is singing the end of the world again,
he has sung it before.
Americans fly over their world and its ghosts,
Americans stare at their own ghosts without
recognition. Invisible the Indian ancestors,
invisible the Mayan-centered
feather industries, invisible the
great buffalo and the buffalo queens,
old ladies of the hip high buffalo grass,
invisible the engineering systems, amphitheaters,
philosophical wholeness in the old
civilizations of the mind.
Occasional sulky sacred bears
stare from the cages of zoos
refusing to acknowledge men as their children.

He dwells in threats of fire, Armageddon, Hiroshima, Saigon,
and Tyre, Berlin, Gomorrah, Hell itself,
the story of fire, his theft of it. "Put
a large wad of flame on
the wand's tip. Wave it,
shouting: Fire, Fire."

The whites of their eyes stare
back at him.
There was a city *here* once, once
there was a city (and now there
is another)

There was a tribe
and now there is another,
there was a nation here once
and now there is another.

He is singing the end of the world again.
He has his song
and I have a long, long
wand like memory.
I remember five worlds
and four have ended.

I see (I can't help it)
buffalo faces in the gloomy white
people of Iowa, waiting slump shouldered
for the light to change,
chanting, "We used to rumble the earth here,
once, with the charge of our electrifying
hooves. Now in the midst of the stolen
golden corn
standing in their fields like sacred groves
surrounded by plenty we are oddly depressed."

He is singing the end of the world, again.
Reincarnated bears
prance and sway in the lowlife bars of
this place calling itself a nation; they
lean, pissing, on the wall in Dallas,
Detroit, Charleston, Denver, hold intellectual
discussings in great roars,

knife each other, make predictions.
They await the Bear god, the Bear Maiden. They
are not concerned with the form this will take,
it is their form, they will take it.

Dancing birds leap out of the young faces
kissing on the streets of San Francisco, Salt
Lake City, Memphis, leaping with an urgent
sky-message; and the lovers call what they
are feeling, "love," "desire," "relationship."
They do not know to call it,
"Birds dancing."
Birds *do* dance, and so do
ghosts, and buffalo.
Spirits line shoulder to
shoulder on the highways shouting
Maya Azteca Aztlan Olympus
Mississippi Valley Seneca Falls Cibola
Shrangri-La, The River Niger, Hollywood,
Tibet. Atlantis. Eden.

There was a nation here, once
and now there is another.
Business people pat each other's pinstripes,
putting their own names on the ancient remedies and
products, systems and understandings. "Let's
design a rocket out of here. Don't forget to
bring the queen of buffaloes. It gives me such
satisfaction knowing she is mine. Let's pretend
that we are doing this for sex,
for money."

He is singing the end of the world again
he has done it before.
He has his firebrand
and his song.
I have a long, long
wand like memory.
I remember five full worlds
and four of them have ended.

Roberta Israeloff
CITY BALL

Pig Iron, No. 9—1982 ("Baseball Issue")
Jim Villani & Rose Sayre, Editors

Moony, who's named for all the obvious reasons—his belly's roughly
spherical, as if he'd once swallowed a barrel of baseballs—usually sits
right there, in his vinyl recliner to the left of the TV, hands clasped behind his head. Each year, as he shrinks a fraction of an inch, his feet rise
slightly off the floor, but it's like the continental drift—you can't see it.
He calls everyone on my favorite team a bum and advises managers against any pitching change whatsoever at any time. And this Saturday,
which should be no different than any other and hasn't been up to this
very minute—in the car we had the same conversations: around exit
three of the Cross Bronx Expressway, Webster Avenue, my mother said,
That's where Neila Thorpman used to live, and two exits later, as we
swung off the highway onto the Grand Concourse she said, I won't even
park, we'll just stay a minute, and I said, We'll park, and she does, but
first she lets me off and I run upstairs (the door is always open) and into
the living room, and there's Moony sitting in his chair—*is* suddenly special: Moony isn't there.

"What do you mean, not here?" I asked my grandmother, Cassie, who
sits with her knees spread as wide apart as the Lincoln Memorial, her
skirt and apron making a lap the size of many tables. In it rest her crocheting, two handkerchiefs, three hair combs, an apple, a nougat candy
and her change purse. "Where is he?" Where could he possibly be? I tried
to remember if I'd seen him walk anywhere recently, especially on a
weekend. We used to go out to dinner once a month to City Island, but
around the second course he'd say he had to go to the toilet and end up
in the kitchen catching the game with the waiters, his food getting cold
and Cassie getting mad.

Cassie indicated the window, which looks out over the Armory. I
crossed the jungle, her tangle of plants with dust-free leaves, and peered
out. There he was, I saw him, Moony and "the kid from downstairs," the
Russian kid, the dark-haired, serious Ivan who's three years older than
me and wears old clothes. He and Moony were looking toward Kingsbridge Road. Moony had his arm on the boy's shoulder. I knew what he
was saying, too: Signals. Signals are the heart of baseball. No one else
knows that, except for me and every major league manager, that's all.
And then Moony told him some signals. Lick your middle finger and
touch the side of your nose, hitch up your pants. And if you don't believe him he'll ask you what you think the manager is doing standing

there on the dugout steps anyway? Why do you think he takes long drinks of water and spits three, clean times? It's all signals. Baseball is a game in code, a game of signs between manager, coach, catcher, pitcher, batter. It's not a lonely game. Unwritten letters, entire encyclopedias of baseball knowledge flutter across the field every minute.

That's not how Moony would say it, that was me. Some fans are more poetic than others.

"I can't believe it," I said, and I couldn't.

"Did you ever ask Moony to teach you to play?" Cassie asked. She was looking into thin air, not at me or the television or what she was doing. If she stopped patrolling for as much as a second, who knew what could happen? A particle of dust could fall, a leaf could drop, a smell could come out of nowhere and embarass her. No, she was always working.

I had never asked him, but that wasn't the point. I never cared about the physical aspect of the game. Not that I wasn't athletic. I made sure I learned how to throw like a boy when I was young, before any of the boys on my block learned. But baseball's subtler side is what hooked me, and for all the years I can remember sprawled on the floor next to the vinyl recliner, listening to Moony digest baseball, I had been hounding him to take me to a game at Yankee Stadium. Cassie and my mother would tell me to lay off, that he was tired, old, fat, too newly into retirement to want to stir. Leave him alone, give him a break, they said. And now he's downstairs with a strange kid.

"I thought we had nothing to do with those Russians," I said. Only last week we were treated to a half hour's harangue on how only poor people cook smelly like the Russians do—this from a woman who doesn't like to use salt—how the husband works two shifts, how their windows face the street, with no shades, how the children are hooligans, murder incorporated, big trouble.

"The girl is wild. His sister, Lana. But the boy is very nice. He comes to visit us some afternoons."

"Oh really." I felt like crying but didn't. It seemed ridiculous to be jealous of my grandfather. When I looked again, I saw Lana, the wild sister, ride her bike toward the field. She jerked the handlebars so it bucked the curb, then gave it a last pedal and levitated off it, abandoned it in midair. The bike, a rusty, clanging racer, ran for a few seconds without her, upright, before crashing into a tree. She ran to the pathetic pile of baseball equipment her brother managed to collect over the months—a broom stick, two tennis balls, two of their father's gloves stuffed one inside the other, fingers sewn together. Then they huddled, all three of them, a conference on the mound. She turned and took 45 paces, turned and threw a pitch. Too high. Not so high, I heard Moony saying. She tried again. Too low. Moony tossed the ball back to her. His arm looked like a tree branch. She scooped the ball out of the dirt. Tried again. This time it came in waist level. Ivan, who'd been waiting with the stick, made a sudden, spastic movement at the last possible second. He twisted his body, his toes came through his sneakers and his shoulder blades sliced through his tee shirt. He smashed the ball, busted its seams, so that as it sailed over the Armory tower it looked like an exploded bird.

Moony wouldn't be saying anything now. He doesn't believe in undue praise.

That's when my mother came up, puffing faintly; she needed to lose some weight. "Where's Moony?" she asked too, first thing.

Cassie indicated the window. "And what's with you," my mother asked, as I moved out of the jungle, steaming, so she could move in and catch a glimpse of her father acting a quarter of his age. I walked to the vinyl chair, looked at it, studied the huge indentation made by Moony, and fell into it. No one expected this. I put my hands behind my head, and moved the seat back so my feet were slightly off the floor. It was the third inning. It always was when we got here. During the commercials I turned to my mother and said, "How's business?"

"Don't be fresh," said Cassie. My mother didn't know whether to laugh or cry. Sometimes she blamed the breakup of her marriage on this one question, asked every week of a surgeon, her husband, who never understood why he should have to apologize to his wife's parents for not having the kind of business Moony meant when he asked, every Saturday at this time, How's business? Business, to Moony, meant sitting on a crate on 8th Avenue and 18th Street, watching lumber supply trucks jockey into driveways, watching Lillie's hands grow arthritic as she works the cash register, watching plumping hardware go up and down the open elevator, watching couriers with mob connections, watching the cops. The kind of business that gets into the folds of the skin of your hands and under your fingernails. The kind you have to change clothes for. Well, my father used to change clothes too, but into cleaner ones than he stepped out of.

Now it's the bottom of the third, that all important inning, says Moony, when the wild pitcher settles down, when the tired pitcher falters. Moony claims you can predict which games will be no hitters in the third. He did just that with Larsen's game, 1956. So he says.

"You shouldn't make fun of your grandfather," said Cassie, out of nowhere.

"How come you're nicer to Moony when he's not here than when he is?" I asked.

"Someday you'll understand." She sat up suddenly, as if she said something impossibly funny, and reached for her daughter's hand. Cassie's always making jokes no one else gets. Mom, meanwhile, dug around in her pockets for the surprise of the afternoon—these big orange, plas-

tic ears she got at the five and ten which have earplugs inside. When she
put them on she looked like something from outer space. "What's the
idea?" asked Cassie.

"I can't stand the baseball announcers, Mother," she said. "You know
that."

"So turn off the sound, I don't care."

"Don't touch it," I roared, just like Moony, and they turned around
to stare at me. I could imitate him to a tee. When Cassie asked if I wanted fruit, I brushed her away with the back of my hand. When she asked How's school, I said "Oke." No one should get in the habit of talking
when the baseball game's on.

Only then we heard crazy footsteps out in the hall, and a wild knocking, then a slower, heavier step that had to be Moony. Lana burst in—
that girl always looked as if centrifugal force tore her apart each night
and she had to shake herself down like a cat to get her limbs on straight
—yelling, "I didn't mean it. Please. We were practicing curves."

Moony stumbled in next, a purple bruise over his right eye. Ivan was
right behind him, as if the boy would have been of any use had Moony
fallen backward. Cassie got up in a flutter but remembered to hold her
apron out so that her things wouldn't fall. She looked like those statues
in rich people's fountains, and she started making those noises which
mean I'm not as concerned as I sound.

"Out of my way, Lady," he said. "I'm fine, just fine. Got brushed
back, that's all." He sank into his chair which I'd kept warm for him.
The cushions gave their familiar whistle at his weight, and the wood
creaked too. "I'm fine," he said again. "What's the matter with you? See
a crowd?"

Lana ran out, but Ivan stayed, trying to explain exactly what happened. He had his mitt with him. Cassie didn't waste a moment. "You had
no business playing ball at all," she scolded her husband. "No business
at all."

He gave her the brush. "What's the score here, Donna?"

So that's what I was good for. The score. "Fourth, top. Two out."

"Yeah? Who's up? Who's ahead?"

"Kaline." Couldn't he tell? I thought that was the point—study the
shadows on the field, the way the umpire makes his calls, who's hanging
around near the water fountain in the dugout, who's on deck—that's
your job, as a fan. Wasn't that what he'd been training me to do? Wasn't
that why he never answered me, completely?

"Yanks ahead by one. Three and two on Kaline."

"Thank you," he said. "What's eating her?"

"Think about it," I said. "You'll figure it out."

"I'm calling the doctor, Moony? You hear me?" That was Cassie,
who else.

He ignored her. She put down the receiver without dialing, and noticed Ivan standing in the foyer, near the cedar chest, which houses Moony's woolen navy jerseys. The boy was still apologizing. In a moment Cassie would ask him if he needed any nice, warm clothing. Then she'd remove all eight objects from the top of the chest, including the dust cover, explaining how she made it herself with fabric from Russia, how lovely it is to have a cedar chest, ask if his mother has one. Then she'd shake out a jersey, make Ivan slip it on, and cluck sorrowfully when it's way too big, too moth-ball smelly.

When that was over, she brought out a folding chair from the bedroom for Ivan to sit on. "Would anyone like some nice fruit?" she asked.

"Quiet, please." Moony said. "The bum is up."

"Lovely language," Cassie sang. She muttered something in Yiddish and got up to get the apples no one wanted, the same ones she brought out last week. I leaned over and said to Moony, "Do you understand her when she speaks Yiddish?" He brushed me away with the back of his hand—no.

"He's lying," Cassie shouted. Her voice was scratchy when she yelled, but she had the best pair of 75 year old ears I'd ever seen.

"Now here's an interesting situation," Moony said. I wasn't sure if he was talking to me or Ivan. We both moved closer, dutifully. "Two men aboard, one and two, one out. Good bunter up. Would you have him sacrifice? Or take?"

"Swing away," said Ivan.

"Sharp kid," said Moony.

"Let him take," said Cassie. The man swings and misses. Moony shrugs.

Now there's a conference on the mound. The one question I always wanted to ask Moony was this: what do they really say during these meetings. I didn't think anyone bothered to mention the pitcher's stuff. Whether the pitcher has his stuff is obvious, anyone can see that, even my mother could. No, I thought they call these conferences because first of all the manager wants to take a stroll, he's getting chilly, and the catcher needs to get up, stretch, flip that mask up over his head, you can go crazy looking through bars all day. And the pitcher wants attention. He's been out there struggling all alone. So the other guys come on out and they have a little conversation that goes like this. How's the wife, kids? Fine, fine, couldn't be better. They here today? Nah, kids had a dentist appointment. Too bad. Yeah. Hey, you about ready for that cold beer? You bet! Then the pitcher steps back, rubs his eyes with his fists like a baby, and spits.

"Do that again," Mom said. "I love it when they spit."

"No, not me, I don't like that part," said Cassie. "I like when they give each other love pats on their behinds."

"Lady, we're trying to watch a baseball game here," Moony said.

I had plenty of questions. Like suppose this next guy strikes out. Will the other players talk to him in the clubhouse? Say you go four for four, five RBIs, but your team loses. Are you allowed to be happy later, in the clubhouse? If your team is behind, bases loaded, two out in the bottom of the ninth and you're on deck, do you pray that the guy ahead of you will end it, any way he can, just so you won't have to deal with the pressure? That's how I'd be. That's why you're not a ballplayer, Moony would say. But those are the kinds of questions I'd like to ask, if I weren't in the habit of only asking those questions I already know the answers to.

"You know, Ivan." Cassie said, crocheting again, "my family originally came from a town near Odessa. That's where you're from?"

"Yes," he said. "It is."

"I used to remember a lot about the village," she went on. "When I was a young girl and couldn't sleep, my grandmother knew it was because I had a big memory. And when my parents decided that we'd go to America, the elders of the village walked me around for days. They'd point to things, and I'd remember them. We walked everywhere, they'd point and say, 'That. And that.' And I put everything into my head, each in its own compartment, until I had to cry, 'Enough! I can't fit any more in.' "

Moony got up, reached the set in a single stride, leaned over like a seesaw, and raised the volume.

"You don't need the sound," Cassie said, "you know all the answers. Anyway my mother and I left soon after that, on a boat for America. It was for 20 days. And I had to keep my head tilted so, because I didn't want anything to slip out. I was afraid to yawn, or sneeze, afraid that something would fly out, like where was Mitya's chicken coop, or the color of the school. I kept my eyes closed until America, when we settled in with cousins on the Lower East Side. And then, no paper, no pencil, no peace and quiet."

She stopped. From my mother's expression I knew she had never heard this story before either. Mickey Mantle was at bat. He had a full count, three and two. No one would ask Cassie what happened next so I did.

"I stole a paper bag from the butcher," she said, "and I found a pencil in the gutter and I sharpened it with my teeth. I tore the bag in half and wrote in the tiniest script you can imagine. I wrote for days, two days and two nights straight, in the little corner next to the kitchen."

Mickey Mantle struck out. Roger Maris was at bat. He was the cleanup hitter. Once I thought the term cleanup referred only to Mick. He was the cleanest looking player I'd ever seen. It looked as if he scrubbed his hair with scouring brushes. His Oklahoman blondness was as exotic as anything from Odessa.

"You wrote it all down?" asked Ivan. "You wrote about your entire village?"

"Yes, I did, and then I had no place to put the pages for safekeeping, so I rolled them into a tube and wrapped my hair around them and fastened them with a hair clip. And when I finished, the second night, I went for a walk to the East River, alone, and that's where I first met Moony."

Moony was squirming in the chair. Maris hit a home run and the Yankees went ahead by five. Moony said, "I told you he'd hit one out of here."

But no one was listening to him. "I walked along the river," Cassie said, "feeling as if a fever had lifted. And there, on a field under a streetlight, a field littered with glass, I saw some boys playing a game that reminded me of a game we played at home, called brennball."

"Brennball, I play that game," Ivan said. He was tremendously excited. "I was brennball champion in my town."

"Only this wasn't brennball," Cassie said, "it was American baseball. And I watched a skinny, red haired man in the field, who used an old leather glove and scrambled to his left, his right. I watched them play the whole night. When it got light and the streetlights went off, the others left. The red head walked toward his bicycle; that's where I was standing. He gave me a ride home on the handlebars."

"Shortstop?" I asked. "You played shortstop?"

"I don't know what she's talking about," Moony said. His hands were gripping the arm rests of the recliner.

"What happened next," Cassie said, "is that I took very sick, very ill, and my mother blamed it on my being out all night. But it wasn't. It was from going into that trance to write out everything that I remembered. She took me to the doctor, who didn't believe me, and they pulled my hair out and all my teeth out, that's what they did in those days, and I came home crying that no one would want to marry me, ever. But Moony did. We called him Moony, then, you know, because his eyes had a far away look, like he was looking for the moon."

"Are you finished?" Moony asked. His eyes didn't look far away now, they looked close, tiny, narrow. He started to get up. He'd never left a game before it was all over. Usually he kept the set on till the game was long over, past the presentation of the Schick player of the day and the Old Spice player of the week, he outlasted all the announcers, the scoreboard, the wrap-up, the theme song—Moony had an affair with televised baseball, usually. He never even got up to go to the bathroom. But now he was on his feet..

"Where're you going, Dad?" My mother sounded concerned. She kept her eyes on him as Cassie started talking again.

"You know how funny it is to think about when we were young. He used to be skinny then. Skinnier than me. Until he got sick and had to stop smoking. That's when he put on all the weight. You know this story, don't you? Oh, god, he was so skinny and his hands were always so dirty I never wanted him to come near me. I was afraid I'd hurt him, you see, and I wanted his hands to be clean. Not for years after we were married could I stand him touching me. It sounds funny to say but it's true."

"You talk too much, lady," Moony said, reappearing with his hat, his jacket.

"Where are you going, Moony?" she cried, "Moony, wait."

He slammed the door shut. "I'm his biggest fan," Cassie said.

"Go after him," my mother said. "Go, follow him."

"He doesn't want me," I said.

"Go," said Cassie, standing up. This time everything rolled out of her lap onto the floor. "Go, of course he wants you. What are you waiting for, a silver invitation with your name engraved? He doesn't want anyone else to go after him but you. Go."

So I went. I ran after him. I wouldn't have been surprised if Cassie had engineered the whole afternoon so that she could throw me and Moony together like this. She knew that was what I wanted more than anything.

I was a good half a block behind him, walking toward the busstop, but he walked slowly and we got on the same bus. I ended up sitting behind him. We didn't acknowledge each other. I wasn't sure where we were going but I had a good idea. We rode under the el tracks. And after about ten minutes I saw it, the beige and blue towers of Yankee Stadium, the giant heart, arising out of nowhere like a modern day castle.

Moony took a few minutes to get his bearings once we were on the street. Then he took off for the ticket windows, all closed now. In fact, people were leaving. I'd lost track of the game, forgot who was winning, couldn't calculate the inning. We kept walking and walking, nearly all around the stadium, until we came to a door marked No Admittance. There Moony stopped and knocked. A man in a cap, with a big stomach, same vintage as Moony, answered, saw Moony, hugged him. They spoke for a few moments, laughed—the man opened the door for Moony and Moony called me. "This is where the players' wives go in," Moony said. "Jake's an old friend of mine."

We walked through a narrow concrete corridor. We passed arrows pointing to the clubhouse, one to the tunnel. "That's it," Moony said. "Want to go?" It was the tunnel I'd always wanted to explore, the one through which pitchers walked from dugout to bullpen and back. It was the best place to get autographs.

"Nope," I said. "I'll go with you." He kept walking in what seemed like circles, but then just ahead I saw some light, and heard noise, and smelled an acrid smell. We passed vendors counting their money, and I turned around to watch them, they winked at me—now there's a job I hadn't thought of; why not, maybe next summer—and when I turned around to find Moony, we were already out there, under a ledge, out, near the field. The base-ball diamond, the players, the bloody dirt basepaths, the grass, everything scrubbed and shorn and raked as clean and perfect as Mickey Mantle's crew-cut. Everything trim as pinstripes, oh it was so lovely. I got dizzy, walked into Moony, who had stopped to get his bearings again. Seats and tiers rose everywhere, people were standing, it must have been the middle of a rally. I heard the crowd roar, and didn't know if I was screaming too, or not.

"I used to like the third base side," Moony said. "That OK with you?"

It sure was. We walked toward left field, along the aisle just above the reserved box seats. We walked until we were at the foul pole, to a pretty deserted section. Moony picked out two seats from which we could see right into the Yankee dugout. Couldn't be better. I had a perfect view of that water cooler.

Next surprise—when the vendor came by Moony ordered two beers. "Don't tell your grandmother," he said. "Go ahead, drink up." I took a sip. Moony just sat there, holding his, as if he wanted simply to feel the heft of the brew, the spongy wet plastic.

"How'd you get us in here?"

"I used to know all those guys. We came here nearly every afternoon, after work, in the summer. With Mike Acre and Johnny Sparrow. This is between you and me, you understand."

I nodded. "It's so quiet here." I couldn't put my finger on what was missing.

"The Voice of the Yankees, that's what's missing," he said. "No one an-nounces here. You have to keep your own score."

"What inning is it? What's going on?"

"I don't know," Moony said. "It never matters as much once you get here. That's the beauty of the thing."

"Well the Yankees are behind by three," said the man sitting in front of us. "Where have you birds been?" Moony and he, Conklin, chewed over the game—Moony was interested after all, I knew it—and I sat back in my seat, looking around. Mickey Mantle's in center field. If I yelled to him he would probably hear me. His neck and thighs were really tremendous, just like they said. But for some reason, everything looked distant, almost more dis-tant than things did on TV. I mean, there I was, in concrete stands, full of city filth and grime—beer and mustard, the seats were sticky, my feet were sticky. And there on the field, on the grass and the most manicured dirt I'd ever seen, stood men dressed like boys, in clean uniforms which were prob-ably dry cleaned in between innings, who never spoke to each other, or heard us. They were in the country and we were in the city, and what a country game it was. And in that country you talk to each other by spit-ting, by patting each other's tails, by taking long drinks from the water cooler, kicking it sometimes, by taking skinny spits, where you always say less than you mean and count on your body to say the rest.

"What's the matter?" Moony asked. "Aren't you having fun? Didn't you hear, this guy Conklin's son is up there, hitting. He was just called up from the farm team yesterday. This here's an exciting game."

The kid looked mighty nervous to me, up there at home plate. Even with his coaches and manager signalling to him, he looked alone and sweaty.

"Don't hit it to Mick," Conklin yelled.

"He's a bum," Moony said.

The kid ran the count to three and two. The runners, on first and second, would be going with the pitch. The kid took a deep breath, you could hear it throughout the stadium, and leaned into the pitch. It took off, rising steadily for enough seconds to lose track of how many. And he broke into a run. If the ball stayed fair he'd have a homer. If it went foul, he'd have another crack. The ball hung in the air for impossible seconds, and then took a turn in our direction. It's coming, I started to say, but never finished. Conklin's eyes widened. Moony stayed in his seat, and the ball came toward us, a gorgeous curve, and landed right in Moony's stomach. Right against his beer, which exploded like a bomb. Moony started gasping, I couldn't tell if he was choking or laughing. He turned blue, the wind knocked out of him, and I was afraid that he would die. On camera. We were on camera, they always turn the cameras to the guy who gets the ball. "Hey," I started yelling, "Hey there, hi." And I waved. And I pointed to Moony, and said, "He's all right," to Cassie and my mother, who I knew were watching. And soon Moony stopped choking, but he didn't stop smiling, and he clutched the ball to his stomach as if it were a baby.

Still, it was a foul ball, and the rookie went on to strike out and the Yankees couldn't get a thing across in the bottom of the ninth and lost. It didn't much matter, they'd already clinched the pennant. One of the things you have to get used to as a Yankee fan is that most of the normal excitement is gone from the game by about July. And here it was August, but I didn't mind. It was the best afternoon I could remember having.

When the game was over, we all stood up and shook hands with the kid's father, who stood around, expecting Moony to give him the ball, I think. But Moony was holding on to it, moving it from one hand to the other, clasping his hands around the seams and releasing them, rubbing it up as if he were going to throw a spitter. Finally, Conklin left, to see if he could get into the dugout. "Go with him, if you want," Moony said, "I'll wait for you right here." But I didn't want to go underground. I wanted to stand where I was and watch the stadium empty like a giant drain. I wanted to think about how it would be when we went home and Moony gave me the ball.

Maybe he would give it to Ivan. What then? I would be too jealous to speak. But Moony wouldn't do that. He was saving it for me. He was biding his time. Like at home, when we waited for the game to be completely, totally over. We watched the batboy, the last one in the dugout, disappear down the tube to the clubhouse. We watched the grounds crew pull the tarp over the bases, and the shadows grow longer in the outfield.

One of Moony's friends, in a cap, came and told us to move on. We started slowly down the ramp, up the aisle, back through the cavern to the street. We had a long, silent wait for the bus. People all around us were full of tips on how the Yankees could have won. Moony never liked to second guess. His only advice: don't change pitchers. It's a man's game to win or lose.

But something happened to Moony on the bus, he got a seat in the back, near the window, and started talking. "There was one night I came here, after work, a Thursday in 1954, 55. Me and Johnny and Mike, we had the bleachers to ourselves. It was late in the game. Maybe it was 56. Anyway DiMaggio was up. He hit a long ball, I mean a long ball, dead away center field, practically right to me. Watch out, they yelled, those guys, what a bunch of clowns, and they hid under their seats. Me, I wasn't afraid of the ball. As I watched it sailing to me, I thought that everything is about right, just as it is, now. I had a job, my family, a roof over my head, it was a late summer evening, I had half a pack of smokes left, and enough money for a beer and the bus home. I thought, That ball is gonna sail on outta here and we'll never have to worry again."

"The ball was caught," he said, "up against the center field wall. And for some dopey reason, nothing was the same after that."

"Really?" We were walking home now, from the busstop. I could see the light on in Cassie's living room. I had just learned about his bad illness, that he had lost fifty pounds, then put on three times as much, that he had lost his own parents within a year—I knew events, I wondered if these were what he meant. I realized how little I knew him, how insignificantly I figured in his life, how I hadn't put in an appearance until he was two thirds of the way out. Suddenly he looked like a dinosaur trudging up the Kingsbridge hill. He was still holding the baseball.

"You should give that ball to Ivan," I said.

"No, I don't think so," Moony said. And then I knew he'd be giving it to me. We climbed the stairs, I went as slowly as he did, and Cassie and my mother met us at the door, telling us how they saw us, how great we looked.

Moony brushed them away, sank into the recliner. It whistled and moaned to welcome him home. He put the ball in his lap. Then he put it in a drawer of the table next to his chair. And I never saw him take it out.

Don Johnson
HOME GAME

Poet & Critic, Vol. 14, No. 1–1982 ("Poems That Tell Stories")
Michael Martone, Editor

Heat lightning silhouettes the hills
beyond the worn-out pasture
where I lob slow pitches toward a flat rock
that no longer gleams like the white rubber plate
of the majors. My father taps soft liners

to my son. Professionally crouched
over burdocks, poised above the looped runners
of morning glories, the boy breaks
with each ring of the new metal bat, stumbles
through sedge and almost catches everything.

Wearing my tattered glove like a badge,
he dreams fences for the open field,
rags the old man to hit the long ball
he could climb the wall for like Yastrzemski.
He is out there where I have been

in the child's sweatless world of fame,
but I would have changed that thunder
building on the river to the first murmur
of applause that lived already as a faint twitch
troubling the sleep of boys throughout Virginia.

My father stole every sign and took my dream
to manage, ran it as he ran me in this very field
at dusk behind his tractor, crying "push, push, push,"
when I let up. In the listening air
his voice seemed to fade toward the waiting house,

to blend with my mother's calling us in
to supper. Now with clouds coming on
like middle age I want to tell my son
that dreams cost more than years,
that a bush league curve will earn

a lifetime's worth of nights in damp motels.
But I wave him back against a stand of pines
and turn in the rain's first spattering
to face my father, still crowding the plate
at sixty. The old game again. He knows

I mean to blow three quick ones by him, win
finally, before the night and the storm's dark
tarpaulin sweep in from deepest center field.
With the boy watching like a deer
from the tree line, I get two strikes clean,

then thunder booms overhead, the sound
of a high hard one splintering barn board
at my ear, bringing back his fatherly words:
"It's all in the delivery,
knowing when to bear down."

On the porch the women wave their white arms,
my mother, my wife, his wife, the boy's mother,
still calling us in as I wind up,
float the fat one down the middle, hearing
the ball peal off the level swing as I whirl

to track the high arc toward the clouds.
My son fades into pine boughs, bent on glory.
I stand here, face masked in rain, knowing
the old man stands at my back, his silver Adirondack
stuck into the storm, daring the lightning down.

Shelley White
THE HEALING

Wild Mustard Press; *Ocean Hiway: 8 Poets In San Diego* (1983)
Paul Dresman, Editor

Autumn, and the lake is down from its spring thaw fill.
The mountains are heavy in the dry air;
they hoard heat for winter and expand as they smother
the valley with their silence.

The woman sits on the rim of the tub in her bathroom,
parting the pink, bloody hair of her son.
He has fallen against the junked De Soto that is rusting
and hollow among harebell and yarrow near the main highway.

Her hand shakes as she wipes at the wound
with an old wash cloth.
There is no one to call and the cut bleeds and washes
over his hair and her hands.

The boy is drowsy and silent.
He matches his breath with hers for something to do as
her hands flutter, then tighten,
open and fly again and again over his head.

She hears the wind that begins in the afternoon
with the coming of horseflies and field dust.

She holds his head between her chest and the washcloth,
lifts him and herself from the edge of the tub.
The sun, the air will dry this streaming and the wind
will blow away the dread.

On the trailer steps, she and the boy sit still and make one
shadow on the door. The wound has dried into a rusty blossom
like those that flower among the sage.
She matches her breath with his for something to do
as he sleeps gathered like rags in her lap.

The leaves of the maple strike their own fires at midnight;
they burn by morning before they die.
But the aspen keeps green
and will not hurry.

Edith Bruck
EQUALITY, FATHER

Milkweed Chronicle, Vol. 3, No. 2—1982
Emilie Buchwald, Editor

Equality, father! Your dream has come true.
I glimpse you dimly, still see you walking
next to Roth the man of property who refused us
a little cottage cheese for the holidays,
Klein the shoemaker who wouldn't resole your only shoes
on credit, Goldberg the butcher
with his trimmed goatee who dragged you
into court for selling meat without a license,
Stein the teacher who gave us Hebrew lessons
in expectation of a heavenly reward and directed us
like a demoniac conductor
breaking dozens of pointers over the heads
of your children, illiterate in Hebrew, destined to hell.
And you, the poorest, most recognizable
by those skinny buttocks! The most agile,
most exploitable in forced labor.
Forward, father! You've been tried by every eventuality,
armed with experience
you know the front lines, rifles, trenches,
the daily struggle even in good times.
You know prison, the hard plank in the dark cell
where you picked off lice, licked your wounds,
unrolled cigarette butts.
You know the taste of blood in your mouth
from a rotten tooth
from a Fascist's fist
from a bullet you caught defending the homeland
you stubbornly believed was yours.

You know death lurking in ambush
the meanness of men
the power game
the bosses' exploitation.
You know the whole gamut of humiliation
the dark street with menacing shadows
ravenous wolves and skittish horses
on sleepless nights during your solitary trips

in the illusion of business deals
doomed to fail
the promises not kept—
except for Jehovah's wrath!

Forward, father! You know the marches,
the cold, hunger! Hold your head high!
You no longer have to hide from your creditors:
they're all there, naked!

Ah, you turn toward me? Don't you know me?
I've grown up, my breasts are firm,
the down on my skin is pure and soft
like mama's when they brought her to you
as a bride. Take me, father!
I'll give you pleasure, not children,
love, not obligations,
love, not reproaches,
love undreamed of by you,
imagined by me. Run:
it is the time of the Apocalypse!
Let us commit a mortal sin
worthy of death.

—translated from the Italian by Ruth Feldman
from Il Tatuaggio

Robert Taylor, Jr.
THE REVEALED LIFE OF COLE YOUNGER

Magazine (Beyond Baroque Fdn.), Vol. 13, No. 3—1983
Jocelyn Fisher, Editor

The Courtship of the Bandit Queen

In prison, Cole is brought word of Belle Starr's death. Down in the Indian Territory she has been killed by a couple of shotgun blasts. The messenger, a reporter who expects a story, watches Cole eagerly, pencil and pad in hand. Cole stands, clears his throat, takes a deep breath, looks absent-mindedly out the small window of his cell where a guard, stubble on his chin silvery in the dim lamplight, looks back in and smiles feebly. Yes, says Cole, I knew the lady slightly, but that was long ago.

The Death of His Father

He sees this as the "key event" in his life, though he does not use precisely this phrase in describing it. He speaks to the guard often on this matter. It was July of 1862, he says, when it happened. He was killed by Captain Irwin Walley's band of marauders and robbed of five hundred dollars. He, Cole, had been riding with Quantrell against the Kansas redlegs. That is what we called them, he says, the *redlegs*. He does not know the origin of the term. Some, he believes, called them jayhawkers, but he always said redlegs. He loved his father. He respected him. We were always a close family, he says. That's all I'm going to say on the subject.

Missouri in Those Days

Cole, says Watkins the guard, what I don't understand is how it was in those times. I grew up in Illinois, you see, son of a dirt farmer.

Ain't nothing wrong with being a dirt farmer. A respectable, honest way to make a living. There's a lot worse than dirt farming.

Was it wild back then?

Wild? Wild? Some would say it was wild. Yes, they would.

And you? What was it like for you?

I'd rather not say.

On Drinking

I don't touch the stuff myself. It's poison. Others might disagree with me. That is their right.

What about Jesse. Did Jesse drink a lot? Was he "in his cups" on some of those raids?

To the best of my knowledge, Jesse did not drink. He was definitely not a drinking man.

And Frank? What about his brother Frank?

The same. These boys were the sons of a preacher and raised right. I never knew them well however.

On the Scout

He remembers the long hot days in the saddle, the gnats, the horse-flies, the way the air clings to your shirt, the monotonous flapping of the holster against your hip. He'd just as soon be elsewhere, yes, indeed. Jesse's jokes soon wear thin. Parmer has the vocabulary of a tree toad. Charley Pitts comes to resemble a hog. If Frank quotes from *Julius Caesar* one more time he feels that he will "lose his beans." It is better when he is by himself. Then he lets his mind wander. Remembers the good old days. Remembers Belle. Belle belonged in the Nations, far away from them that would civilize the daylights out of her, her with them little round bird eyes, that hawk nose, hair dark as a Indian's, hands strong as many a man's. He wonders, besieged by the inquiring ladies of North-field, whatever become of her. But he wouldn't care to be on the scout again, no.

What Became of Charley Pitts

Watkins tells Cole what became of Charley Pitts. They cut off his ear, he says, and put it on display in Northfield. A Doctor got the rest of him, soaked the skeleton in a pond for darn near a year just so's the bones'd get good and white. Then hung old Charley up in his office. Good for the business.

Crazy, Cole says, the things people will do.

With Charley Quantrell in Lawrence

It wasn't so bad as people said, Cole says. You have got to remember what old Jim Lane and his redlegs had been up to in Missouri, raiding people's homes and robbing and looting and burning. There are the Times to be taken into consideration. We killed, sure, maybe two hundred on that raid. Took the town by surprise. That was always Quant-rell's way, you see. Take them by surprise. But remember: we didn't harm the hair on the head of a single female. No, sir. And we was provoked too!

Hiding Out in Caves

Cole gets a laugh at this one. We had no use for caves, he says, not when we had the cash to spend on hotels. Give me a hotel any day over a cave. The bed's better.

continued

His Brother's Suicide

He doesn't know how to explain this. He hates to see men die and has himself long made it a practice to avoid death. In prison he notes Jim's strangeness, the wild look in his eyes, the talk of a "workers' revolution" that will right all wrongs, the slouch, the way he has of sneering when he looks at you across the supper table. Why, he looks like a wolf, just as crafty and haggard! Charley Pitts, Jim says, we're all like Charley Pitts. The capitalists'll find a way to make a profit off of us. That's the way it is.

Compassion

In prison he becomes a nurse, in fact the head nurse. He washes the men's wounds, gives them what comfort he can. His brother Bob dies, while in prison, from his shot-up lungs, and the event moves Cole to a steely resolve. If I can prevent a needless death, he tells himself, I will do it. Jim laughs. There's no saving them, he tells Cole. They're going to pick us all to pieces just like they did Charley Pitts. Cole begs to differ. You do what you have to do, what you *can* do!

Prison Visitors from the St. Paul Women's Club

The ladies are permitted to call on him in the library, where he has for some time been head librarian. He looks up from his desk to see four dark-gowned, veiled, silk-gloved, ostrich-feathered figures bearing down upon him. One of them, her plumes quivering, cheeks reddening, announces the purpose of their mission. It is to hold an interview with him.

He assumes they have the permission of the Warden.

He stands, takes off his wide-brimmed straw hat.

Please be seated, ladies. If the Warden says it's okay, then it's okay by me.

They ask about his feelings when his father was killed by the redlegs. They wonder if his mother ever spoke of joining the "cause." Was it true that he saved many lives during the raid on Lawrence. This Captain Quantrell, they wonder, was he the ladies' man they say he was. What a lot of questions!

The Death of Belle Starr

Oh, yes, he reckons he knew her all right. My God, how he knew her! His Belle! He has a keen memory of her skin, feels it right at the tips of his fingers at the most inopportune times, while lettering the spine of a book, while thumbing through its pages in search of telltale marks. It's distracting, downright distracting. She was Belle Shirley then. It was Texas. Scyene. Her daddy fled here from Missouri during the conflict.

Good stock, the Shirleys, none better, Belle the best of the lot, hot-blooded and clean of limb. A fine rider. A keen shot. And when you touched her just right, just so—Lordy have mercy!

Revisiting the Scene of His Birth and Childhood

He is a big man yet, and retains some of his youthful charm, but when he steps down from the buggy his shoulders suddenly seem to slump and the sunlight flashes so bright that his bald head gleams. Are you sure, he asks us, that this is the place?

Cole, you have to remember that you've been away over twenty-five years.

He looks around, squinting. Everything, he says, was so different then.

The Outlaw Mentality

Look, Cole says, no man alive could possibly have done all that I am accused of. I am a peace-loving man at heart, like everybody else. I'm of a loving and peaceful disposition.

Caddo Gap, Arkansas

While hiding out in the Ozarks, Cole happens to meet an eye-doctor, one of the traveling kind, all his equipment in a wagon. The man is friendly enough, but Cole quickly perceives that he is a thief, taking advantage of the gullible hill folk. They don't know no better, the man says. You mean, Cole asks, that these glasses you sell to them are no good? Why, no, says the man, just that they ain't quite as good as I make them out to be, you see. I see, says Cole, and are they good enough to give away? The man looks puzzled. Why, yes, he says. I reckon they is plenty good enough for *that*! Well, then, says Cole, I reckon that's what we'll do. Now the man is genuinely flustered. Here is this calm, smooth-talking stranger, too hefty to pick a fight with, telling him to give away his product, if, that is, he understands him correctly.

You do, Cole says. Now you clear out of here and leave that wagon with me. I can see you're too skittish for this business. I'll take over for you.

That is how Cole became an eye-doctor in Arkansas for two weeks. When the glasses did no good, his patients must wash out their eyes every evening with sassafras tea, a remedy he has from his mother back in Missouri.

Asked about the truth in this story, Cole just grins, says he doesn't recollect ever being in Arkansas.

continued

Dime Novels

Cole comes across these now and then. Yes, he says, it amazes him sometimes what people will read for entertainment. You'd think they'd want the truth, but no, they like these potboiler stories that tell about the daring James-Younger gang and their narrow escapes, make it all sound like a lot of fun.

Mr. Younger, the ladies ask, do you regret leading the life you led?

Yes, ma'am, he says. I'd take it all back in a minute. I regret just about all of it, yes. I'd do most everything different if I had another chance. Ladies, I am overcome with regret.

His Brother's Suicide

We had been out of prison only a few months, you see. Twenty-five years in that place! Maybe it was just too much for him. Things had changed, you know. We wasn't allowed to leave Minnesota and so had to take whatever job we could get. We hired out as salesmen. A man wanted us to travel about the state persuading folks they had best buy their tombstones now, because sure as heck no one was going to buy one for them later! It helps to make jokes, the man told us. And we wasn't to call them "tombstones" but say "memorials." Jim never took to this, I reckon, though I liked it well enough all right. At least you were in the out-of-doors, and it was honest work, and folks was friendly even if they didn't agree that they needed a stone. But Jim, he's always having bad luck. A horse knocked him over and he took to bed, holed up in a hotel in St. Paul. I hired out as a police detective, and the next I knew, Jim was dead, shot by his own hand. I had him shipped back to Missouri then, and he's buried in the family plot.

Charley Quantrell

There is a reunion of Quantrell's men once a year. When Cole's pardon is made unconditional, he returns to Missouri and attends one of these picnics. He doesn't remember the men who attend, though several greet him as though they are long-lost friends. They exchange memories, these men. What became of Bob, they ask, what happened to Jim. He stands in the midst of them, trying to place the faces. But only the framed portrait of Captain Quantrell looks familiar to him. He can see Quantrell as clearly as though the man paraded before the old rebel guerillas on his shining black charger, once again urging them to take up arms in the defense of "your women, your homes, all you hold most dear." A dark-eyed, smiling man, tall and of slender build. Looked like a schoolteacher.

The Cole Younger-Frank James Wild West Show

It was a lulu while it lasted. One hundred and twenty riders: cowboys, Indians, and Cossacks. Frank, thinner by far than he used to be and stoop-shouldered, rides and shoots to the delight of the crowd, but Cole, prohibited in the terms of his parole from exhibiting himself for profit, only strolls around the arena in a black top hat and tails, now and then returning the inevitable greetings from small children and old men. They may look at him if they wish, but he will not encourage it. He is putting aside as much of his earnings as possible, saving to buy a house in Missouri. Later, he is permitted to accept an occasional invitation to deliver a public lecture. His theme: Crime Doesn't Pay.

Rain

When it rains, Cole turns moody. He takes to his rocker, looks glumly at the wall. Rain, he tells us one day, is what done us in. If it hadn't been raining that day in those woods in Minnesota, you see if any of us'd been caught by that posse! The rain made everything boggy. You'd a'thought we was in a swamp. It was disspiriting, no weather to run in. And we all knew it was just a matter of time, which it was. I tell you, I hate rain. I want to see the sun shine!

The Reason Jim Killed Himself

The Younger family explains it this way: it was a question of love. Jim, after his release from prison, fell deeply in love and desired to marry. It was only natural. It would have saved his life. By the terms of the parole, however, the marriage could not be arranged, and so his will to live was broken. He died for love, the lack of it, the being deprived of it. This is the way the family explains it, Cole nodding in assent from his rocker on the big front porch, sucking his clay pipe. Yes, he says, such circumstances would kill any man. Later he adds, But there was more to it than that.

Repentance

He doesn't place much stock in preachers. In 1903, two years after his parole, he answers the question, "Do you attend church?" Yes, he says, *once*. But the years wear thin. He makes jokes about his low spirits, saying he reckons it's all that lead that's been pumped into him. Feels heavy, that's all. Takes to the lecture circuit in earnest, travels to New Mexico, Texas, Oklahoma, Kansas, Arkansas, and Kentucky. He feels he must make the small boys understand. Maybe he's just wearing out. He reckons it's the lead. Fourteen bullets, maybe

more! Back in Lee's Summit, Missouri, he allows his niece to persuade him to attend a revival meeting being held just outside of
town. It's rough going, but he goes back the second night. And the
third. Nora, his niece, watches him closely during the services. So
does everybody else. He appears to be listening intently, the hym-
nal always open on his lap. One morning he tells her—this out of
the blue, in response to no question—that Jesse James could not
carry a tune. He doesn't know how it's gotten around that Jesse
sang hymns in a beautiful clear tenor, but he wants her to know
that there's no truth in that story. Then he laughs and says no
more. It is that evening that he comes forward. He rises from his
seat slowly, walks slowly to the front, every sinner's eye upon him.
I want to repent my sins, he says. Everybody stands and applauds.
Even the preacher claps. This is a true story.

Politics

He admires Theodore Roosevelt, but will never support a Re-
publican. Europe is a mystery. Why get worked up over what goes
on over there? Kings are a thing of the past, that much he knows.
It was fine the way Spain was put in its place, but what is all this
to-do over Germany.

Dreams

He finds himself in desperate straits. He rides horses until they
die beneath him, and still can't get away. He dives into deep rivers,
comes up on the sidewalks of cities. Buildings rise around him like
so many angry marshals with warrants for his arrest. His father
calls to him, says, Coleman, come over this way. Belle appears, usually laughing, pulling him by the hand from one path to another,
through thorny bottomland along the jutting banks of deep creeks.
Where are we going, he asks. The mountains, she says. Then he de-
sires her. He's a young man again, his bald pate tufted with thick
curls, his skin tawny, muscles taut and aripple. Belle, he says, this
here looks like a fine spot to rest a spell. She walks just ahead of
him. So *now* you want me, she says. She allows him to hold her
hand. His gratitude knows no bounds.

Northfield

Jim's jaw is all shot away, Charley Pitts dead, Cole full of lead, Bob too, but Bob can stand and so Cole says, do it. Stand and surrender or we'll all be dead like Charley here. Cole, towards the end, has been able to walk only with the aid of a staff, and even that gets shot out from under him. We're through, Bob shouts. Cole remembers the dampness of the ground, how slippery the fallen leaves feel against his cheek, how loud the thudding of the approaching footsteps. Step softly, damn it, he wants to shout. Why, he's asked later, did you boys come all the way up here to Minnesota. To get even, says Cole. Everything we ever done, during the war and since, was to get even. And the two who got away, was they the James Boys? That wasn't the name they went by, no.

Modern Times

The year everything turned topsy-turvy, he feels, was not 1876. 1876 was the year of his capture and imprisonment for the Northfield bank holdup. It was also the year of the Battle of the Little Big Horn. No, he thinks 1889 is the year of the big changes. That is when, he reminds us, the Oklahoma Territory was opened for settlement. All that used to be Indian land, you see. Why, he reckons if he had been anywhere else but in prison, he'd have been one of those lined up and waiting for the signal to chase across all that broad prairie and stake himself a claim. Reckons he could have held that claim too. 1889. Year brother Bob died too. Yes, that was some year. Year Belle Starr died too, wasn't it, Cole. He smiles, He believes that is correct.

Prison Life

He has twenty-five years of it. Can he comment on it, please. Tell us what it's like. Well, he says, most likely its biggest drawback is the absence—total absence, mind you—of female companionship. Otherwise you get along. There is time to read, to broaden your horizons through the printed word. Not for nothing was he a librarian while he put in his time! He reckons, though, that it's worse for some than it is for others. He stops talking, looks out the window. There's nothing out there, just trees leaning in the wind, but he seems to see something. He's no longer smiling. His eyes glaze over now. Now he begins to sob. You'll have to excuse me, he says.

Love

We need it, we want it, we go after it, we got to have it. We
need more of it than we can ever get. That's the way it seems to
him. In his later years, he is often astonished, discovering himself
in the grip of a strong passion. He recognizes the feeling. He is
floating, he is sinking, he reaches out to touch, there is only air, a
chilly wind blowing.

His Brother Jim

They are on the road, in a buggy, the illustrations of tombstones packed up in a leather case and kept right between them
on the seat so that it can be quickly taken out, unfastened, the
11 x 17 sheets unfolded and handed to the client. The company
does not believe it necessary for the Younger brothers to carry
along a sample stone. I think we should have one, says Jim, but
Cole, laughing, says he agrees with the policy of the company.
Jim is quarrelsome, moody. At one farmhouse he takes advantage
of the hospitality, helping himself to chunks of fresh-baked white
bread and taking great gulps of sweet milk, then begins to lecture
on death. I'm dying, he says among other things, and so are you.
The woman smiles, refilling the bread basket. Are you men kin to
the famous outlaws, she asks. Remotely, says Jim. Another time
Jim astonishes Cole by grasping the hand of a child, a plump red-
faced lad, perhaps eleven years old, and saying to the boy, whose
parents look on from their front porch, now child, you can say
you've met the merchants of death. That may be true enough,
Cole tells him later, but saying it won't sell us any memorials.

The State of His Soul

He comes to see that, in spite of the best intentions, he has not
improved. There are moments of searing illumination, scorching
vision. Out of prison, he craves a sky that confines. On his front
porch in Lee's Summit he rocks crazily, sucking on his clay pipe
as though for sweeter air. Nora says, Uncle, are you all right. He
thinks it a strange question. He's on horseback, it seems, much of

the time, trees soaring around him. In the house the walls creep
outwards. I've repented, he whispers, I've repented. Doesn't that
count for nothing? Who's firing at him now, who's crawling towards him in the underbrush. You'd think they'd let a fellow rest,
forget what he's been, help him remember what he wants to be,
whatever in the world has become of him.

photograph by Michael Kenna; *River Styx*, No. 13—1983
Jan Garden Castro, Editor

David Henson
THE LAST ATLANTEAN

The Pikestaff Forum, No. 2–1978
Robert D. Sutherland et al, Editors

Atlantis Without Birds

Marble women in gardens used to
reach into the sky and gather
birds by the armful.

The last raindrops brought them
down in scores to swallow
worms they turned into wingbeats.

You could set aside a cut
of hot bread for just a moment,
and its crumbs would end up
scenting the highest branches.

Wind gusting in their blood
must have told them to flee...

At about this time every evening,
they'd glide into the trees
like night air filling your lungs.

The Moon from Atlantis

The moon is what's hauling
the sea over this land
according to our scientists.

For years I've watched the same moon
heave itself over the mountains.
I've seen flat leaves on cornstalks
and even the arc of a leaping dolphin
black against it.

I've held it in palmsful
of shining, wet sand.

Under its soft light I've buried
my head in my hands
and rubbed the lines from my face.

Tonight, so full the sky creaks,
it lumbers through the trees
breaking off the branches.

The Ships Leaving

Today,
as the others
left,
I watched
the horizon slowly
eat their sails.
They saw it
swallowing
a continent.

Jo McDougall
REPORTING BACK

Coyote Love Press; *Women Who Marry Houses* (1983), by Jo McDougall
George Benington, Editor

There has been an accident.
A bridge has broken. The water under it
Has taken a bus, a car, a truck.
For days we watch a picture
Of the one survivor
Who fell with his truck tucked around him, two hundred feet,
Bounced off a passing freighter,
Was pulled back.
The man will not talk with reporters
Or answer his phone

Some who see what they see will never tell
Say they don't remember
Say what somebody said they said.
Buy this man a drink.
Ask him
What did you think of going down?
Hydrangeas? Your mother? A fox?
"A fox," he says.

Michael Rink Cameron
AND THE HUNTER HOME FROM THE HILL

Epoch, Vol. 32, No. 1–1982
C.S. Griscombe, Editor

The poolroom was in the Federation Building, downstairs, in the basement. You had to walk down steps to get there. You could walk right in off the street. Anyone could. They left the doors open and on a Thursday evening early in the spring, about March or April of 1951 while the Korean War was on, anybody, any boy or kid or man or just anyone could walk right down to where the two tables with the scarred balls and roughed-up felt and scratched-from-belt-buckle-leaning-over wood were standing. The Federation building was run and owned by some Jews of Chemung. It was red public brick with maybe marble sills on the windows or maybe just fake marble sills, and none of us kids in the basement art class knew what was upstairs or had ever been there.

The night when the hunter home from the hill came into the basement pool room was one of the first soft spring, snow-melting nights and at seven o'clock Chemung was dimming, the street lights getting ready to glow, supper over for the working people; the Kennedy Valve and the country bars on Water Street tuning up for the night shift. The night was going to be clean and easy, with the dishes done after supper, the fathers lighting up cigars and unfolding in the easy chair the Star-Gazette with the right hand columns picturing maybe one blurry photo of the new Mig-15 taken from one of our Sabre jets which had followed the Mig up to fifteen thousand feet. The kids were done with the roller skating on the slate sidewalks outside and it was now too dark to do that anymore. The early evening tension was mild like the weather and the lights were on in the showroom of the Chevy dealer and someone had spit-shined the black Chevy sedan in there so that it glowed like a serviceman's shoe. The hunter was fourteen years old and had been mistaken for eighteen years old and enlisted in the army and got away with it, a brave, dangerous feat, and had been sent to the real Korea and was now back, walking down the steps that led to the Federation Building basement where the pool tables were and where some of us kids attended an art class given by two ladies. He was an unphenomenal person, a boy-man of indeterminate age whose face would look the same at six or sixty, but had done a phenomenal thing—had been to the fabled Korea we and our fathers could only approach in the newspapers, where the Migs and Sabres dogfought in the sky and long lines of communist Chinese trooped down mountain passes in the snow in bulky suits with their earflaps down and their fingers frozen to their rifles.

I, on the way to art class with Palmer, had stopped in the unlocked, never-locked bathroom of a closed gas station to wet my comb in the sink and slickwave my hair up over my brow. Palmer was content to let his brown bangs lie even though there were girls at the art class, even possibly dirty, unknown, pretty ones from the Diven school in another part of town. The two nice, hectic ladies would be responsible for our art and our behavior, both uncontrollable, and in the public basement room with steam pipes high near the ceiling an early-matured talented boy built like a boxer was going to draw a charcoal likeness of a girl and also accurately picture the bare bulb which hung on its wire above her head. We were going to laugh at the bulb in his picture because of its suggestion of the funkiness of this basement room where we were to produce art. One of the ladies who was beautiful and concerned was going to have an honest laugh at the big kid's bare bulb, too, realizing that the bulb was the truth though the fly he had drawn circling it was not. It was too early in the New York spring for flies.

No one's father was in Korea. Our fathers were too old for that and it was unlikely that any of the school kids' older brothers were old enough. We were nine and ten and the older brothers were only thirteen or at most fourteen.

The hunter was only fourteen. He didn't have one of the gaudy satin jackets sewn in Japan with a picture of a Korean dragon and a Korean map in purple and orange on the back. These jackets were sent home or brought home by the older brothers of kids older than us. The hunter didn't have one.

Palmer had started me on model airplanes and I had a P-51 Mustang framed out in balsa at home on a card table. I was having trouble getting the tissue paper covering onto the wings at the time, 1951. Palmer's father was a small, dark intense half-German man who could walk like Charlie Chaplin when serious and when he didn't know we were watching him. We had found rubbers in the glove compartment of his car and this had matured us much, we thought, as had drinking the corners out of stale whiskey pints from Decker's Alley, behind the garages. And there were the girls,

possibly dirty, from Diven school to be met, punched and snick-
ered at tonight. We were coming along, Palmer and I. It was pretty sophisticated to be downtown at the Federation Building after
dark where there were pool tables. It was pretty sophisticated of
me to carry a comb, too, and to walk right into an unlocked gas
station men's room like I had. We were coming along.

The hunter had no credentials. I remember seeing him, a slight
boy in nondescript clothes with a pool cue in his hand, bent splay-
fingered over the table, not even playing anyone, just banging the
balls off the cushions in his own good time. There were other kids
in the basement as we came in, and a little rumor had got started,
which we listened to. He had, it was said, been sent to Korea and
made it to the front lines before they found him out and shipped
him home to Chemung. He had, it was said, gone all through the
basic training of the U.S. infantry. He had carried a rifle, had shot
it, had killed Koreans in the Korean War, it was said. We looked
over at him. Solitary. No uniform. No identifying badges. Banging
cue, cracked and yellow, into the seven ball. Clack.

During that Thursday evening's art class we made a business
out of kneading gum erasers into balls that we could throw up and
down the length of the long, shabby room. Our targets were each
other and the dirtier of the girls from Diven school. There was
one, in particular, that I liked, and Palmer liked her too, and she
knew it. She acknowledged the erasers bouncing around her with
sly, inward smiles and spent a lot of time arranging her barrettes.
Later on, leaving, when the class was done and the nice ladies were
tired and the Chemung street lights were burning haloes into the
fresh dark sky, we got to jostle the girl and her friend around a
little on the sidewalk before we parted for our homes in opposite
ends of town. They were pretty and sly, but not as dirty as we
had hoped.

The world was huge and it was a spring night, and the arrows
of our hopes darted out of us as we ran the streets home. Soon
we were going to learn how to drive the spit-shined Chevies and
wear the rubbers and jostle the Diven girls expertly and with deep
meaning. And we were going to learn earth's lies and maybe like
them better than this pure, raw night—better than Charles Mekos'
fly-around-the-light-bulb.

The hunter had been finally approached by one kid bolder than
the rest of us who had dared to ask him if he had got a chance to

shoot any North Koreans. The hunter home from the hill looked up, mild-eyed, from where his cue stick lay across a dirty knuckle.

"You can't see if you hit anybody," he said. "There's a whole line of guys firin'."

He seemed to be waiting then, with that face full of some odd kind of wisdom and resignation, for another question, a further demand, but none came.

Kala Ladenheim
MOKELE MBEMBE

Dog Ear Press; *Not Far From The Mountains Of The Moon* (1983), by K. Ladenheim
Mark Melnicove, Editor

The cryptozoologist was born too late to seek the Patagonian giant sloth. Kraken turned out to be a nauseating polyp. Even the Yeti, still undiscovered, eluded him in a climate that tended to frostbite. He decided to pursue rumors among the Pygmies.

If you see Mokele Mbembe and tell of it, you shall die.

A Greek trader he had met in a card game in Beni took him to a village at the head of a trail where there had been stories recently. For a cigarette, the headman agreed to introduce him to the next village. The Greek handed the explorer two extra packets of cigarettes and warned him not to trust the man. "They're not dangerous, but they're terrible thieves."

Along the road, small people stood around waiting for an event. Cleverly woven baskets hung beside long sticks on which a forest animal like a large rat had been impaled. They offered to trade the sticks, baskets or rats, for salt. Nails. Cigarettes. They knew the trails like a gang knows alleys.

The first village was full of people who told him about someone's great-uncle who had heard of a man who saw Mokele Mbembe and told his wife and was never seen again. It was as large as a hippopotamus, more huge than an elephant. It had a crest like a rooster. It had ten legs, or it walked upright like a man. The villagers brought him pieces of bone carved into napkin rings according to a design the missionaries had taught them.

When he came to a village where no one talked about it, he knew Mokele Mbembe had been seen. He dropped hints, posed questions outright. The men turned away and pretended not to hear him. They stared at an ordinary bird perched impudently on a branch nearby and commented on it as if they had never seen the like before. They walked off without answering.

He knew he had found the trail.

The curiously symmetrical volcanic hills were like scarified breasts. Bamboo grew in clumps on the lower slopes. The flame-trees were in bloom. He found a mass of branches trampled into the low cleft of a tree and recognized the nest; once triple-named mountain ape, *Gorilla gorilla gorilla*, was considered a myth. The region was full of fabulous creatures that had finally been seen. Shy okapi had seemed a fantasy of zebra and gnu. The Pygmies themselves had seemed a traveller's invention.

When the giant Watusi neighbors fought them, they were fables for Pliny. Now camera safaris caught them posing, bought curios from them. They approached the jeeps, threatening, like bears in Yellowstone.

On his fourth day into the bush he saw a white man in a suit walking towards him with a trunk on his back. He waited till the apparition reached him. The man was at least two meters tall. He set the footlocker down, upended it, and sat on it.

"I am a Prussian," he said at once, and smiled amiably. He had heard all about the cryptozoologist. "I trade with them." He pulled back a sleeve to display a dozen watches. "They want salt. I am introducing them to mirrors. Any iron is precious, but I am cautious about trading them knives and axes. They make tiny blades from nails. Mischievous people. Watch out for their women. There's a nasty strain of gonorrhea. I'm just recovering."

The trader took a small polaroid camera out of his pocket and snapped the zoologist's picture. "They like these. I always take the headman's picture when I come to a village and give it back to him when I'm ready to leave. They'll be glad to know I've captured you." He laughed confidently. "Your trip will be that much easier." He passed the print over. It was not drying in the humid air. He waved it futilely to speed the process.

The German pulled a packet of pictures from the pocket over his heart. "Here is my girlfriend in that last village. This woman here is Masai, my wife. This is my wife in Karamojong. Two in Kisangani. Here I am with my favorite; the other one snapped it. Here is my wife in Germany. I go back there for two months every year and sell what I've traded here and buy more trade goods. I always make just enough to come back. Now with so many tourists, the Pygmies were getting spoiled and lazy. I have to go deep in the bush. A few years ago I bought a braided girdle for a box of matches. Now they don't do good work anyway, and to buy something like that I have to pay a mirror, some cloth, even a razor blade. It's a good thing the prices for the work are going up in Europe. As long as I make enough to come back, I'm happy. I believe you are headed in the right direction. At least two more days, that way." He hoisted the trunk on his shoulder and continued in the direction the zoologist had come from.

That week he reached a village where no one had ever heard of Mokele Mbembe. He was sure the creature was in earshot. Even the old men stared at him without a sign as he described the creature. He had learned several euphemisms that were used by people who didn't want to anger the forest demon. He invoked them. The men spat on the ground and offered him a piece of root to chew. He squatted beside them and tried some other names. They shrugged and spoke quickly to one another, making a joke in a dialect he didn't understand. He couldn't hide his excitement. In every village in the region, he eventually heard stories about it. No one in this village would even hint at it. They must think it was listening to them now. He would wait.

After he had loitered in the village a few days, it was clear he was going to be a pest. A foreigner who had come from the west during the last fighting with the Belgians, and had married a woman who had hitherto been sterile, was recruited to guide the white man. The outlander spoke a little pidgin French and was not afraid to name the creature. He had been all the way to Kisangani once when it was still Stanleyville. He didn't believe the stories the old men told. In his village, the old men had leopard magic to make bullets run away, but when the Belgians came their magic was stronger. He was angry and wanted the old men to pay back what he had spent on their worthless protection. His wife and her family hid him from the men and made him leave. Well, he would show the White Man this thing in the woods. In exchange he wanted something special: the same medicine he took himself.

The bargain was struck for a week's supply of antimalarial tablets. He took three days' worth of Chloroquine as earnest, swallowing them at once. Then he went home to see how effective they were. Since she was only a Pygmy, he didn't mind having been cheated for his wife. He had not beaten her and thrown her out when he realized she was sterile. Instead he had taken to siring children on the other wives in her father's family. All the women were curious about the outsized foreigner, even though his children might be difficult to bear.

When his wife understood he had agreed to hunt Mokele Mbembe, she put her hands over her ears so she wouldn't have to hear that unlucky name. She mourned as if she were already back in her father's compound, taking care of her husband's bastards. He was too good a husband for such an unlucky woman. He had told her he was cursed by his witchmen and couldn't return to his own country till they died, but she didn't care. He didn't talk well, but he told her wonderful things in his funny accent. He said one day they would go to a city in the west; it was like a thousand villages. All the men would want her for a wife. They would give her metal and she could take it and buy beautiful cloths. Now her man would see Mokele Mbembe, and she would never see all the magical things he had promised her. They were gone like a dream. He didn't believe in anything so he wouldn't take the right precautions. She pulled hairs out of his head, and when he slapped her she cried and prayed even louder. It was too bad for her.

The two men left the next day. The guide wanted to carry a gun. The zoologist didn't trust him. He wanted to capture the animal alive.

"Mokele Mbembe," he repeated, elated at finding someone who would talk about it here. "You've seen it? What does it look like?"

His guide kept up a steady pace. It had seemed slow at daybreak, but

after four hours without a rest it was proving to be a killer. "Great creature. He eats the dead. Eyes that shoot fire. He kills by looking at you.
He doesn't like to hear people gossip about him. Better not to talk now."
"Have you seen it yourself? You know where to find it, eh? How
come you live with the Pygmies? Do you usually hunt alone?"

There were stories of tribes who hunted elephant, but the tiny bows
and arrows the band he lived in used could barely bring down the jungle
chickens that ran whooping in surprise as they crashed along the trail.
The foreigner preferred to use a spear that was taller than he was, and he
owned the treasure of a knife. He was known as a brave man, but not
trustworthy. Although all his actions since he joined the band had been
honest and correct, one never knew. He was not invited to join in their
hunt because everyone knew he was sure to do something wrong one day
when it counted most.

"I hunt alone. They are little men. You and I, we hunt big animals
because we are big men, real people. We are afraid of nothing, even Mokele Mbembe." He stuttered over the name. "You have your book. You
write spells in it, yes? This is important. The leopard men do not know
this kind of magic."

The tribe liked it when he hunted alone because he could kill animals
that were forbidden to them. When their own prey was scarce, they
could come and share his full pot. Then it was just meat. Game was getting scarce and the village would have to move soon, maybe in the direction they were taking. Except for the chickens, he hadn't seen anything worth hunting all day.

They made camp where the vegetation ended at the crest of a sudden
hill. Smoke gathered in the cup of the crater, then oozed over the lip,
trailing sulfur into the resurgent jungle. The guide neither ate nor slept.
He built a fire and refused the rice the hunter cooked over it. Instead of
lying down himself when the white man spread his sleeping bag and
yawned, he said he would stand guard. In the middle of the night a sound
woke the zoologist. The guide was sitting on the other side of the fire,
eyes fixed out on darkness. He was about to offer to take a turn on
watch, but fell asleep again, to his shame, and woke at dawn. There was
still a small fire. The rice was untouched. When he opened his eyes the
guide said, "We go now."

He tagged behind the African, prattling about the creature. He repeated all the stories he'd heard about it. Was this the same thing they were
after? When did he see it last? Now his guide was silent, as if this near
the beast he had finally fallen under its spell. "You hunt something for
so many years," the cryptozoologist chattered, "and you get so you feel
when you're near it. Last year I traced a sighting, but the trail was a
month old before I got there, and the stories were all confused. How
long have you lived with the Pygmies?"

The guide raised a hand to warn him. They stopped. He panted loudly in the silence, catching his breath from the pace the other set. Was there something else breathing? His heart was too loud. He couldn't hear anything over it. Even the jungle was silent, as if refusing to repeat the name. *Where no one will talk of it, know it is nearby.*

They started again, walking carefully, stalking something he couldn't sense. He felt the heat for the first time in weeks. His own body stank. His clothes rustled. The gun turned awkward and caught on branches.

"Mokele Mbembe?" he sighed, as if calling to a lover. His guide was running now, graceful and silent, along a path he could barely make out for himself. Something was nearby. The air flattened against his face as if it were used up. The guide was gone. Should he wait, or keep on in the same direction? The path was a parting of vines. He could follow it by finding where the air moved. There was a clearing ahead; light broke through the canopy. A flash like water, or metal. A downed plane?

The roots of the last tree before the opening formed a niche. It held a wooden form studded with nails and beads and rags. He should collect it for a museum. It was beautiful. The wood was oily from being touched. How many years of handling to get such a patina?

There was a flash of movement as the branches swayed shut across the other side of the clearing. The guide was moving on into the woods there. The path he took was invisible. In the clearing the sun echoed on neat stacks of metal. Sheets of aluminum had been peeled away like sections of an orange. Cloth and sticks were sorted and arranged. White sticks. Bones, they had not been left where they had fallen. A formal rock garden. Fillings in the teeth, moulder of uniforms. Not pygmies here. Glass fragments meticulously sorted and heaped. Canteens stacked like moons. The circumference of the boneyard was unbroken.

The guide felt the old medicine fly up out of him as he moved towards home. The leopard men had not been wrong after all. It was a very slow medicine. The bullets return on themselves. He had thought it would be fast, like bullets. The old power is restored. Behind him, in the clearing, he heard the white man fluttering like a bird that has flown into a hut. He had not realized yet that he was alone.

"Mokele Mbembe?" His voice was white like a bird. "Mokele Mbembe?" he called once more.

William Stafford
LOST IN THE CENTURIES

Memphis State Review, Vol. 2, No. 1—1981
William Page, Editor

I went out on a week end. Quiet had come back—
a river can't keep a farm alive
all alone; pig fences can't hold a hillside.
I hacked with my stick at weeds crowded
by the front step looking into a window. "Earl!
Ruby!" I called, only because
I wanted to hear those names again.
One quail was all that answered. There are
silences too loud for what you think
when you stop at an old farm on Sunday.

Paul Fericano

POEM FOR WILLIAM RUMMEL
SERVING A LIFE SENTENCE IN A TEXAS PRISON
FOR NOT FIXING AN AIR CONDITIONER

Poor Souls Press/Scaramouche Books; *Commercial Break* (1982), by P. Fericano
Paul Fericano, Editor

they grabbed him in 1972
he took $120.75 for the labor
but he didn't fix it

that did it
Texas wasn't going to take this shit

first it was $80
on a stolen credit card in 1963
for 4 tires

then it was $28.36
on a forged check in 1969
for a motel room

and now this
his third felony in 9 years
an obvious threat to society

with such a record
the prosecution nailed him
3 felonies: habitual criminal
the judge agreed
3 felonies: life imprisonment

his final appeal
reached the Supreme Court in 1980
and by a vote of 5 to 4
the majority said:
fuck you
Texas is hot
you should've fixed the air conditioner

Bruce Cutler
DOING JUSTICE

Juniper Press; *The Doctrine Of Selective Depravity* (1980), by Bruce Cutler
John Judson, Editor

In this State's Twenty-eighth
Circuit Court, Juvenile Division,
semper eadem: assume the kids'
innocence, ask the difficult questions
where were the parents? why?
who were the teachers? when?
what about counselors? how?
The list goes on. When we do not get
the answers, we send out officers we trust
to bring them back. Our staff compile
the data. They validate with psychometrics.
1) the kids are not of legal age.
2) they cannot comprehend society. Nor
3) have they had the chances they deserve.
And 4) the disabilities: dysphasia,
anaphylaxis, bone disorders,
sickle cell, *et cetera*.
Plus the social structure. And the law
enforcement system. Plus the trail
of infrastructures, and the interface.

There is more to say, of course. Now
we will be fair to ourselves: long
hours, crowded calendars, but
most of all, the data: difficult
at best. Respondents who are never there
or who volunteer the facts we cannot use.
People who know, who will not talk.
People who talk, with nothing we want to know.
Bringing it in on forms, checked off
as "yes" and "no" to questions we
must ask. And also answer.
So then we must decide: 1) to send away
for therapy; 2) ditto, for correction;
3) to place on probation; 4) dispose of, otherwise.
Nothing is easy—keeping their names
out of the papers, keeping information

away from the police. I mean as much
as we can, keeping it all professional.
A kind of game of yes and no,
that once begun, consumes us.

Comes one William Thomas Shank
before the bench: charged with delinquency
(murder in the first degree), delinquency
(arson in the second degree), delinquency
(five felony counts of larceny).
Previous offenses known now total ten.
Previous interventions of this court: release
on recognizance of parents, release to officer
for supervision, sentence to Boyville,
sentence revision, sentence prolonged
for aggravated assault, psychiatric supervision,
charged with rape, sentence forfeit,
sentence revised, appeal for clemency,
appeal denied, appeal revised,
remanded, parents apprised, reminded,
removal of family from flat for fire,
temporary transfer to Nation of Islam,
mother asserts that the boy is incorrigible,
father asserts that he isn't, wasn't.
Rearrest, petition. Redisposition of request.

Statements. *One.* "The victim, Walter
Stover, severely beaten, died
of apparent fracture of the skull. Dog
was likewise beaten. Victim's apartment
ransacked also. Unknown amount
of cash and property removed."
Two. "Yes, I think we really
tried. I always had some kind
of job. We sent the boy to school.
Everything you told us, we did do."
Three. "No, I don't know.
I don't know why. He was the best baby.
Never gave me trouble. Always
doing what I asked. I don't know why."
Four. "Shank had a way of sitting
there in class and being someplace else.
At first, imagination. Like a trip,
you know? Then he was really someplace else."

Five. "I first arrested Shank
for setting fire to a wino in an alley."

From diagnostic inventory: "So difficult
to say. Some evidence of Oedipal
fixation. The stable family sometimes
makes this more acute. Fondness
for fire as an index of displacement. Quote,
'I burned the wino because I felt bored.
Nothing to do. I don't like winos.
Smell. Making problems on the streets.' "
Later: "With sedation, Shank revealed
a fantasy of self as capable of flight.
Familiar to the last detail: 'I never
have to think of pissing when I fly,' unquote.
Says he likes to live in rooms where stuff
is piled on either side of bed.
Quote, 'They're like wings, I mean they make me feel
good about sleeping. And waking up
is nice.' Has a tendency to laugh at fantasies
without revealing content. 'Just my own
kind of cool.' Prognosis deferred."
Referral to the Center for Perception Research.

Handwritten note: *In the covenant between
your God and you, this clause is clear:
I am the sole Creator. I
created you. Not you, who created
Me. This is why I am a jealous God.
Why to be a man you must rebel
against your father. Although I say
you must not do it. Do not do
it, for if you do, you make your father
Me. So as I say, you must not do
it. Your father is a likeness of my Self, since he
created you. To think of him as Me is right
but wrong. He is your father. But he is not Me.
Taking him for Me you have a moment
when you think you face Me: kill us and you are then
a Man. Not kill us and you may become the Other.
So then, would you want to do it? Try?
Kill the father-Me so as to become the Other?
Or not knowing, not knowing Me,
never know the Other? Do not do it. No.*

We shall soon find that Shank is guilty.
This is conditional, however: conditional
upon assumptions that we make. Assume
he wanted Stover's money, TV,
anything—at age 15, how much
could anyone know about effect (death)
and the spur of cause? Know, we mean,
the way that law and custom dictate:
know the way that Adam knew
by knowing Eve, putting on a knowledge
neither of them really knew until too
late. Meaning power, as the hand
will know the purchase of a hammer-
handle, but not the force of hammerhead.
No, we must consider innocence
not as absence or as ignorance, but rather
as the act—a distance, trajectory if you will—
bridging what the body whispers *Do*
and the Other of the waiting, unknown world.
Knowledge is the spark of word on world.

We also note the following: that night,
Shank surprised one of his companions
at the *labia majora* of a Candy Hippworth,
minor female. The rest of the restraints
he might have felt were then removed.
Pattern of the violence that ensued reveals
degree to which he cannot yet connect
effects with cause. *Re* burning down
the family's apartment: arresting officer
Kudirka, "Standing out on pavement,
littler one, Devlin, pointed out
this Shank as arsonist. I thought he was,
because the crowd would not defend him."
Note: "Shank did not resist
arrest." We know that this is not
extenuating: it simply amplifies
the known regarding what must mostly be
unknown. Nor does it explain
Shank's assault within a week on Devlin
in an alley on East Thirty-first Street.

Handwritten note: *In love, at the beginning,*
she was my life. I needed her. She would give
me back my life. But instead
I gave it to her. And when we finished,
separation. Lying there. I could imagine
my life, inside, enclosed. That way.
Taken from me, held. Growing,
they say. But somewhere else. Not me,
but a child. They say. Or would it be me,
but in the time I was borning?
But that—that was before, before
anything I know I am, and only
something Others say. Who knows? Not
the Others, they can only say about it.
Only God will know. I would like to know.
Undoing. Know by the outing-in
where you can glimpse a last thread
of what was taken, what you left.
Make yourself a Man. Show
them. Make your mark. A Hit. Your name.

In pronouncing sentence, the Court declares
that Shank by virtue of his age shall be
remanded to our officer for supervision. At age
15, the law declares that he shall not
be subject to incarceration. Let us explain:
by saying this, we simply give
the juvenile a chance. Another chance,
before the weight of a six-digit number
falls on his back. But hasn't he killed?
you ask. And burned, and stolen? Yes.
He has done more than most of us would dare
in peacetime, less than what necessity
would lead us to in war. But the test
of what we stand for comes just here,
just at this point, where virtue once
tested contemplates its failure,
meditates the restoration of its state.
The law compels this moment of decision;
the citizen cannot slough it off.
We see him see it through to doing.

continued

Subjoined: Officer to ensure this minor
will be kept away from others who might
influence him. Continued counseling. Efforts
to assess his innter state. Friendly
overtures to family for some medication
under Chief Surgeon's supervision.
Alert to P.D. Precinct Five
re juvenile's release. Contact with sympathetic
media on problems of high jobless
rate among his peers. Release
of certain data to both HEW and LEAP
as part of grant proposal for a study,
"X-Quantities as variables in crime rates
among the urban poor," or the like.
Set in statistical perspective: in 1830s
ten thousand prostitutes were plying
trade in New York City, something
like a quarter of the females 15 years
to 45. America as promise.
The greening and the greenback. Myth and monolith.

Handwritten note: *we can perceive*
each instant because we can expend
it. Paradox. Consumption of our life
as mode: life consumed leads
to new life. The past as fossil fuel:
we burn, we burn it. Behind the ancient
thing we burn is a thing we must believe
in. Hardening of forests, forest behind
forest: heat that warms my hands
today is consummation of three
hundred million years of forests.
Hand I touch today is hand
that holds a pen, a chalk, a stylus,
staff, and stone. Or that merely raises
in a sign. Or moves. That hand,
before the life of Man, before
existence on the earth, something
remote in galaxies, we can know as Other.
Because in fact. Once existent.
Once another. You. Me.

Dumile Feni, from *Somehow We Survive* 1982), ed. by Sterling Plumpp
Thunder's Mouth Press; Neil Ortenberg, Editor

Marianne Ware
UNDERSTANDING GUYANA

Doris Green Editions; *Bodies Nearly Touching* (1982), by Marianne Ware
Pat Nolan, Editor

for Gerrye Payne

I remember when we lived on 112th Street in New York City
During the housing shortage of the late 1940s.
We shared one room, the three of us, in a decrepit old building,
Just half a block and around the corner
From the famous Cathedral of St. John the Divine.
There was a toilet in a closet;
Our beds were nearly touching,
A community kitchen down the hallway,
I'd get lost in the corridors looking for the showers.
My father, a dyed-in-the-blood-red radical,
A believer in, "The nobility of the common man,"
Reveled in that atmosphere:
The inconveniences and lack of privacy,
Our beds nearly touching.
My mother swore it was a privilege to live with him,
To work all day at a terrible job
So he could be free to, "make a better world for everyone."
But I was four years past the age of seven so I doubted her.

Then one evening in December
When I walked the slushy streets with him,
Down among the multitudes,
We saw twisted, legless wonders
Trussed in carts along the sidewalk, selling pencils.
And I asked to give them money,
But he said, "No! We have to change the system;
Charity perpetuates the scourge of Capitalism."
"Oh Please," I begged. "It's cold; right now it's cold.
My God they must be hungry."
Which made him turn his wrath on me, to rage
That Heaven would be made on earth, in time, by men like him,
And I must never take that name in vain (the Lord's)
Because it meant I thought He lived, was not a myth.
Angry Father, righteous Father,
Spewed his doctrine, leftwing gospel, on the pavement,
Struck me blind and mute and once more unaccountable

In the chill of my eleventh winter,
A Baptism, then, of ice instead of fire,
Down the street, half a block, around the corner
From the famous Cathedral of St. John the Divine.

Frigid, rigid, pious Father,
Was there forgiveness in his teachings,
Opiates for someone small and weak and disenfranchised?
Not until I took communion:
Bit the hook, the Party line and Manifesto with the wafer.
Then I could worship him at midnight
When his fellows had departed,
Wise yet furtive in their travels,
See him haloed in the half-light
As he strained against my mother,
While our beds were nearly touching.

I remember in the '50s on the West Coast
Where we'd come to find escape from a tribunal
Led by someone named McCarthy,
How my Father, martyred Father
Gave his relatively young life
For the true Cause and to cancer,
How my mother, sainted mother,
Seemed resigned and then unburdened at his passing,
How it took me so much longer
To become a disbeliever
See our beds no longer touching.

Now I'm older, cured of visions
Of a true church up the block, around the corner,
Or a great and holy Father
Turning chaos into order.
But there are children, little children
Always looking for a Savior
As they tremble in the corridors.
Suffer children, suffer children;
He is risen in the Jungle
Where they've fallen with their bodies nearly touching.

Ron Wallace
1001 NIGHTS

Wisconsin Academy Review, June 1983
Patricia Powell, Editor

Each night I read you stories—
Sinbad, Aladdin, Periebanou, Periezade—
in that strange exotic language
you cannot possibly understand:
countenance, repast, bequeathed, nuptial,
what can these words be telling you?
What can they signify?
That I love you? That it's time to sleep?
Keep safe throughout this night?
And yet you will not let me simplify,
get angry if I explain,
and hang on every word as if
our lives depended on it.
Perhaps they do.
One day the stories will fail us,
there will be nothing left to tell,
another hand will rub your back,
another genii will rise.
But for now, sleep tight, sleep tight,
and dream of the singing tree,
the speaking bird, the golden water,
the stone that was your father
restored by morning light.

photo by Joanne Leonard; *Kalliope*, Vol. 5, No. 1—1983
Peggy Friedmann et al, Editors

Susan Wood
WITNESS

Crazyhorse, No. 23–1982
David Jauss et al, Editors

It would be summer, Saturday—the only day
a man can relax, my father said—
and in less than ten minutes
everybody's shirt would be stuck to the upholstery.
Wedged between grown-ups in the Buick, bored,
I tested my father's temper or watched
for Burma Shave signs. They never changed.
It seemed to me then that nothing would.
Not the bleached-blond haze of summer nor the car
turning off the highway, dust spun from its wheels
slurring everything behind us. Not slaps,
nor looks exchanged between parents,
nor an only child, too fat, who talked too much
and wanted too soon to be grown.

Freed from the backseat, I followed the men
down to the green pond, brim-stocked and scummed
with growth, and begged to go in the boat.
They teased they would pay me a penny
each minute I was quiet and could I keep my word?
My father threw out his line, waited
for its tug and pull. A snake sunned itself
at the pond's edge. Water moccasin, he said,
soft and quiet as an Indian's shoe.
He looked at us, each one, and smiled
as if surprised to be there and who he was.
This is some life, he said. Some life.
We caught fish after fish while the light lasted,
until it seeped into the pond like ink
spilled on a rug and the women called,
Time to come in, come in now.

Supper over, summer dark, they sat at the table
laughing at somebody's joke,
the women hoarse with cigarettes, Doc's giggle.
Brad, handsome as Ernest Hemingway, bellowed
when he laughed. My father wiped his eyes.
Half my life, or more, has disappeared like theirs.
I think I know now that everything changes
and nothing does, that someone is left
who remembers and then there is no one.

I know as little as the hot breath of a summer night
without a breeze when it is late and a child hopes
no one will notice and send her off to bed.
Ours were the only lights for miles.
We are here, *this place*, I thought, and no one
can see us. This is a question asked in a book:
If a tree falls in a forest and no one hears...
And if someone had happened by that night,
what would they have seen?
A child lifted in her father's arms,
slowly giving in to sleep.

Sue Standing
CELLAR DOOR

Zephyr Press; *Amphibious Weather* (1981), by Sue Standing
Ed Hogan, Leora Zeitlin et al, Editors

A room to go to—
not lapidary windows,
but jars which hold the light of fruit,
the taste of summer, and my mother's labor.
In winter, I open the knotty pine door,
hide from sister and brothers,
read *Little Women* and *The Secret Garden*.

My mother stands at the sink all summer
as the fruits succeed each other—
strawberries, cherries, peaches, apricots, apples.
The huge blue enamelled cauldron
steams on the stove.
She wipes the sweat from her forehead
with a dishcloth.

At the center of all this ripeness,
her hands of fruit and sun.
Spearmint strained through cheesecloth.
Scalded mason jars lined up on the embroidered tablecloth.
Stacks of shiny metal lids and sealing rings
(used for gypsy bracelets at Halloween).
I sneak sweet froth skimmed from the top of jams.

Her hands stained and nicked
from all the peeling, cutting, blanching—
beautiful how she touched things,
how quickly she could thread a needle.
I'm not supposed to love her for this—
smoothing our hair, sewing our clothes,
or on her knees waxing the floor.

I see the blur of her smile,
her smile that hid so much.
I saw her cry only a few times,
when she could not hold us after her operations,
and when she told me once she was afraid,
and I could not look at her
for fear of her fear.

I remember the sound of the jars sealing at night
as if something were alive in each,
kicking to get out: first one jar, then another,
then a chorus of pops and smacks like frogs on a pond.
Then the careful carrying down to cellar,
and the winter choosing of fruit for breakfast.
When I chose, I chose by color not by taste.

I open the door so slowly,
feel the knots in the wood.
She told me here one day that I should cultivate desire.
I was surprised.
I had never connected my mother with desire,
and could not ask her if she meant a strong will,
or an earthly passion, or a clear heart.

I come to this room
where there is no longer fruit on the shelves,
just cases of tin-canned goods,
gallon drums of wheat and emergency water,
a strong smell of must.
I wish I could find just one jar overlooked,
one jar of clearest mint.

A flickering leaf-veined pattern
falls on the floor
like a hand in front of a candle flame,
her hand on my forehead,
as if the last rooms of memory
hold only light.

Richard Behm
A MESSAGE FOR SUMMER IN THE SUBURBS

Nit & Wit, July/August 1983
G. Jurek Polanski, Editor

In summer's twilight wind that parries
Treetops, and the shadows growing long
And longer, stretching like tentacles
Of black rubber, we absolve ourselves
With small tasks: weeding the garden,
Making salad, rinsing dishes.

A solitude enfolds us, as if we could be
Kept from harm, kept safe forever
From the mad, starving world, the angry boil
Of narrow streets, the lines of yellow refugees,
The officially beaten, the subway sleepers,
Our own dark selves.

Angelus splashes blue notes over housetops,
Drooping sun sets windows ablaze,
Sprinklers whir over emerald lawns,
Wind subsides to soft equivocations,
Dark gathers in the east. It may storm tonight.
In fragile houses, we sit, waiting.

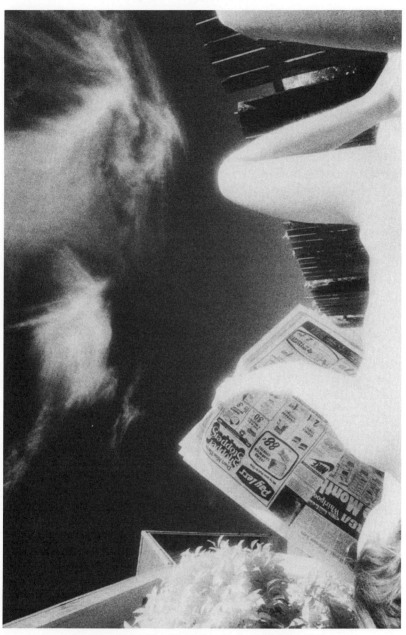

photograph by Dennis Moler; *Fedora*, No. 3—1981
John Hawkes, Editor

Benny Andersen
THE PHONE CALL

Curbstone Press; *The Pillows* (1983), by Benny Andersen
Alexander Taylor & Judy Doyle et al, Editors

"You have to promise me, not a word to anyone," said Frans. "They are for purely internal use. If the company found out that I'd taken them home with me, I'd be tossed out at once."

Palle spread the pictures out in front of him, five six large photographs.

"Look, it's all here, from all possible angles. It's the police photographer who takes stuff like this and then our company makes inquiries, if it's a client that something's happened to, and asks for copies—for insurance purposes, you understand. Sometimes there's a question whether it's suicide or accidental, there can be a great deal of money at stake. If it's premeditated suicide, there's no payment to the survivors. But there's no question here. We're just not allowed to show them."

"No, there's no doubt here," Palle admitted. The pictures showed a soldier who lay on a plank floor, probably in an Army barracks. He had taken his boot and sock off one foot—only one—and had stuck a carbine in his mouth, pulled the trigger with his big toe and blown his brains out. Seen from the front, or more correctly, from above—there wasn't anything remarkable except for a pool of blood by the side of his head, even his face was undamaged, very pale, nearly chalk-white, but maybe a flashlight was used. The eyes were rigid and wide open, the mouth half open. In another picture, you saw the neck, or more correctly the gaping hole on one side of the back of the head. Just a dark crater with some wispy hair around it. In the third picture the brain lay in a little pool of blood, it was intact and looking quite like a brain. Palle was amazed that it was whole. In the fourth picture you saw the ceiling with bloodstains, and then there were a few pictures of the carbine and of the fragment of the cranium with sticky hair on it.

"If only it had been in color," Frans said. "Agh, we have some that are much better. A man who strangled his five children while his wife was at work. The youngest was scarcely a year old. They were laid in a row. Jesus, it was something else. But I can't get ahold of them, it's too risky. Jesus, you should just see them—these here are nothing."

Palle looked for a long time at the pictures. He had never seen a dead person. He'd seen pictures of dead people, of course, but it could just as well have been someone who was sleeping or had fainted. But with the soldier there was no doubt: This man was dead, stone cold dead. It was the closest Palle had ever been to a dead person. He couldn't take his eyes off the pictures, and in order to gain time before Frans took them back again, he asked:

"Does anyone know why he did it?"

"I guess it was something about a girl who had broken off with him, or maybe she was going to have a child, I can't remember. Anyway, it had something to do with a girl."

Palle laid his hand lightly over the picture, he still had to keep hold of it a little longer, try to imagine the soldier as living, with ordinary eyes, with a more closed mouth, smiling, looking, talking. It didn't work. The soldier wouldn't close his mouth, the eyes kept on staring rigidly. Strange that anyone could react so strongly, take his life so to heart that he died of it. Palle was simultaneously moved and envious.

The door opened and Birte came in, Frans hurriedly began shovelling the pictures down into his briefcase. Palle blushed.

"Well now, that's certainly something I'm not supposed to have seen, isn't it? Dirty pictures, my God, haven't you outgrown them? As if I hadn't seen things like that before. Can't you remember our honeymoon, Palle, when we proceeded according to the French postcards you'd gotten from your brother-in-law. It was the most tiring period in my life, and it irritated me that right in the middle of it all you incessantly had to consult the cards and see whether it was correct now, whether it was my right leg that should be up over your left ear or the reverse."

Frans had quickly regained his composure: "Dear Birte, I truly believe I could teach you something new, but bear with a poor bachelor and amateur—and now I have to withdraw."

Birte showed him to the door.

"We're going to the movies. A war film, for a change."

Palle didn't like the film. There was a welter of corpses, bombs, ruins, arms and legs, but that was all right for that matter if there hadn't been a speaker who unctuously advocated peace the whole time: Look how terrible war is, all of us must do our best to avoid a third world war, it would be even worse! In the beginning you swallowed it, but soon it was apparent that the peace message was a thin excuse for wallowing in blood, mud, misery.

However there were a few documentary sections, which Palle couldn't shake off afterwards. Some refugee faces, staring children, homeless dogs, a bathtub hanging out of a halved house. And particularly one from the German retreat in Italy. A group of young soldiers in a roadside ditch. They sat smoking during a pause in the allied bombing attack on the highways. You could see they were young, still their faces looked old. One of them stared right into the camera, as if he were thinking: Can't we at least be allowed to rot in peace without being stared at?

209

They were home a little after eleven. At the foot of the staircase they heard the telephone.

"I think it's ours," Birte said.

"Who'd call us up this time of the night?"

Birte was already on her way up, her heels bobbed up and down in front of him.

"It's more likely for her downstairs, she gets phone calls at the strangest..."

Palle was about to lose his breath, he wanted to keep on following those heels, they looked good after all the tanks. One ate too much, was too well off. He came along behind, the thick winter coat made him heavy, but now or never, he took the last three steps at one time, slipped and went down into a split, of which he would never have thought himself capable.

Birte thoughtfully pretended she hadn't seen it, and he was up again at once, stood behind her and filtered his breathlessness out through his nose so that she wouldn't believe the few stairs had done him in. She rummaged in her purse. It was still ringing in there, it *was* for them.

"Oof, I haven't got my keys with me—give me yours."

Palle was still not able to talk normally, silently handed her the keys, but yet didn't let go of them and opened the door himself.

As the door sprang open, the sound died away, and Palle got a prickling feeling that the last deadline had run out. He leaped into the room and tore off the receiver. Dial tone.

Birte turned on the light and turned up the heat again.

"Who could that possibly have been anyway." she said.

She took off her coat and hung it up.

"Who it could possibly have been—What do you mean by that—it was someone by God!"

"It could have been a wrong number."

Birte went into the kitchen and put the water on for tea.

Palle looked at the telephone dial. Guess—guess, make your bet. DA—FA—OB—SO—and then the numbers. And all the fully automatic... Christ. He went out to Birte.

She was tapping the crisp bread with her nail to see if it was crisp enough.

"Well, maybe they'll call again," she said.

"Who?"

"Whoever it was, if there was anyone."

They drank their tea with just the table lamp lit.

"How do you like the caraway cheese?" she asked.

"Unsurpassed. Ask for it next time. What's it called? I mean if I'm the one to do the shopping?"

"You can't count on that anyway. I've had it all explained, it's not the name, it's something about the seasoning, it comes out quite differently every time."

"Pure chance then?"

"You have to enjoy it while you have it, and hope it shows up again before your taste changes."

"Well then, I won't change my taste any more from today on—it's just the thing I want for the rest of my days."

"Ten years ago you couldn't stand caraway cheese or seasoned cheese or any cheese at all, except the school cheese in a red rind."

"Ten years ago I didn't understand a damn thing—not even you."

"Thanks a lot. Maybe you do now?"

"Maybe it's done you good to be seasoned a little, too."

She kicked him on the shin, but it was with her slipper and painless.

"Not to mention your caraway taste," he smiled and pulled his chair out on time—"even though you can turn out differently from time to time, too..."

She sprang up, her eyes flashing lightning. It was probably an act, but you couldn't tell it from real lightning. He had burned himself a few times before, so he remained on guard.

She sat down again quietly. So it was just exhibition lightning. He wondered how she would look when she was completely beside herself so she couldn't even flash lightning...

She buttered a piece of crisp-bread for him. When he brought it up to his mouth it snapped in two, it was only held together by the butter and cheese.

"It wasn't intentional," she said (excuse me didn't appear in her vocabulary), "I thought I had patched it carefully. Give it to me."

But he had already laid the pieces together and bit crunchingly into them. The rattle of the diaphragm, Asta, Eva, Minerva.

"Are you still thinking about the telephone," she asked.

"Well, maybe..."

"Who could it possibly have been?"

"You don't think there's anyone who cares to call us?"

"At this hour, I mean."

"But frankly speaking," Palle quickly finished his mouthful, "does anyone care to call us?"

"I think you're just tired."

"Naturally people call us up. But seriously now... is there anyone who really cares about us, aside from just hearing how things are going, or to say they've bought a car, or that they're taking a little trip, or whether we've saved the paper from the seventeenth, for there was something there they wanted to see, and they've happened to throw theirs away."

"What had you imagined? Should they pour out the story of their lives to you—or ask for yours? What is it you expect, all in all?"

Palle bit into the folded up bread again. EXPECT—expect. No, it wasn't like that . . .

"Why do you always leave a little in the bottom of the cup? It's the same with your milk at breakfast."

"Excuse me, I've never thought about it."

He hastened to drink the cold bitter dregs, while he smiled bravely at her. Aegir, Amager, Nora—Amager, Poul . . . but why should it be him in particular?

She stood with her green slacks over her arm and the hanger in her mouth, she'd learned that from him. Marriage, habit or profit. The slacks were hanging down so he couldn't see her from the front, but in a moment she'd turn and go in. He swung around in the chair so as not to miss the sight, threw one leg over the arm of the chair.

"It could have been my mother," he tossed out, "maybe something's wrong with Dad."

"So call her up," she said as she turned her back to him. He sat so low that he could both see where her thighs met and sense where they parted again below her buttocks.

"Not at this time of night."

"But she can call you?"

"Well, no one's saying that it had to have been her."

"Do as you like, I'm going to bed now anyway."

She hung the hanger with the trousers in the built-in closet, went over and turned down the heat, and went into the other room to fuss with the sofa bed.

Palle sat up straight in the chair again. If there was something wrong with his father, there was nothing he could do about it anyway, and then besides he'd find out about it in the morning. He turned up the heat again a little. Remember to turn it down. Buttoned up his shirt and sat back.

Suddenly it struck him that if he phoned, there could be someone else phoning him at the same time. He was tied hand and foot. He sat up with a jolt and began biting his nails. If he was going to call, it had to be soon, it was after twelve, one couldn't in all decency . . . there was nothing to do but take the chance. No, he'd give the telephone a chance first, five . . . no, four minutes: if it didn't ring again within four minutes, he would call someone or other and then hope for a bite, or at least not be called himself meanwhile. He began on the nails on his left hand while he watched the clock.

When the four minutes were up, he dialed AM and gave the number. A long time passed. College prep course, excursion to the morain formations in the Deer Park, where Poul failed to appear; he had dropped out the day before, and the teacher's comments beneath the beech tree: "He was congenial and charming as a person, but was unfit for scientific work. This has been an obituary and it was well-meant."

Early untidy spring some place on North Falster, everything had gone to hell, but they took a walk in hell together, Poul failed some entrance exam or other and he himself frightened out here in the province by Birte's plans to take a job in a home in England or France before they got married. Poul and he walked slowly along the beach and caught sight of a fishing stake that had washed up on the beach. With a joint effort, they got it afloat nicely and gave it a shove outwards. Poul stumbled and fell headlong in the shallow water, but remained lying completely still and soaked until the pole turned out into the current and went east.

"At last," said Poul then, "that was wonderful, by God."

And Palle remembered the relief he had felt at the other's relief, from now on everything would inevitably go better. And things had gone very well for him, too, but for Poul?

Finally he heard a voice: "Hah?"

"Yes, is it you Poul, it's Palle—Jesus, please excuse me for calling at this crazy hour—had you gone to bed? Oh, that's too bad—no, it was only—someone telephoned me, but I don't know who it was."

"Didn't you ask who it was?" came the sleepdrowned reply from Poul.

"Yes, of course—that is, no—you see ... I didn't talk to the person in question at all—"

"Did either of you say anything?"

"The thing is, the telephone rang just as we were on our way up the stairs, so I didn't get ..."

A strange hollow sound came out of the telephone, the poor man was obviously in his bare feet, freezing. Palle hastened to finish his explanation:

"And so I thought it might have been you, but I can see that it wasn't, please excuse me, but if it had been something important, you see—well, good night, Poul—and ... hey, Poul? Are you still there—won't you stop by someday, it's been a long time ..."

"Oh, yes," there came despairingly.

"But we can give you a call about that, now hurry back to bed again, and excuse me for waking you this way. Give our regards ..."

Palle stood listening a little while without hearing the click.

"Good night, Poul, hurry in now to ... oh ... be sure to get in under the quilts."

He heard a shiver: "Heww—huhh—good night ..."

Finally the click came.

Palle slapped the receiver back and stared at the telephone. Not a sound. He looked at his watch, nearly three minutes. There could well have been a call in the meantime.

"You're not sitting there calling up people at this time of night?" Birte stood in her pink pajamas with toothpaste foam at the corners of her mouth.

"I've been thinking over what you said. You're right, actually, who should ever conceivably call us, really, at all? It's always we who call them, isn't it? Does anyone ever call, on their own?"

"You're tired. Come on to bed."

"You're the one who's tired." Palle straightened up. "Anyway, I can't go to sleep before I've figured this out."

Birte pulled her chair over in front of him and sat down with her bare toes on his thigh.

"What is it you want to figure out, then?"

"What friends we have anymore, real friends, people who ... who would really be distressed if we got sick or ... went away for a long time."

"Why don't you think about whether there's anyone we'd be distressed to see leave?"

"It's always us who call."

"Yes, but then what do we call about—do we *really* call as you say, don't we just call and arrange something, too, are we seriously concerned about their welfare on the phone, do we confide ... I don't know what it is you want people to use the telephone for, there are things, after all, people have to talk about *without* it—sit and chat together in the same room."

"Good, but then what do we talk about when we're in the same room —work, children, troubles, politics, books, the future ..."

"Good gracious, isn't that more than enough? What else do you expect?"

Expect—expect, back to that again. It wasn't something that could be defined in a word or two, and if one finally found a word for it, at the same time it meant something entirely different which didn't have anything to do with the matter. Friendship, contact, intellectual rewards, oh Jesus, all of it was the kind of stuff that was in the pamphlets and church magazines that came in through the mail slot certain days of the week and which they'd pounced upon when they first got the apartment because it was something for *them* that had come to their residence, someone had ferreted out that they were living here and actually sent something to them—but now they tossed it unread into the wastebasket.

"You should unbutton your jacket when you sit in the easy chair. You get such ugly folds across your stomach one would think you had a car."

Birte tried to unbutton the jacket with her toes. Palle took it off and threw it across a chair, it happened to hang crooked, looked like a scarecrow with broken arms.

"I could understand if we had moved in from the country," Palle continued, "but we were born here in the city. We have known a lot of people. I must have played with a dozen children before I went to school, have attended classes with, let me see . . . twenty some in grammar school —yes, all in all half a hundred. To that add the college prep course, twenty, thirty others, and then later on—but where the hell have they gone— who's left?"

"We do have each other. Aren't we left?"

Birte tickled him in the side with her toes, but he had no desire to laugh now, and so it only hurt.

"Who could it have been."

Palle went at the remains of his fingernails.

She got up without answering, rocked up on the balls of her feet a few times for her flatfootedness. Then she went to bed.

Palle turned slowly to the phone. Dumb and shapeless it looked, the receiver hung down over each side as if the whole thing had melted together. There was something more vigilant about the first telephones where the receiver hung on one side and you had to turn a starting crank as if you were winding up the imminent conversation. Plant the short receiver in your ear instead of settling your head against this wheedling bakelite sausage.

He took a piece of paper and began writing names down. Hans, Ellinor, Thygesen, Onkel, Janus. Sat a while staring at the names. They made no sense to him. It was like a rote list of words he had learned, durch fur gegen ohne wider um . . . he'd forgotten how they should be used, what they governed. On with it, there had to be more lists, someplace or other there had to be a hole—Kristensen, Markussen, Christensen with Ch, did he know anyone by that name or anyone with Kr, he sat weaving random names in, the hell with it, on, better systematically, alphabetically: A, Abel, Asger, Arild—that was the one with time, Arild's time—Bent, Bitten, Borge, Balle, . . . Balle. Could that be possible. Balle, he was the one who didn't like to ask for the return of a loan if it was under ten kroner, as they cunningly figured out and so they always borrowed five or seven seventy-five and amounts like that until one day some idiot tried to put him on and asked to borrow 9.99. From that time on he never lent anything less than ten kroner and began to keep accounts, too.—Balle with the runaway sandwich maid, who drank up his money, and cheated on him with others. Should I marry her, Palle, I think she needs a fixed point in her life (balling point, thought Palle), a home, then she'd stop with the others, don't you think I should jump into it, damn, I think I'll do it! That's the way Balle could take it into his head to call him in the middle of the night, maybe it had been precisely him, he probably hadn't finally decided yet.

Palle dialed the number, then happened to think that Balle had probably gone to Greenland, it had been five years since they'd spoken together, they were probably complete strangers to each other, really he had no desire to talk with Balle. Did he want to talk with anyone at all? Was it he himself there was something wrong with?

He put down the receiver. He wished he could call the soldier without the neck and ask how things were with him during the last hours before he took his shoe and sock off. Or talk with the young soldier with the old face and the hopeless look in the roadside ditch, ask what he had seen, and whether he had later come to look on existence differently.

He went to bed. He felt that she lay awake beside him, but didn't take any notice. He couldn't sleep. They both lay there awake.

Then the telephone rang.

"Aren't you going to get it?" she asked.

Palle didn't answer. His whole body was stiff as a board.

"Are you asleep?" Birte touched his arm—"What's wrong with you? You're shaking. Is there something wrong?"

"It must be a wrong number. Someone we don't know. At this time of night."

"Would you rather I answered it?" She tried to get up, suddenly he could move, he took her in his arms.

"Just stay here."

She lay down again. He could feel that she lay looking at him.

"What is it like to die," he said.

"Why do you ask about that," she answered after a long pause.

"I want to know. Do you ever think about death?"

"No. Only when it's someone in the family that dies. It's been a long time. But I myself tried to die once for that matter . . . that was a long time ago, too."

"I never heard that."

"I never told anyone about it. When we were in Norway. You remember that I sprained my foot when I ran into a boulder?"

"Yes."

"Actually, I died."

Birte lay on her back looking up at the ceiling.

"You remember, I skied down ahead, I was to warn the rest of you when there were any dangerous turns or drops, because I was already familiar with the ski run. I really wasn't worth a tinker's damn because it had been a year since I'd tried it, and everything looked different, the snow cover was hard as glass. And then what I feared came, a slope so steep and long that I realized you others wouldn't escape unhurt. If I'd been alone I probably would have taken it, but then I just managed to turn off. I was going so fast that I couldn't brake quickly enough and I steered right toward a huge, snowcovered boulder. I didn't even have time to react, I barely had time to think: Now you'll die, be smashed against the stone, never get to warn Palle and the others. Then there came a flash of fire, dazzling snow or sun.

I'd probably been lying unconscious with open eyes for a long time. I lay and saw only: my ski boots, the skis, some thin branches and an inconceivably blue sky. I lay for a long time, looking without thinking about what I saw. It was the strongest thing I've ever experienced, but I didn't think about that until later, I just lay there and was there, looked, lay, without thoughts, without a soul, totally empty. It was only later that the question popped up: Why is the sky where the earth should be, why are there branches and blue sky between my skis, where has the earth gone, how did I get here.

I had flown through the rock by a miracle. I had after all myself seen how I steered right into it, and now I lay on my back with my skis up in some branch thicket. In some way or other death had opened itself ajar for me and let me slip out on the other side. What I now lay looking at was something I shouldn't have seen. If it had happened right, I should have stopped seeing the instant I was smashed against the boulder. Everything here was something I shouldn't have experienced at all, everything that happened from now on was something extra, gifts, a bargain.

With great difficulty I freed my feet from the bindings and got up on my feet. It turned out that the boulder had been covered with a huge, sloping snow-pillow. The skis had actually only brushed the side of the boulder and tore through the snow-pillow which I thought was the upper part of the boulder. I'd only hurt my left ankle. The whole thing had probably only taken four minutes. So I hurried over to the trail and called to you, and heard you answer from above, "We're coming!" It was as if your voice struck me in the stomach, I doubled over and pressed both hands against my navel. I burst into tears and wet my pants. It's the shock, I said all the while to myself. Straighten up now, Palle's alive, you're just in shock. How good it was that you were the first one to reach me. I was very fond of you back then, but from that moment it was something completely different. You were the first person."

"And now?"

Birte turned over on her side and laid one leg over his.

"It's strange you made me remember it. I haven't thought about it for a long time. I never thought that I'd forget it. I believed fully and completely that every moment in the whole future would become a gift, I would never ask for anything. But one forgets how it is to die. One forgets how much you love each other. You mustn't think it's gone—I only forget it because of so much else, I'm sorry about it. But it's just like it comes back when one speaks of it. Otherwise I wouldn't have spoken of it. How did you get me to speak of it?

Palle seized her with all fours.

—tr. from the Danish by Judith Doyle, Alexander Taylor, Cynthia Andersen & Benny Andersen

Dannie Abse
OF ITZIG AND HIS DOG

The Iowa Review, Vol. 11, No. 1–1980
David Hamilton, Editor

To pray for the impossible,
says Itzig, is disgraceful.
I prefer, when I'm on my own,
when I'm only with my dog,
when I can't go out
because of the weather
because of my shoes,
to talk very intimately to God.

> Itzig, they nag, why do that,
> what's the point of that?
> God never replies surely?

Such ignorance! Am I at the Western Wall?
Am I on spacious Mount Sinai?
Is there a thornbush in this murky room?
God may never say a word,
may never even whisper, Itzig, hullo.

But when I'm talking away
to the right and to the left,
when it's raining outside,
when there's rain on the glass,
when I say please God this
and thank God that,
then God always makes, believe me,
the dog's tail wag.

construction by Suzan Pitt; *Helicon Nine*, Vol. 2, No. 1–1980
Gloria Vando Hickok, Editor

R.T. Smith
MAKING THE SNOWSHOES

Black Jack, No. 13–1983 ("Rural Cream" issue)
Art Cuelho, Editor

She sits by the lodge fire
bending hickory limbs, shaping
lithe saplings cut on the north side
for slower growth and firmness.
A Crow woman from South Dakota, she forms
two hoops and ties them tight
with hide strips she has chewed soft.
Her hair reflects luster of a raven's flight.
The wind drifts flakes against the lodge.
She learned this skill at her mother's side.
Lacing split strips of pale wood,
she weaves a loose web, thinks
of her man out hunting game, leaving
blue prints as he stumbles
over the earth's white mask.
How long ago did she leave the land
where her fathers slew buffalo?
How long have her hands bled with effort,
moving like wounded animals in the shadows?
Knotting the thongs, she blesses
each flat basket, waves the feathered
medicine stick and makes a small song.
Her eyes hold the color of smoke.
Her voice keeps the gold of the fire.
The ancient strength of hickory,
speed of the wild beast whose skin
secures the withes that will spread
his weight, carry him into winter,
make the hunter of doe and stag,
the comfort of her frozen nights,
float like a shaman over burning snow.
Her skill will bring him home.

AUCTION

After farming poetry for twenty-five years I am retiring and will auction off my poetry farm and all implements next Saturday. Drive five miles north on state highway, turn at sewage lagoon and go west until you reach the old dump site, then turn south on gravel road and go past the rendering plant and follow direction signs from there.

SATURDAY 2:00

Diesel translator

Prose poem combine

Antique iambic cultivator

Carton of hand-made cliche filters

750 bales of couplets

Stainless steel inward image dip-stick

12' x 24' brooding house

300 gallon aluminum free verse tank

14' hog and poet feeder with grantmonger trough

12 packages of objective correlatives

Acme Easy Effort Electronic Alliterator

Epic compressor

Genuine leather surrealism harness

12 gauge oxymoron, like new

Hand-forged image chisel

4 h.p. metaphor pump

Tractor with hydraulic rhyme lift

16' sonnet silo

50 gallon drum of critical solvent

4 barrels doggerel detergent

Cast iron allegory funnel

Imported philosophical throttle

Gas powered internal rhymer

Self-propelled versifier with manure bucket

Panegyric syringe

Heavy duty revisor, needs work

Used palindrome, live and evil

Roll of transparent logic

50 lb. hexameter sledge

Line cutter with carbide tip blade

Galvanized simile dipper

Pun pen

Other items too numerous to mention

Coffee will be served on the grounds

ALEX ANDRINE ESTATE

broadside by Don Olsen; Ox Head Press (1981)
Don Olsen, Editor

cover art by William Tunberg; *Mississippi Mud*, No. 19—1979
Joel Weinstein, Editor

Bill Wilson
DISCOVERABLE LAWS

Tamarisk Press; *Fundamental Car* (1981), by Bill Wilson
Dennis Barone, Editor

Yeah,
I was thorough. I learned the schedule by both heart and mind, in case one failed. With my backup systems in place, I kept watch for any crack or deviance—it's always there that things get busy, look at the sidewalks. Same as with Horatio Alger, my patience got rewarded. Certain discoverable laws surrendered themselves up to me and I was careful to allot them slots in my personal home-made laminated shrine of truth, to clasp the clasp and slip it into its carrying case and then walk around with it everywhere, like when I was a crazy kid with my collection of 45s. At last I came to a point of as they say absolute knowledge, so why was I still hungry? Why because I'll tell you why that was the kind of blah-blah absolute knowledge fit for crank callers to radio talk shows, a quaint Waldorf salad of fix-it-yourself manuals paperback Nietzsche and the Daily News. I had become one of those people who gives extemp speeches on the F train, who spits and drools all over himself and everybody recoils like the sides of a dish pulling back from the rotten pudding it contains. I got locked onto being maybe nineteen, twenty years old, running around beside some railroad tracks trying to think of a big answer. I should have stayed more quiet in myself and let it roll off my back. Live and learn.

Finally the day came to dismiss the bag lunches and the thermoses of ovaltine that had sustained long days in the metropolitan libraries. I took the train to Coney Island and smashed my inadequate shrine fitfully among the concession stands, leaving no ghosts. (Actually there was one small animal ghost, hamster-sized, but it crawled off under the rubbish of that landscape.) Boy, was I ever sick. A whole summer ahead of me like a soggy cardboard box. I wanted to both dissolve and keep going, a shrunken but equally complete universe running in tune with the larger one. Fat chance, sucker! said the sash-weights and the streaked plates, the dull blue Oldsmobiles pulling away from under sealed windows where air conditioners dripped. I thought—stupidly—that I had no choice. I allowed necessity to book me a seat on the quasi-immutable wheel that would at last return me to the gears of circumstance.

One day you meet me on 7th Ave., my face mask of endurance maintaining itself above the revolving door of identity, the fan-tan boredoms. You would be the kind to notice the book in my back pocket, *Ball Four*. I happened to be laughing to myself about the part where Casey Stengel doesn't have time to take a call from Eisenhower. Of course, as we both know, that part never happens, but it sure felt good pretending it had. Then you ask me, "Hey, whatever happened to that shrine of truth you used to carry around?" "Oh, that thing," I say, a little embarrassed. "I lost it one day on the subway and nobody turn-ed it in. Anyway, I found out I'm better off without it. These days I'm throwing away as much as I can, so when I step up to the plate I feel light, clean, and ready to connect." I demonstrate with a practice swing. February becomes March.

In dreams we cross the tracks to ma-and-pa restaurants where good hot meals can still be got cheap. In the meantime I'm asking you please mister to forget: these wax-paper cut-outs in the frames of my glasses.

William Dickey
JANUARY WHITE SALE

New England Review/Bread Loaf Quarterly, Vol. III, No. 3—1981
Jim Schley et al, Editors

The men are different this year in
the January white sale catalog.
For one thing, they are there, they
used not to be: a white sale
was a very blonde lady in a peignoir.
Now men can sell sheets.

All of the men are dark, and they have,
as far as I can see, distinct body hair.
I can see, because the men
in this year's catalog do not wear pajamas.
Dark and naked, they are
more intimate with the sheets.

The sheets, of course, have been changing
for years. Except in hospitals
and the homes of very old people
there are no white sheets. There are sheets
patterned like bamboo, patterned like tigers.
To be in bed is to suggest the jungle.

I wonder, idly, whether somewhere
in the mid-West, there is a home
for beautiful blonde women with only the faintest
suggestion of cleavage, for lovely blond men
with chests that would be hairless if they showed,
but do not show because of their pajamas.

It would be, as it once was, white on white.
Snow drifting gently outside the white drapes
that are reduced in price, and that look
pure, simple, unlaundered.
There would be bedspreads in white chenille.
The experience would be, as it once was, virgin.

But I remember my mother's friend,
when my brother, young and inexperienced in these things
was sent to a white sale, how she
snatched the sheets out of another woman's grasp
and handed them to him, saying:
"Your mother wants these."

He bought them. He was young, and she was right.
So he began to learn what we all learn,
what these naked men and their jungle have come to tell us,
how we darken, how patterns are laid,
beautifully, but inevitably, upon us.

Barbara Stafford-Wilson; *Smoke's Way* (1983), by William Stafford
Graywolf Press; Scott Walker, Editor

Barbara A. Banks
MISS ESTHER'S LAND

Kitchen Table: Women of Color Press; *Home Girls* (anthology; 1983)
Barbara Smith et al, Editors

The crying of a distant trucker's air brakes slashed into the night, set the yard dogs to barking, and snatched Esther uneasy from a fitful slumber. A cow lowed and its mournful sound wrapped about a dull, heavy ache inside Esther's chest. Sitting up, she stared past the digital clock that glowed 2:15, and through the window down at a long, menacing shadow. The shadow sharpened into lines and Esther remembered it was the aged and crippled apple tree lying prone across the bricked walkway, its infant apples turning brown against a ridiculously green front lawn.

Esther sighed. The feeling had begun day before yesterday, the same day the tree tumbled over during a not-unusual June shower. No lightning. No thunder. No reason for the falling tree. Its roots simply eased up out of the sodden Virginia clay and gave up the grip they'd held so long.

It should've died years ago, Esther thought. It was only a nuissance, each spring teasing with its thousands of pink-white promises, only to bear each summer fruit too puny, too bitter to be eaten and savored.

A soft shower began. If it were not raining she'd go out into the fields to walk along the white taut fence rows, bend to scoop a handful of soil, her soil, and roll its rich texture between her fingers. The land. Its fully stocked ponds. Its carefully cultivated fields. Its hundreds of white-washed fence posts stationed as so many sentinels to protect all that was hers. Such thoughts usually brought comfort, but were lacking this morning. There was no solace in recalling the special spot, kept hidden from everyone, including Molly, by a barricade of trees she never cut. Nor was there comfort in knowing that despite her seventy-five years, and the broken hip that never quite healed, she still supervised everything within her land's boundaries, boundaries that extended to the edge of the river, and beyond sight of the house on the other three sides. This was her domain, and the new will would see it was protected even after death. But something was wrong.

She listened for Molly's soft snoring as had been her custom since they'd grown old. Reassured, she thought, Molly's health is good. She'll outlive me by years. I did the right thing with the will. Molly will keep my land from white men and any others who'd clutter my fields with factories and gutted cars and squalid little houses filled with those who would defile it. In afterthought, she added, and Molly will have a home for the rest of her days. My grasping son will have to wait longer to cash in on the land.

The ache throbbed. Perhaps the feeling had something to do with his visit later on today. She wanted to tell him not to bother, but quickly shook the thought away as she was not of the generation of women who felt free to demand their own "space." A celebration, he'd said. A special gift, he'd hinted. She knew what he wanted but could not expose his deceit as she was trapped by her own. She could no more tell her son and his family to stay away than she could tell them she didn't want the new electric stove (that she'd wound up paying for) or the fading curtains her daughter-in-law dumped on her and Molly each spring, or the dutiful Sunday afternoon telephone calls, conversations made vague by her own faulty hearing.

When you're old, she sighed, you lie. You pretend pleasure no matter what you feel because that's what old women are expected to do. And I've been old, it seems, for as long as I can remember.

The dogs quieted. She could hear the swish of tires up on Route 60, drivers impatient with the rain, pushing faster and faster through her Piedmont region, hurrying up, into, and through the Blue Ridge.

Urgency is part of what I'm feeling too, she mused, but they, the nighttime drivers, they know what their impatience is about, unlike this indefinable beast that winds itself tight inside me, a feeling that I have not done something, but what, and is there time, and why do I think there isn't.

It came to Esther suddenly that the feeling was familiar. It had been inside her a long time, steady, dormant, waiting to burst and spill over as it had begun to soon after the signing of the will, the paper she'd been holding at almost the very moment the tree fell, the tree she'd coddled and cajoled long after she'd realized its fruits were gifts only unto itself.

The ominous thing began to surge, rising and swelling, frightening Esther into a loud gasp. She slid her hand across the sheet to clutch a fistful of Molly's gown. The gesture's reward, once passion, was now reassurance as she put the puzzling anxiety aside for a moment in her gratitude for the good health of Molly, Molly who slept beside her in the huge four-poster bed they'd shared secretly for forty years.

Molly leaned over, listened for Esther's steady breathing and eased from under the covers.

"No you don't," said Esther, reaching over to tuck the quilts tightly about Molly's thighs. "Stay put. It's not even 5:30. As damp as it is, you'll catch cold, or worse yet, your arthritis'll have you so crippled you won't be able to run around here taking care of Harold and whoever else turns up to plague us today. Wait 'til I build your cookstove fire when I go out to feed. Let the fire knock the dampness out of the house first." Molly's arthritis was no better than her own. When had they begun to act in caricature of the genuine?

"Happy birthday, you old grouch," Molly said. Her thin face cracked into a wrinkled smile.

Esther grunted. "Can't see how it's going to be that happy with young Harold and his bunch showing up. Just more work for us. You don't think this is going to be an every-year occasion, do you? Why couldn't they stick to coming once a year at Christmas? Why couldn't they give me the best birthday present of all by staying away and giving us some peace?"

Molly smiled again. "What's the matter? I could feel you worrying all night."

"Ah, maybe it's that I'm just tired, tired of being old, and tired of getting older. And I'm not in the mood for all the sweetness we're about to be stuck with once my son gets here. Maybe they won't stay long. Remind me to call the Adams' boys to come remove that tree. I don't want to look at it a minute longer than I have to."

"I'll take care of it. You just relax. This is going to be a big day. The kids have planned a glorious celebration. Contacting all those people, putting together a money tree..."

"What people? What money tree? Jesus H. Christ, Molly, why didn't you stop them? You know how I feel about money trees. Mocking a living thing. The folks who get the things usually don't need the money, or die before they can spend it. Celebration. No need for any fuss. I didn't do anything special to reach seventy-five except not die."

"Es, you've done more for this community than you realize. Everyone who lives here owes you something, and if people want to show their appreciation—"

"Then I wish they'd show it by leaving me alone."

"And, Es," Molly began modestly, "after breakfast, I'd appreciate your help in carrying my personal items down to my old room."

"That's something else I'm tired of this morning, Molly. Don't you ever get tired of these moves you've been making every time somebody shows up for the night? Forty years of lugging your combs and brushes and gowns and colognes and jewelry up and down the steps. Shit!"

Molly, ever the prim schoolteacher, flinched at the profanity, but now was not the time to anger Esther, not with the celebration so near, not with the reward for so many years' hard work near. Still, Esther had never before complained about their secrecy.

"What happens between us is our own personal business, Es. What earthly good would it do anyone to know? Why after all these years are you making an issue of it?"

"And why not? I'm seventy-five years old today. You're sixty-nine. And I suspect that makes us old enough to do as we damned well please."

"What happens in the privacy of one's own...I really don't know why you want to—"

" 'Come-out' is the word you're looking for, Molly."

"Tell others about it. I mean, people defecate, but they certainly don't go around talking about it."

Esther swung her lanky body out of bed. She snatched the paisley housedress, apron and underwear from the chair where she'd laid them out the night before.

"Es, wait."

But Esther was already limping quickly across the floor. The anger felt good, but it did not, as expected, replace the nameless thing that gnawed inside her, frightened her with its intensity. Instead, it began to define it.

Esther stopped at the door. "Defecate? You mean to tell me, Miss Molly, that you've been comparing what we've been doing for the past forty years with shitting?"

She stormed out of the room, stomped down the steps and down the long hallway into the bathroom. "Defecate," she mumbled when she came out and leaned against the wall to tug on the tall gum boots.

In the kitchen, she snatched the eyes off the wood cookstove. She splashed kerosene over the stack of kindling and green wood inside. Carelessly, she threw a lit match into the stove. Flames leaped up quickly, singed her hair. "Talk about shit, Miss Molly, you better start using the new electric stove because I'm getting tired of this shit," she shouted.

At the kitchen door, she paused, then retraced her steps through the dining room, past the bathroom and through the hallway until she stood at the front door near the foot of the stairs. "Not that I care," she yelled, "but you better stay up there until the fire dries some of this dampness 'cause if you get sick, you'll find out what shit really is when you're up a certain creek without a paddle, Miss Molly, 'cause I'm not going to nurse you."

"Defecate," she grumbled as she stepped out the front door to be met by the fallen apple tree which only enraged her more. "Shit," she said half-heartedly, "I'm so tired."

And Miss Esther went back to bed.

Esther lay fully clothed. She didn't mean that, she thought. I know she didn't. It's just that I'm so tired. Sure wish this feeling would go a-way. But the feeling nagged. She looked out the windows and was surprised at how much she could see now that the tree no longer blocked the view. Fields of corn and wheat and clover and tobacco in various shades of green contrasted with the purplish-blue of the post-storm sky. She followed the gradual slopes of the fields from the muddy James River in the east to the tall trees that hid her special spot in the west. She wished she could see that spot again, the place she'd been tempted to share with Molly but never had. Would she ever go there again? Was it the same? So pure. Untouched, and she liked to think, unseen by man. A shame nobody loved the farm as she did. Well, maybe Molly did. She *had* helped her hold onto the place.

Molly appeared in the window's lower left corner. She leaned on a tobacco stick and picked her way carefully around the puddles in the path that led to the outbuildings, the pig pen and the chicken coops and yard. The hounds approached the frail, birdlike figure. Unused to anyone but Esther carrying the slop buckets, they suspiciously sniffed the boots of Esther's Molly wore, were puzzled but followed anyway.

When Molly went into the corn house, Esther fumbled inside her nightstand drawer for a crumpled package of forbidden cigarettes. Her jaws ached for the long-retired pipe stem. Damn doctors. Molly would smell the smoke when she returned, but she wouldn't say anything, just as Esther never mentioned the bottles of brandy that kept appearing in the back of the cedar closet. Why hadn't she mentioned the will to Molly? It didn't use to be this way. All the secrets. When had they begun? And why *is* that traffic so loud up on that highway? When once she'd complained about the highway noise to Molly, Molly'd said, "Don't forget, that highway brought me to you." And Esther remembered clearly the fall of '38.

Beneath the shadow of a Dr. Pepper sign that sagged, rusted against the side of Williard's cinderblock store at the edge of Route 60, stood a thin young woman who patted her foot impatiently. Esther prodded the mules that pulled her wagon across the newly-paved road. Damn. The bus got in early.

Sharing her home with a stranger didn't set too well with Esther, and the idea of sharing anything with this high-yella, serious-looking woman who obviously was the boarder made Esther wonder how much she needed the money. She wondered if she could back out of the agreement she'd made with the school superintendent, but then she remembered that taxes were due.

The woman looked warily from the approaching team of mules to the tall, handsome black-skinned woman who leaned from the wagon, pipe-stem stuck between her teeth, grinning.

"I'm Esther Watts. You're to board with me."

"I'm Molly Simpson. Pleased to meet you."

"You don't look so sure of that," Esther laughed.

And so they met.

When Esther realized Molly was being intimidated by the mothers of the children she taught, she quietly set the women straight. And when Molly saw how Esther struggled with the farm accounts and ledgers, she offered help and gradually took over all the farm's bookkeeping.

Molly was shocked that Esther was so nonchalant about making a profit from the farm. She seemed to only care about making things grow and holding onto the land. Molly saw the awe on Esther's face when she stared out over the flourishing fields, and she heard her walk the floors at night, worrying over bills run up by her late husband, Big Harold.

When Molly discovered Esther was having trouble meeting the increased taxes the year all the money crops failed because of the drought, she suggested Esther allow the white men's hunt club to hunt along the game-rich river banks in exchange for their payment of the yearly farm taxes. The club agreed, and Esther sighed in relief.

But that's not all Molly did. She introduced Esther to the world of books, books written by people who loved land as Esther did. Esther was impressed by the strangers who could articulate the things she did not know, and never would know how to say.

But the fourth summer after Molly came was the finest, the summer Molly didn't go away to North Carolina for her regular summer job. Molly stayed right there on the farm, cooking and cleaning and smiling from those great hazel eyes that watched Esther knowingly, though neither of them knew just yet what it was those unsettling eyes knew.

On Esther's thirty-fifth birthday, Molly rushed in flushed from running, hair spilling from its proper bun. She carried a spindly out-of-season apple tree. The gift stirred Esther. She yearned for something she did not quite understand. Molly, who had always appeared serious and angular in the gray and black frocks she wore on alternate days to school, seemed soft and smooth and lovely in the violet spray of late evening that filtered through the curtains.

Esther kissed her. She pressed her mouth softly upon Molly's and was struck still by the newness of the thing, by her own naivete. She did not know how to touch her, was not sure if she should, was afraid she'd spoil this wonderful thing by making it carnal. Frustrated, she stammered, "Now what do I do?"

By morning, the issue had been resolved.

But it was never about sex, Esther thought, never about sex, not when it was good, so good did Molly taste of Eagle Brand cream with just a hint of cinnamon. And Esther, astute, rejoiced because in Molly lay her survival which was to her the survival of the land. And that was paramount though it *was* made sweeter because the sex was good, that in this expected-to-be-awkward coupling there could be grace and beauty and power—an incredible sense of power she had not known before, not even with the land that always strained against her in the constant struggle that would always make her love it best. But with Molly, there was no struggle, Molly moved as she moved, my God, the first taste of possession can be so very sweet.

So in the summers, Esther rushed from the fields at noon, laughing, filling her mouth with bread Molly baked, repeating the latest jokes the hands told. They joked a lot in those days, knowing they'd be paid on time. And sometimes while the men waited in the fields for Esther's return, she'd pull Molly to her, murmuring into her cheek, "You really love me, better than God or anybody, don't you?" and then would wallow shamelessly in her own good fortune when Molly whispered, "Yes."

And when the winters came and heavy snows covered the fields, and there was no school, Esther would awaken before dawn, dress quietly in the dark, rush to feed, milk, and cut firewood, and by seven, be sitting across from Molly at the bleached-white oak table eating sausages and eggs from the farm Molly saved. And when the dishes were washed and dried, they'd take thick mugs of steaming coffee back to bed where they'd lie most of the day, isolated by the snow—Esther praising the land and Molly raging against the Jim Crow school—neither of them knowing which they preferred, to touch or to talk.

It was good then. Where had it gone? The snowbirds red, bright red, everything was brighter then. And the lilacs and wild yellow roses, transplanted from the fence rows to the edge of the yard because Molly liked flowers all over the place, because Molly felt life should burst in flaming celebration of itself. Where had it gone, and when, leaving behind the nagging truth that there are no flowers in the front yard now, and the apple tree is dead?

"Es? Are you awake, Dear? It's after ten. I'm sorry for what I said. A poor choice of words."

"It's okay. I saw you going out to feed. Did you throw two buckets of nubbins to the hogs, and broadcast loose corn up on the high ground for the chickens?"

"Certainly did."

"Thanks for doing my chores. I'll get up in a bit. I'm just too tired right now. I'll help you take your things down in a while."

"I took them down while you dozed."

"Oh?"

"And, Es, please try to feel better soon. I know you don't like a fuss, but this celebration means a lot to me."

"Yeah. Close the door on your way out, please."

When Molly was gone, Esther lighted another cigarette. Why hadn't she told her about the new will yet, the will leaving everything to her except the token amount to Harold?

It began to rain again. The river was rising, and Esther wondered if it'd overflow its banks again. It was already swollen, spilling into the bottom land, and Esther remembered another day long past when the river threatened the crops that grew along its edge.

On a day when the river flowed thick like a fat brown worm, stretching and winding its way through the Piedmont lowland, lavishing its lushness along the banks, Molly packed her bags and left. She just upped and left.

For weeks she'd been quiet and distant, talking only when she tried to interest Esther in the ledgers. Once she became so irritated, she threw up her hands and said, "How will you ever manage if something happens to me?" Esther just laughed and said, "Then I'll throw myself into the grave behind you." And Molly quietly asked, "And leave the land?"

But Esther paid no attention. Tobacco beds had to be burned and sowed. The barns had to be cleaned, and anyway, Molly always got moody when something upset her at school. It wasn't that she was insensitive to Molly's needs. It was simply that she never believed, as Molly did, that through books and learning, one could "pull one's self up by the bootstraps." Freedom came with owning the boots. She'd watched Molly struggle with torn and out-of-date textbooks, and the white school superintendent who ignored the dozen or so colored schools spread out over the county. And though she'd often held Molly in her arms while Molly raged against the unfairness of it all, Esther privately blamed the parents of Molly's students for their plight. After all, they'd sold their land to white folks for piddling sums, and that was why their rootless children were doomed. Once, half asleep, she'd snapped at Molly to quit bitching about the school and quit the damned job. She was more useful on the farm anyway.

But she never thought Molly would go. That she would leave the person she loved better than God? No. Never. She hadn't even believed it when she came in from the fields expecting her dinner hot, and found Molly packing. When she asked why, Molly said, "You don't know why? Well, let's just say I'm not happy here, not anymore."

Esther was numb. But the river was rising. The cows had to be moved. And she went back to the bottom land thinking by the time she came in, Molly's things would be put back neatly in the first and third bureau drawers.

When she came in and Molly was not there, she kept thinking, she'll be back. She'll get over what's bothering her and she'll be back. But in the late evening when the dogs hunched their bodies into open-ended balls beneath the glider on the long front porch and whippoorwills provided music for dancing fireflies, Esther rose from the creaking glider, and went back into the dark house where she did not light a lamp. She placed her single cup into the sink and heavily mounted the stairs. Inside the room where she now lay, she looked at the empty bed and wailed, clutched her own thick black hair and wailed, "My God, my God, she's gone," and then was still.

But the land was there, needing, unfailing in its needs, and Esther responded woodenly at first. She spent her days taciturn with the hands who wondered at her change, and her nights brushing her hair, trying not to remember how beautiful Molly said it was. She came in late from the fields, laid her clothes out for the morrow and slept dreamless in the half-empty bed. At first she had trouble sleeping, but in a week, she forced herself to sleep. She had to get her rest. The land had its needs. And it would not fail her.

Esther awakened to the buzzing of a power saw. Molly must have called someone about the tree. Well, she wouldn't have to look at that anymore.

Through the east window she watched the workmen. In the background was the graveyard where Big Harold's lone tombstone stood. She could see the pinkish marble stone clearly though it was partially shaded by a spreading cedar tree on a knoll overlooking the river. Time to mow the grass out there again. She wondered why she'd begun to groom the graveyard. It had been ignored for so long. Now a border of lilies grew just inside the fence that protected it from the cows. The feeling came back, but this time she would not run from it. Maybe if she followed the thought that brought the feeling, it would take her back to its meaning. Then maybe it would go away. She'd learned to do that after Molly left.

When Big Harold plunged, drunk and unsteady, from the barn roof he was tarring, Esther chose to bury him on the farm rather than in the church cemetery. He'd never set foot in church and it seemed hypocritical to bury him on the church grounds. But that was where it should have ended. Weeds should've been allowed to overtake the grave.

She'd married Big Harold Watts when she was barely fifteen because she was tired and scared and because it was expected. She was tired of people stopping her on the road to ooh and aah over what a strong, independent young thing she was, taking over the farm as she had after her folks died, and then hearing them say as soon as she walked away that she'd lose the farm before the year was out. A woman couldn't run a farm alone, not four hundred acres. Esther was afraid they were right. She worried over taxes, and poor crops, and hands half-doing their jobs, exasperating her into firing them, or having them quit because she couldn't always pay. And the land had to be saved, no matter what. So when Big Harold showed up, looking for work, she'd looked him over as a mule she was thinking of buying. He was big and strong, and maybe the hands would listen to him.

Harold did not work out. And she couldn't fire a husband. At first he laughed and dreamed a lot. Later he took to drink and gambling.

Once Molly asked if she'd turned to her instead of a man because she'd had a bad marriage. After thinking a while, Esther answered, "No. It wasn't a bad marriage. It just wasn't any kind of marriage at all. He never understood what was important to me. No one has except you."

And Molly had smiled sadly out of those knowing eyes and changed the subject.

So when Big Harold fell to his death sixteen years after they'd wed, Esther was almost relieved. She generously acknowledged privately that Big Harold had done her two enormous favors: he'd given her a male child who would love the land as she did, and he'd died before running up more debts. But the summer of his death, young Harold ran away to join the navy, and Esther discovered just how deeply in debt her dead husband had plunged her. She didn't know what she'd have done if Molly hadn't come along then. So when Molly came back and suggested she mow the graveyard grass because "people might talk and then they might suspect," naturally she did.

In late August, when the fields were whipped dry by an unrelenting sun, and the corn had hardened ready for harvest, and the first of the apple tree's bitter fruit lay in rotting heaps in the tangled front yard, Molly came back.

When she tried to explain why she'd gone, Esther gently discouraged her by saying, "If you tell me nothing, there'll be no lies between us."

Molly spent the first week straightening up the account books that Esther'd filled with doodles and great blobs of ink, dusting the house from top to bottom using red oil recklessly, and when she wasn't being bookkeeper/housekeeper/real contrite, she was frenzied in her passion, dragging Esther back to bed at all hours murmuring, "I love you, I love you, better than God or anybody, better than God, Miss Esther, better than God I love you, Miss Esther."

But Esther had retreated into her now analytical mind, the mind she'd honed during long lonely evenings in the half-empty four-poster bed where she now thought Molly certainly no lady. And where once there'd been a kind of holy delight, Esther longed for her silent fields, felt exploited and somehow cheated as she pondered the frantic desperation in Molly's newly-grown long fingernails.

Molly never again complained about the school system, just ticked off the years until early retirement. She joined all the civic clubs, even created a few—all of which were aimed at "uplifting the race." When she wasn't working on her committees (she declined all offices saying she was, after all, an "outsider"), she threw herself into making Esther a wealthy woman whose wealth was recognized in the county seat. Not only did she handle the ledgers, but she began suggesting more lucrative money crops and investments. And when the adjoining hundred acres of river land came up for sale, she urged Esther to buy it because it held a right of way through her own acreage, an arrangement that bothered Esther though no one had ever abused the arrangement before. Esther bought the land, but as a gift for Molly.

Sometimes, in the months that followed Molly's return, Esther would look up suddenly to catch a look of loss in Molly's eyes, but that was rare. They were both so busy. Molly with her quest, and Esther with the land. Whenever Molly needed money for this one's bail, or that one's dinner, for this cause or that, she went to Esther who still cared nothing for money and gave freely. It was a small price to pay for what Molly had given her, the freedom to own outright the land her ex-slave grandpa had begun buying two months after the end of official slavery.

Sixty cents a day he worked for, slaving still from sunup to sundown, clearing off white men's land, and never getting more than a few sections of his own cleared. When Esther was five, the old man had taken her by the hand to the special spot, watched her face and said, "Gal, you got the love, you got what none of my own chllun has, you got the love to keep this land from white men, and as long as you do, you free."

But she'd never told this to anyone, not to her son and not to Molly because to fully explain the importance of that moment, she'd have to tell of the special spot, a place more beautiful to her than any music, any book, or any person. You see, it was a place for herself, a reflection of her nakedness.

"Es, please get up. It's past dinnertime. The guests should start arriving about two. You've got to get dressed. Don't lie there sulking. I apologized."

"Did they haul away the tree?"

"Yes, the darnedest thing. Jesse said it was all hollowed out, cleaner than a bone. The only thing he could figure was ants. He saw a few around the tree, said you probably ought to spray out there. Is that what's been on your mind? That tree? My lands, it never even produced one decent apple, did it?"

"You ought to know, Molly, you gave it to me, remember?"

"So I did, didn't I? Es, wear your blue. Here, I'll just take it down to press it."

"Molly, I've been wondering about something. Why'd you come back the summer you left me?"

"Es, we don't have time to talk about that now. My goodness, that was more than thirty-five years ago, and I was only gone three months. Why're you thinking about that now?"

"Please, Molly, I need to know."

"Because I loved you."

"That's not enough."

"It never was."

Today has something to do with my land, Esther thought as she bathed. Harold wouldn't be making that long drive if there wasn't something it for him. White folks don't come out to praise an old Black woman who has given money only to her own kind. And everything in my life has somehow been connected to the land. But Molly, what has Molly got to do with all this? Have I made a mistake about the will?

"Es, are you dressed? Harold isn't here yet, but the mayor is downstairs already. Lots of other people. Thank goodness it stopped raining. We're going to have quite a crowd."

"Molly, what has all this got to do with my land?"

"What? Oh, Esther, those people downstairs want to repay you for all your years of community good, they want to put up a monument to your generosity, your commitment to the betterment of our people—"

"Save the fancy words, Molly, about my land."

"Please, Es, I hear more cars..."

"About my land, Molly."

"All right. I'm not saying this celebration has anything to do with it, but there are some who want you to sell the hundred acres of river land. I've agreed to sell them mine. So has Jake Barnes. They'll pay you well. They want to build a planned community for our people, Es. Just think, something I've worked and dreamed of for years. Good schools, decent housing, even a library. Don't worry, they won't build any houses on your section. I've seen to that. That'll be a park, Es, a park, where children can play. And Es, they'll name it after you, the whole thing—"

"They knew better than to come to me, so they came to you, and you agreed. Why, Molly, why? I thought you loved the land as I do."

"You can't love things that can't love you back. Now, please, Es, hurry."

"The answer is no."

"Please, Esther, for me."

"For you? Do it for you? What have I done in the past forty years that was not for you? You say people are waiting down there to honor me for holding civil rights meetings in my home, for bailing out sit-in demonstrators, for feeding bastard children of slovens, for forcing the school board to buy new books, but you deserve that credit. Anything I've done was for you. Go celebrate. My God, Molly, how could you, knowing the one thing in the world I loved was—"

"Your land? Go ahead and say it, Es. I've always known it."

"Yes, dammit, I love my land."

"Without me, you'd have lost it."

"Maybe. But now I pay dearly. Why did you *ever* come back?"

"Because I loved you then. Why haven't you ever asked why I left?"

"Damn why you left. My land. My land. The right of way. You want money? Take the money off that damned tree downstairs on your way off my land. Get off! Get off!"

"Es, look at me. It wasn't money. Didn't you hear anything I said? It's because I wanted to make things better for a change for people who didn't have a chance. But I couldn't change things. I had no power. Look at me! I was just a colored teacher whose main responsibility was making sure the pickaninnies looked well-groomed with vaselined legs and freshly pressed hair on the one day a year the superintendent deigned to appear. Those children didn't stand a chance in hell, and there was nothing I could do. I had no power. But there was power in your land. It stood for money and it could make money, something whites had to respect. But you never saw that. To you the land was an end unto itself. You and the land. Inseparable. Selfish. One. No wonder you mourn that tree. I left you because—look at me, dammit!—because I was tired of being used by you to save the land."

"But you came back—"

"Because of the land. Oh, maybe it was an excuse then. I loved you, and any excuse was good enough. But when I got back, you were completely closed to me. So I decided if I were to be the servant of the land, I'd unleash its power and use it for some unselfish good."

"Then it hasn't been all 'shit' to you then, these forty years? Well, Molly, how do you think those people downstairs will feel about honoring you through me if they knew about us?"

"Oh, Es, maybe in the beginning it was important to pretend to be what we weren't. I thought it was. But not now. What makes you think they don't know it anyway? If any one of them has ever thought about it, they know. But people are wonderful at ignoring things when it's to their advantage. You've been a master of that. You want to go down there to tell them? Go ahead. They'll just look at each other and nod silently that ole Miss Esther is getting senile. They want the land, and they'll have it, if not today, then when you die. Harold will surely sell it. And remember, they've got the right of way. If you don't sell it to them, Es, there'll be no park. Houses will go up down on your acreage too. Either way you lose. Why not lose gracefully and gain something?"

Esther sagged against the dresser. The thing inside was bursting.

"Just get out of my sight, Molly. You've won, no need to gloat."

"Es, I'm sorry. We'll talk later. Try to be happy for me. Try to think of someone other than yourself for a change."

While the guests in the back parlor taped dollar bills to a retrieved branch of the apple tree, Esther laid the will upon Molly's nightstand and quietly slipped from the house. She paused at the gaping hole in the front yard where the apple tree had been. A wry smile crossed her face and then was gone. The dogs came up whining, wagging their tails. They followed her to the corn house where she got a hoe. She locked the dogs in. Then she walked through the wet fields as quickly as the bad hip would permit.

At the bottom of the hill below the barn, she paused at a fresh water spring, wiped spider webs from a rusted, dented dipper that hung from a nearby tree. Crawdads scurried along the bottom of the ice cool pool as she scooped a final drink. She rose then and followed the spring's overflow until it deepened into the stream that would lead her to the special spot. Please let it be the same.

Honeysuckle vines hung in a dripping arc over the path she followed. She carried the hoe poised to strike and paralyze any moccasin or rattlesnake that dared slither beneath the leaves upon which she stepped. Nothing must stop her from reaching the top of the hill where she could rest, feel whole again. It must be the same.

The widening stream became the swimming hole of her youth. A smiling young Molly swam naked beneath the water's surface. She shook her head to clear it of all visions of Molly, past or present. Nothing mattered except getting to the special spot.

By now they knew she was gone. Soon they would come looking. It wasn't far now. Just a few hundred yards to the thick clump of trees that grew trunk to trunk, so close they could not expand in girth so they grew taller and taller stretching toward the sky and breathing room, concealing the hill and its plateau.

At the trees she started to turn for one last glimpse of the house, but didn't. None of that mattered any more. There was not much time, and soon they would begin to search.

Stooping, she hoisted her dress and squeezed between two trees and two horizontal lines of rusting barbed wire. She stepped inside where it was cool and green and safe.

It was the same!

It was still the same huge room with its ceiling of thick leafy branches of oak, hickory, ash and black walnut trees which grew so evenly spaced, their planting appeared planned.

The floor upon which she walked was a pungent carpet of layers and layers of moist decaying leaves that stretched flat for a quarter of an acre, then was dissected by a twisting stream of clear spring water that rippled softly over pale flat stones.

She knelt upon the scarab green moss at the stream's edge, stuck her left hand into the cooling water. The pain in her chest now extended down her arm and into her fingers. She knew she could not tarry long. She sloshed through the stream and continued over more of the soft carpet until it abruptly ascended the hill that rose swiftly, almost perpendicular to the ground upon which she stood. The soft patter of a fresh shower fell upon the roof of leaves. They would not find her now.

Once she would have run madly up the steep incline to get to the twin trees in the center of the plateau, but now she walked slowly around to the hill's far side to climb its gradual slope. She climbed steadily, slowly.

Finally. She was there. Standing between the twin dogwood trees. The green roof overhead. The muted orange, brown, yellow leaf-covered earth beneath her feet. The blue lupine, the violets, May apple and morning-glory growing wild in the scattered cones of sunlight.

She looked out over winged green leaves and bright red bells of trumpet vines that grew along the plateau's ridge, and down into the valley where the stream rippled quietly. She grew heady in the musk of damp rich earth and wild flowers. The animals, no longer frightened by her presence, reappeared. Squirrels leaped from tree to tree. A doe and two spotted fawns paused to take long sips from the stream. A rabbit took tentative steps in her direction. A bird began to sing. Esther wondered at its haunting melody that brought a vision of a young Molly carrying a twig of an apple tree. The vision shimmered, then was gone.

A whisper of a thought. Perhaps if you'd shared this with Molly . . . .

No, she could not have borne betrayal of the special spot. It was part of herself that was pure and good and free, and as long as she kept it from others, it was the source of her strength, as long as it was kept sacred, secret, *nothing* that happened outside the barricade of trees that grew trunk to trunk could destroy her. Big Harold, Young Harold. Molly . . . yes, Molly too. That was the worst. Couldn't have stood up under that without . . . . None of that mattered here. She laughed out loud. She was God here. She and God and the land. The trinity. This was her church, the place where she worshipped her own self, filled herself with strength at an altar of trumpet vines. She laughed again.

And what was Molly, a sacrificial lamb?

Enough of that, she thought. With or without her, I'd have saved my land. Besides, she got as much as she gave. Esther marveled at how clearly she could see things here. It's fitting that this place die with me. It's the best part of me, she thought.

She leaned back into the hollow of the intertwined trees, the backrest of her throne. Something glittered in the leaves at her feet. She uncovered it with the hoe. It was a crumpled, still shining beer can. And Esther raged.

She rose, jabbed the hoe furiously toward the sky, ranted, raved, shook in her wrath, and was storming off the hill toward the house when the ominous thing inside her burst into a massive implosion.

The mourning dove ended its clear elegy.

Ernesto Cardenal
TAHIRASSAWICHI IN WASHINGTON

Unicorn Press; *Poets Of Nicaragua* (1982), Ed. & tr. by Steven F. White
Teo Savory, Editor

In 1898 Tahirassawichi went to Washington
"only to speak about religion"
      (as he said to the American government)
      only to preserve the prayers.
And the Capitol did not impress him.
The Library of Congress was all right
but it did not serve to keep the sacred objects
that only could be kept in their mud lodge
              (that was falling down).
When they asked him at the Washington Monument
if he wanted to take the elevator or the stairs
he replied: "I will not go up. The white man makes piles of stones
to go up them. I will not go up.
      I have gone up the mountains made by Tirawa."
And Tahirassawichi said to the Department of State:
"Tirawa's Lodge is the round blue sky
      (we do not like it when there are clouds between Tirawa and us)
The first thing that has to be done
is to choose a sacred place to live,
a place consecrated to Tirawa, where man
can live in silence and meditation.
Our round lodge represents the nest
      (the nest where we can be together and keep the small children)
In the center is the fire that joins us into a single family.
The door is for anyone to enter
and for visions to enter.
Blue is the color of Tirawa's Lodge
and we mix blue earth with riverwater
because the river represents the life that flows
without stopping, through the generations.
The pot of blue paint is the dome of the sky
and we paint an ear of corn that is the power of the earth.
But that power comes from above, from Tirawa.
That is why we paint the corn the color of Tirawa.
Then we offer tobacco smoke to Tirawa.

Before, one did not smoke for pleasure, only in prayer.
The white man taught the people to profane tobacco.
On the paths we greet all things with songs,
because Tirawa is in all things. We greet the rivers:
from far away the rivers are a line of trees
     and we sing those trees
closer, we see the line of water, and we hear its sound
and we sing the water that flows with its song.
And we sing the buffaloes, but not on the prairies.
We sing the *Song of the Buffaloes* in the lodge
because there are no longer any buffaloes.
And we sing the mountains because Tirawa made them.
We go alone up the mountains when we wish to pray.
From there one sees if there are enemies. Or if friends are coming.
The mountains are good for man, that is why we sing them.
And we sing the mesas, but we sing them in the lodge
because we have not seen mesas,
     those mountains flat on top
but they have told us that our fathers saw many mesas
and we remember what they saw so far away in their journeys.
And we sing the dawn when it comes in the east
and all life renews itself
(this is very mysterious, I speak to you
     of something very sacred)
We sing the morning star
the star is like a man and is painted red,
     the color of life.
We sing when the animals wake
and come from their hiding places where they slept.
The doe comes first, followed by her fawn.
We sing when the sun enters the door of the lodge
and when it reaches the edge of the skylight in the center of the lodge
and later in the afternoon when there is no sun in the lodge
and the sun is on the edge of the mountains that are like a wall
of a great round lodge where all the people live.
We sing in the night when dreams come.
Because visions visit us more easily at night.
They travel more easily over the sleeping earth.
They draw near the lodge, filling it completely.
If it were not the truth that those dreams came
we would have abandoned the songs a long time ago.
And we sing in the night when the Pleiades rise.

more

The seven stars are always together
and guide the one who is lost, far from his village
(and they teach man to be as united as they are).
Tirawa is the father of all our dreams
and prolongs the tribe through our children.
With blue water we paint the sign of Tirawa
(an arch and in its center a descending line)
on the face of a child.
    The arch on the forehead and the cheeks
    and the straight line on the nose.
(the arch is the blue dome where Tirawa lives
and the straight line his breath that descends and gives us life)
The face of the child represents the new generation
and the riverwater is the passing of generations
and the blue earth that we mix is Tirawa's sky
(and the blue drawing drawn like this is Tirawa's face).
Later, we make the child watch the riverwater
and he, watching the water, sees his own image as well
as seeing in his face his children and his children's children,
but he is also seeing Tirawa's blue face
portrayed in his face and in the future generations.
Our lodge, I told you, is shaped like a nest
and if you go up a mountain and look around you
you will see that the sky surrounds all the land
and the land is round and is shaped like a nest
so that all the tribes can live together in unity.
The storm can knock down the eagle's nest
but the nest of the golden oriole only rocks in the wind and nothing
    happens to it."

Tahirassawichi, I suppose, has said nothing to the Department of
    State.

—translated from the Spanish by Steven F. White

photocollage by Steven D. Foster; *TriQuarterly*, No. 55—1982
Reginald Gibbons, Editor

Lloyd Davis
BOB HOSEY IS DEAD

Annex 21, No. 4–1982
P.W. Gray, Editor

His brother calls to tell me
just before class
but the afternoon
is taken up with talk
and I don't think about it.

In the car on my way home
at dusk
I do.
It's the middle of March,
three weeks
before the opening
of trout season.

When I get to the airport
the landing lights
are like two lines of blue marbles.
Over the trees
at the end of the runway
a Convair is coming in.

As I take the curve to the left
the plane is opposite my right window.
I see the prop blades turning.
The cabin lights are on.

Then, just before touchdown,
a crosswind lifts the wing.
But at the last second
it holds
level
and steady.

Frank Stewart
TO A FRIEND

The Paper, May-July—1981
Patricia Matsueda, Editor

killed in Dragon Valley, Vietnam

Under other circumstances—you didn't
know me then—I sat with such a blistering
lamp as this beside my face and wrote
those letters that you've found. The full moon,
like a white, disembodied ear, would leap up
above the city, like this one, and hang listening
to the pencil scratch. A chill on the glass.

August. October. You lie there, second wife,
and fall asleep in the white debris reading
the ones returned, all from a friend
who wrote about the moon on a southern ocean,
falling in love in foreign bars, the roar
of a thousand trees snapping at once,
and how it rained on certain sweet autumn
nights something like grease and vinegar.

That's all. Or maybe that time deceives.
I copied out the weather in return, my loss of heart,
friends, and wife, how it ages me, but that I wouldn't die.
The sky's small as a lamp now. The window intimate
as a cheek. A table, a pool of light to extinguish.
When I lie down next to you the pages crackle
like little fires in an enormous field surrounding
us, that makes a mystery out of space, out of
closeness, and who is listening and who is burning.

W.D. Ehrhart
Chapter 1 of VIETNAM-PERKASIE

McFarland & Co.; 1983
Robert Franklin, Editor

All I wanted was a cup of coffee. I was just sitting there, waiting for the water to boil, taking an occasional potshot out the window—and suddenly the world was in pieces. I never heard the explosion. Only the impact registered.

Sprawled out on the floor in a confusion of dust and debris and shredded clothing, I couldn't understand why I hadn't heard anything. "I'm hit bad," I thought, "sonofabitch, they finally got me," while another part of my brain kept screaming, "Jusus fucking Christ, not now, not now, not after all I've been through, oh please not now!" I almost threw up.

I'd been in Vietnam nearly twelve months to the day, and I'd been through one hell of a lot of shit during a year in a Marine infantry battalion: fifteen major combat operations, battalion scouts, patrols and ambushes and night listening posts, rocket attacks and mortar attacks and firefights and even a month at Con Thien—and I hadn't gotten a scratch.

I didn't even have to be on this operation. I was too short, had too little time left in-country: I was due to go home in less than a month. "What the hell," I'd thought, "Can't do diddly-squat back in the rear but sit around on my thumbs and mark days off my short-time calendar. Might as well be with my buddies."

Every Marine sent to Vietnam was supposed to serve there for thirteen months, unless he got a million-dollar wound or a bullet in the head first. When you got down to around ninety days left to go, you got your hands on a *Playboy* centerfold and drew ninety little numbered squares on her body. Each day you filled in one of the little squares on your short-time girl, and when all the little squares were filled in, you were supposed to take your short-time girl back to The World and trade her in for a real one. The morning Captain Broderick told me I didn't have to go on this operation, I had about thirty-five days left on my calendar. "What the hell," I'd said, "Might as well be with my buddies."

It wasn't quite as simple as all that, I suppose. In Vietnam, there were few things worse than having time on your hands—time to think about what you'd been doing and what was going on around you; time to compare the America you'd enlisted for with the one you saw blowing up villages, and tearing up rice fields with tanks and amphibious tractors, and bullying old men and women, and generally running around with your rifle and your name shooting anything that moved; time to think about those articles you kept reading in *Time* and *Stars 'n' Stripes* about protest marches and Vietcong flags in Times Square and Allen Ginsberg trying to levitate the Pentagon; time to imagine what miniskirts looked like on real girls, and wonder if the high school sweetheart you'd gotten a Dear John letter from five months ago was wearing one while every filthy bearded hippie in Trenton fucked her eyeballs out, and her loving every minute of it with flowers in her hair. It could drive you stark raving bonkers. I was more afraid of slack time than I ever was of combat.

And I guess there was more than a little macho in it. You know: "I'm a Marine, I ain't scared of a good fight, and even if I am, you'll be the last one to know about it." Whistling in the dark. One more test.

And anyway, I wouldn't have felt right letting my buddies go without me. It's like when you were a kid and the whole gang trashes old Mr. Bowen's garage, and everybody gets caught but you, and they all have to clean up the garage—and you feel so guilty watching them from your hiding place that you clamber out of the bushes and shuffle over and pitch in without anybody saying a word. Besides, nobody realized it was going to be this bad.

We were going to bail out the U.S. Army again. Our battalion had come down to Phu Bai three or four days earlier from up around the Demilitarized Zone. We'd just spent four straight months in the field, and we'd been sent to the rear to give us a chance to rest and refit. And then the army MACV compound in Hue City radios down to Phu Bai one morning that they're taking incoming small arms and light mortar fire, nothing heavy, but can we send up a relief column and check it out? So we saddled up two companies and a command group, loaded into trucks, and headed up Highway 1 toward Hue.

That was about 0430 hours on January 31, 1968. By the time any of the Americans in Vietnam realized that a major North Vietnamese assault was underway from one end of the country to the other, our little relief column had been caught in one outrageous motherfucker of an ambush barely half of us would survive. Jesus, what a set-up.

Hue is built in two parts, north and south, bisected by the River of Perfumes. As we approached the south side of the city, North Vietnamese Army regulars—NVA—opened up at point blank range from concealed positions on either side of the highway with rockets, mortars, recoilless rifles and heavy machineguns. Marines began dropping like Samoans on iceskates. A lot of them never got up. But I wasn't hit.

And I mean everybody was getting hit. Captain Braithewaite, Alpha Company commander, got a .50-caliber machinegun bullet through both thighs in the first burst of fire. Major Miles, the operations officer, got killed trying to load dead and wounded back onto the trucks. That first day, we lost almost half our fighting strength. It took us nearly fourteen hours to fight our way six blocks north from the edge of the city to the MACV compound one block south of the river—and when we got there, we had a few choice words for the goddamned Army and their goddamned light sniper fire.

We actually got across the river briefly, charging over the long narrow bridge behind our two quad-.50 machinegun trucks. But the quad-.50s got knocked out almost immediately, and we had to fall back to the south side before sundown while we still had anybody left alive. And even then I wasn't hit. Not that day, or the next day, or the next day, or the next day. And everybody was getting hit, some guys two or three times. One gunner from Alpha Company got hit three times in less than an hour.

After that first adrenalin charge across the bridge, most of the fighting in the next two weeks took place on the south side of the river, the side opposite the old city that contained the Citadel of the ancient Annamese emperors. It was the Citadel that later got all the coverage on the six o'clock news, but in the early going, we couldn't even get close to it. We had to set up operations in the MACV compound, a few hundred Marines in a tiny pocket of a city teeming with 2,000 well-dug-in NVA regulars. From there, we slowly began to extend our tenuous hold on the city, one building at a time.

By the third day, the battalion scouts had managed to take a building right across the street from the MACV compound. It was kind of beat up at the moment, but it was a really nice house just the same: three-story concrete and stone construction, a big yard with a low stone wall around it, canopied beds, a wine cellar, oil paintings on the walls, iron bars on the windows to keep out satchel charges. Definitely not your run-of-the-mill Vietnamese hooch. Probably the mayor's residence or the provincial governor's mansion, it was altogether a fine place to set up shop for awhile.

Which was a lucky break for us because for the next two days we couldn't get any farther. Or rather, we couldn't hold anything we took. Come daylight, we'd dash across the street to the next block, fight our way through it house by house: kick open a door, flip in a grenade, leap in shooting, go on to the next floor, then on to the next house—the NVA giving ground slowly and stubbornly, just waiting for nightfall. Then all in one big push, with their overwhelmingly superior numbers, they'd drive us back through the block, across the street, and right back into the mayor's house. Net gain: nothing. Casualties: heavy.

After two days of this, the battalion commander finally decided, "Bullshit, this is crazy. Let's get some flame tanks and do this right." Hooray for the colonel. And we meant it.

That's why I wanted a cup of coffee. There wasn't much else to do on the morning of February fifth because the flame tanks were over by the stadium supporting Alpha Company, and we couldn't have them until they'd cooked all the NVA holding the stadium. So I was just relaxing. Passing time. Enjoying the pleasures of urban warfare.

For a whole year I'd fought in the boondocks. With a few exceptions like Hue, Danang and Saigon, all of Vietnam was the boonies. Thatched-roof hamlets set among rice fields, water buffalo, dirt trails, sand barrens, bamboo jungles, abandoned plantations long overgrown, mangrove swamps—right out of *National Geographic*.

Then, suddenly, a real city. Not New York or Philadelphia, but a city nonetheless, with paved streets and concrete houses, a university, a stadium, big cathedrals, shops and stores, and all the assorted goodies that accumulate in cities. We even found a beer store that hadn't been looted yet, and had warm Vietnamese beer coming out of our ears.

This house-to-house stuff was a new kind of fighting, and we paid dearly for our on-the-job training. But there definitely were amenities, and I was enjoying several of them that morning. Most notably the roof over my head and the overstuffed armchair I was sitting in while I waited for the water to boil. When I'd found out we were going to stay put and do nothing for awhile, I just pulled that big easy chair over to a second-story window in the governor's mansion and sat down to watch the war. I hadn't had much sleep lately and I started getting drowsy. A nice cup of coffee was just what I needed.

Every C-ration meal comes with a lot of things, but five of the things you get are a packet of coffee, a can opener, a plastic spoon, a big can (maybe with crackers and jam and cocoa inside), and a little can (maybe bread or date pudding). To make coffee, you empty the big can (eat the contents if you're hungry, or put them in your pocket for later), bend the lid back into a handle, and fill it with water from your canteen. Then you take your can opener and make a few air holes around the bottom of the little can, which you've also emptied. You bend the little can slightly at the open top end so the big can will sit on it, and that's your stove. You're supposed to get a heat tab with each meal, but usually you don't, so you just take a little piece of C-4 plastic explosive—it won't blow up if it's not under pressure—put that in your stove instead, and light it. You get up-wind of it so the fumes from the C-4 don't kill half your brain cells, put the big can on top of the little can, and when the water boils, you pour in the packet of coffee and give it a good stir with your plastic spoon. I was just about ready to pour in the coffee when the world came apart. Things were fine. Then they weren't. Just like that.

Most of the casualties we took in Vietnam got it in their first few months in-country, or their last few months. Guys got it in their first few months because they simply hadn't yet learned enough to avoid getting it. But guys got it in their last few months because they got stupid in a way that the new guys never could.

Because they couldn't suppress just a little longer the intoxicating illusion that they were actually going to get out of the game ahead. Because they couldn't stop thinking about that big Freedom Bird full of plump stewardesses leaping off the runway out of Danang, next stop: The World. About Mom and Dad, and hot running water, and cold beer from the tap in the tavern down the street anytime you wanted it. About clean socks and clean sheets, and cruising through town in your own car on Saturday night, and never jerking off again because little Suzie Creamcheese is gonna sit on your face till the cows come home, and who knows what all the hell else can make a man who's come so far just that once forget completely everything he's ever learned about staying alive, plop himself down in a big easy chair like it was his own kitchen back on the block, shrug his shoulders, and try to fix a nice cup of coffee.

Luke Breit
SACRAMENTO

Pinchpenny, June 1983
Thomas E. Miner, Editor

The movement of air northward
flutters and turns the pages of the seasons.
In another time, I would by now
be preparing for winter. At dusk,
when the heat of the day
had begun to seep into the ground,
I would be splitting the great logs
of oak and madrone, redwood and cedar,
piling them peacefully one atop the other,
the brilliant flame hidden in the heart of each.
Mornings, I would check the roof
for obvious leaks, the walls for wind tunnels,
the stove chimney for clogs
that could force fire from its seams
out to join the passionate wood walls.
The store of good books would already be
settling in under the eaves
of the coming, private time.

Here, the change is barely noticeable.
A slight drop in temperature,
the breeze cooling the evening off,
jackets in the darkening streets.
But there is no sense of urgency,
of important tasks undone
and the weather about to unbuckle the world.
Here, there are thermostats
that will lock winter outside
to swirl and howl aimlessly about.
The worst winter storm
will not even make the lights flicker
nor interrupt the glaze of the new television season.
Instead of the homes of friends and neighbors,
there are the bars, the restaurants,
where we sit so close to each other
our sleeves kiss in moments

when the waiter's back is turned,
while their occupants never meet.

Here, in winter, our houses ride it out
without the need of our participation.
Temperatures target themselves
towards our maximum comfort.
When things go wrong,
there are telephone numbers to call,
experts to make repairs.
Only the unexpected knocks on the door
are the ones to fear.
No one has been out in the cold
picking berries all day,
standing outside your door in the frosty air,
both her breath and the warm pie she carries
steaming in the pale moonlit night.

Michael Spence
THE LOST PEOPLE

Hiram Poetry Review, No. 30—1981
Hale Chatfield, Editor

Where are all the people in your poems? —Editor

Look, *there*: one just ran past the corner
Of that rough shack, wild sea oats still trembling.
Tilting on the edge of a rail, a cigaret—growing
Its fingernail of ash—flips backward onto the porch.
Inside, the stove is hot, bacon spattering its smell
And beads of grease. A door squeaks: is it wind
Or someone hiding? Outside on the beach, you find
A footprint—a tiny stream of sand from its rim
Crumbles down. Then a rock arcs into the surf, its splash
Like a voice. Who threw it? On a clothesline, dresses
And shirts shake their thin bodies of air, beckoning
You, perhaps, or warning you off. Two swallows call,
Flapping from a hemlock. Something scared them,
Didn't it? By blackberry vines tangled as green cables,
An orange plastic bucket lies overturned, as if dropped:
Bits of pebbly fruit tumble out, dark juice spreading
Its stain in the sand. Listen—was that a cough
Or a laugh? Climbing over a dune, you start panting;
Sweatdrops trickle down your brow, annoying as flies.
You wipe them; grains of sand cling to your face.
Where *are* they? you ask the last rim of sun, the tide
Going out. Night begins, and still you search the beach.
Now, you are one of them.

photo by Clyde Munz; *Black Mountain II Review*, Vol. II, No. 1—1982
Stephanie A. Weisman, Editor

Victoria Rathbun
UNCOOL

Punk, No. 1—1978
G.P. Skratz, Editor

Broke drunk &
listening to the white-boy blues
cigarette burns down &
it's like forever   Oh how uncool.
You're not even a regular, you're a
social dinosaur. Maybe you had envisioned
something different, like
the sun splintering on a sea of passion
& logic
the ice in your glass turning to diamonds
or cruising in your
Ford Galaxie
just off work & diligently happy
with the radio on
knowing everything there is to know
& letting it just
fly out the window.

Tim Jeffrey
HABITS OF CONTACT

Samisdat, No. 101–1980
Merritt Clifton, Editor

After work, Howard put some Brubeck jams on the Magnavox portable. He shaved, wearing only a pressed pair of Gatsby baggies. His thin-muscled chest was as taut as drum parchment, a light cream-coffee brown sensuously highlighted in the shadowed hollows of his biceps and rib cage. These Howard felt moved to inspect further in the full-length mirror of his mother's room.

Muffin poked her head through the hank of heavy drape he used in lieu of a bedroom door. He didn't bother to remove the joint from his mouth. "I smell sumpthin." At thirteen, she was the baby of the family.

"You don't smell shit. Get outa my be'room, girl." He pulled on a white, open-necked disco shirt, made of an indeterminate silk-like fabric, without removing the joint.

"Mama say, feed Blackwell."

"I done fed Blackwell, fool. Now what else you want, 'cause I'm fittin' t'step and you in my room."

"Didn't feed no Blackwell, How'd."

"Nigger, you a lie, too." He changed the record to some 'Earth, Wind and Fire.' "I done thu the muthufucka scraps outside, bitch, and if you goes an' axim, dumb dog probably burp on y'ass."

He picked out his hair all nice and round, put on some tassled gray leather Sibley shoes with moderate heels, and splashed on some English Leather. He changed records again. The speaker crackled and popped like an old fire. A dull bass leading in, getting stronger, calling in some horns that fell in smooth. Violins. An orchestral section of brass pounced, repeating the rhythm line. He lay on the bed. The singer growled in, flew up to his highest note, a sustained wail, banked it, circling the musicians, then dropped perfectly into the sweep of the music's climb.

Definitely sweet.

Howard groaned with the singer, "Leeme all alo-aww baby ..." taking up the time on the bed with his hands "... way y'domay, bay-bay, awwwdomay ... "

Muffin again.

"Chu want?"

"You goin out wi'Deke? He call you."

"What he say? He ain't goin now or somethin'?

"He just callin' see if you was." She caught his look. "I tole him you was."

"All right. Get out my face."

She backed almost all the way out, holding only her face through the drape. "Deke say 'Tell 'at dumbass nigger Train on his dumb black self.'"

Howard stared back for a moment. The record needle clicked on the empty track between songs.

"Train after you?"

"Ain't checkin' me out. If he do, I be takin' a ride on his train." This was very funny to Howard. Muffin watched him. He stopped laughing. "I am cool," he said. "Ain't I? Move, girl."

When the curtain fell back, he stared out at the yard through a dingy window, no longer moving his feet or hands to the music. What it was, Train had come up with some nice Columbian weed and offered an excellent deal on a half a pound to Howard. Howard agreed, but the month's money got all wrong and he conned a white dude into buying it straight off Train. Train let the jellyfish walk on a promise, evidently, something Howard would have never done with a honky, something no nigger would have done, not and let anyone know. Everyone knew. So Train planned to front-up Howard. "Gimme gimme gimme some sweet thang baybay, doncha ugh, domay, ugh, say you do—"

Fuck Train.

Eight-thirty, Howard was jumped sharp. Deke had been out front in the car for five minutes or so. He hadn't bothered to beep or come up. He never did: when Deke said he'd come, Deke was there. Howard thumped down the wooden steps slow, studiously cool, and as he walked, added the coup d'grace, a pair of thirty-dollar rose-tint wire-rims, gazing everywhere but at the car, arms pinned rigid, hands crippled back so the wrists looked like stubs. The fact that Deke hadn't honked, and Howard's preoccupation with his walk, were part of an unspoken, visceral familiarity between two who prided themselves on the demonstration. Howard climbed in. "S'happenin."

"What it is." Hooked fingers, fists tapped clean and tight, done with the affectionless ritual movements of habit.

"You got it."

"All right, den."

Both looked off, Deke into the rear view mirror as he started the car, Howard straight ahead. Howard's high was easing away. "What it actually is," he said as Deke headed the car up the street toward Dexter, "is some 'lumbo, so it ain't what it is, it's where it is, so's I can be where you is." This was funny to Howard.

"Glove compartment, man." Howard snapped the compartment open and took out the cellophane bag. Deke appeared lost in thought. Although, more than anything, he was concentrating on driving the car. No one put as much into the act. His shoulders were back, he was leaning a little with his elbow on the armrest wearing his severe expression, seemingly but not at all oblivious to other bloods who checked him on his roll-by; he knew what the red Buick Riviera would look like, two extremely aloof brothers inside. Even the guys who didn't catch the looks on their ladies' faces, they pretended to look beyond it, checking it glancingly so as not to appear interested.

Howard used his own papers to roll, one, then another, which he stashed in his pocket. He used the dash lighter to gun up the third, toked, and handed it over to Deke. "Reefer, reefer," Howard said, gasping it in. He sniffed, then exhaled. "All 'round my soul."

Deke stopped a cautious distance from the cars ahead at every light. Howard slumped against the window, watching. They passed a young woman with straightened hair, in a cool green leather, waiting at the opening of the bus stop enclosure. Deke lethargically craned back at her, then fell back into his preoccupation at the wheel. Howard made as if he hadn't seen her. Weed always turned the floor to velvet under his shoes. "Whose deal this we goin' to?"

"Brother-in-law house," Deke mumbled.

"I was wonderin' why y'all jump so cool."

Deke smiled. "Hey now. You sayin' I don't always be lookin' good?"

"Talk louder, man. You did a deb or sumthin?"

"Mean a deb? Nigger, ain't did a deb in so long. Been listenin' to yourself all day, why you can't hear shit? Listen this fool. A deb."

"Hear you now, nigger. Must be you gotta have someone come upside yo'head once in a while." He backhanded Deke's outstretched palm. Howard chewed on an uncracked, nut-hard seed from the joint. They passed a gas station which, from all its appearance of disrepair would have seemed abandoned but for a man in greasy overalls and some friends standing about the pump island amid crooked cracks. A German shepherd, still as a picture, stared out an empty pane in the service bay door. The men laughed, slapped hands, pointed at each other. "Yeah," said Howard, drifting, "Somebody got to get on y'ass." He took the seed off his tongue with the pad of an index finger.

"Fact, this ain't shahp," Deke said. "This ain't nowheres near halfway neither."

"Kiss ma dick."

Howard laugh-hacked. He pointed to the seed on the finger. "Want some? Get you high."

Abandoned cars in the heavily-leafed weeded lots littered with explo-

ded diamonds of windshield glass, lots they passed so irretrievably soaked in motor oil as to be hardened to an unnatural industrial sheen ap-
proximating asphalt, mullen and lamb's quarter edging wastes of gray
board fences covered in torn-away layers of posters, scrawled over with
spray-painted obscenities, store windows frosted with street soot.

"Detroit fucked, man." Howard said.

"Heard that."

They banged over railroad tracks that gave, to either side, into rotting storehouse docks on rusting, overgrown spurs. "Shit look like Germany, man. Been won by the Allies."

"They gonna be some Allies at the party tonight, so don't be bogue
now."

"Goodness gracious, Chauncey, I would not have white peoples think
poorly of me and mines." This time Howard put out his palm to catch
Deke's backhand. "Cool huh? I gots mucho linguistics."

"Is this place anyway?" he asked after a while. "New York?"

"On down Grand River. Whyn'chu punch some jams."

Past the deep multiple-flat dwellings, some boarded up; flowerless
trellises, stashed in porch lattices. Taking Grand River west then, storefront churches and drycleaners, discount shoes, the usual bars, repuss-
essed furniture stores, rib and pizza shops. Every sight memorized. Howard let his arm dangle out the window. "Check m'man. Think he the
bomb. Check it out, Deke."

Deke disturbed his poise for a second to scope the young dude deck-
ed in upholstered heels, a Barcelona hat and a red walking suit. Howard
laughed. "Ooh boy, tickle me. Niggers is extremely flamboyant."

"Gonna get me somethin' on the up-and-up," Howard said afterwards. "Get me a business and jump ship on the ghetto."

Deke shot him a sarcastic smile. "The fuck kinna work you do?"

"See 'at drugstore?"

"Shei-hit."

"Hey now. Drug store right up my alley. Deke's and Howard's Discount Drugs. You dispenses with the money for the drugs, and we
counts it. Sound cool, bro?" He burst into the consumptive laugh, worked himself up. He spit out the window. He slapped the dashboard. "Pre-
posterous, man."

They passed Leroy's U.S. Star Bar. People were parking in lots across
Grand River, all gotten up for some dancing at Leroy's, crossing through
traffic in couples and groups of males. Two blocks beyond, Deke turned down a street. "Train be there tonight," he said.

"Makes you think that ring a bell with me?" Howard snapped quickly. He had been thinking the same. Train almost always made it to the

Star sometime on Friday, sometimes alone, sometimes with a couple of his boys tagging.

"Muffin tell you I call?"

"Yeah, she telt me. She telt me Train lookin for me, too. I say like, hey, the fuck that to me? He goin' the Star, hey, I wish the muthufucka ha' himself a marvelous time, man. Hope he get some pussy. If the muthufuckin' trick can."

"'At ain't cool in the least."

"You see me scart? Shoot. Don't owe his monkey ass nothin'."

"You tell him that."

"I'll tell'm."

"You tell him then."

"Where this place, man? You gettin' me mad."

"Down the street," said Deke. "Where you think?"

"All right den, cool." Two cars could barely pass in the narrow corridor between the lines of parked cars at the curbs. They had to wait behind others in the lane, stopping and starting again. Howard said, "I'm leavin' that shit downtown pretty soon anyways, man. Foolin' with dope pushers come up on me say, 'you owes me,' shit, I don't even be needin' that. See maybe I can get me a cool job, lay up for a minute, get me a ride."

"Work at the factory, man. I done told you that."

"Naw, man."

"You talkin' 'bout a ride," Deke tapped the steering wheel. "Make some long-ass money in a car factory, bro."

"Done already worked in one o' them." Howard snorted, sat up, put the bag of grass away. "Wondered, what is these muthufuckas makin', man? They's manufacturin' nigger complexes."

The streetlight in the middle of the block was out. Houses large and looming close to the street in the darkness of great crowding trees. Deke said, "The fuck that spose't mean?"

"Ain't about nothin', anyways." He slumped back against the door. "Got some crazy-ass nigger on my ass for sumthin' I ain't even did. My habits o' contact ain't shit. I'm in a, like, extremely questionable element, man."

"What's that got to do with factories, answer me that?" Deke asked, as if speaking angrily to a child.

"It don't." Train. Always some fool badder than somebody else. Howard knew he had more intelligence than anyone, even more than Deke, and that he would outsmart Train. Had to. "I means like everybody down here on a reservation. And they don't know it. But they likes it."

"Uh-huh."

"That's it." But Deke wouldn't slap his hand.

"But you cool."

"Look, they either dressin' like muthufuckin' zebras or they talkin' like, hey, we gonna get over brother. Revolution. Ain't heard no plan yet." Howard waved in the general direction of several parked cars. Drivin' Cadillacs like the script say niggers should, and Marks, and Deuces . . ."

"But you don't want no Mark, now . . ."

"Heyall naw. The fuck for?"

"Listen this boo-shit."

"You know, like people in this town either buildin' cars, stealin' cars, or parkin' them in lots so's they can get stolen." He paused. "Called the assembly line." This was funny to Howard. The car stopped completely.

"Got an attitude, man. All the time you talkin' shit." Howard started to reply but Deke overrode him: "Ya'll be talkin', but what you is, you just another nigger tryin' get over runnin' your mouf like you ain't and put y'foot knee deep in y'peoples' ass."

"Ain't mines. Maybe they yours."

"Aww man. They y'brothers and sisters—"

Howard put a bad drum run on the dashboard. "Hey, like sometimes my brothers is sisters."

"Fuck you."

"I appreciate y'all lookin' out for my better interest, now. It's the bomb. Mean to thank you."

They stopped across the street from a brick home on the corner that had been divided into flats. They climbed out and composed themselves, putting their hair in place and checking their belts and the pleats of their pants. The flat was upstairs. At the door they were greeted by Deke's brother-in-law, a sturdy, intelligent-looking man in gold-rimmed spectacles and a clean tight natural that engaged the carpet of his beard so uninterruptedly even Howard admired it, self-consciously touching a small constellation of shaving bumps on his neck.

"Billy Charles. It's a pleasure." Billy Charles diplomatically let slide the second stage of intricate handplay, urbanely patting Howard, instead, on the shoulder, and ushering the two inside.

First of all, there were white people, nine of them exactly. They had some connection to Billy Charles' work. Whoever else he was speaking to at first, Howard could not keep his eyes off them, laying for the opportunity to look back at them. It seemed a kind of confirmation that the white women sat on their chairs or the couch edge and rarely moved, waiting on drinks from their boys like southern belles, feet planted together, eyes either moving quickly about them or evidencing the same type of unease by laughing inordinately at any simple remark by a black person. He watched the black men, instantly rebuking in his mind any who spoke to the white women, scrutinizing their looks and gestures from his remove. Talk ranged between business and Pan-Africanism.

Another cheap scam.

It was a small place and as the guests milled there was the confused jockeying for space, the undulant atmospheres of conversation—college talk, near as he could tell. Howard found himself standing off a good deal, attempting to appear preoccupied without drawing any eyes. Several times Billy Charles invited him to mingle, to help himself to anything. Others inquired about his job, his education, though it never occurred to him to ask the same of anyone else. Managing a civil air in the midst of all the hale goodfellow cheery part talk wore on him. He wanted to find a night club. Deke was ever immersed, however, with several brothers, in talk about sports, money, plans.

"I can see you looking out the window there," Billy Charles said from behind, obviously having cultivated an affinity for him Howard could not have been responsible for encouraging. "Every Friday night, or nearly—you see that streetlight?—there's some guy, usually he's drunk, who comes down the street from this way here. You can hear him singing. Then he stops out there in the streetlight. You can't see him awfully good through the tree branches. He'll stop cars if he has to, but he'll put on one bad show. We get a kick out of him. Weirdest thing, dude gets into it."

"That right?" said Howard, rubbing an eye. "That's beautiful, you know."

"I swear," said Billy Charles.

"Incredible," said someone from behind, a white, who had been listening. "Love it."

After Billy Charles' preliminary introductions, Billy moved away, leaving the white man with Howard. To no avail, without even succeeding in getting Howard to turn from the window and acknowledge his presence, the man asked, "You're with Deke, right? Your name is Gibson, Billy said?"

In his best nigger drawl, Howard replied, "We's all name Gibson, man."

The rest of the evening improved little. No one again made the mistake of addressing Howard. That none of them danced, that this was supposed to be a party and no one even brought it up, appalled him. When he could get Deke aside, he told him, "These macaronis talkin' politics and smoothin' down the road like muthufuckin' cotton salesmen, Deke. Le's hit it. This shit make me sick. You done put in your 'pearance."

"Better lay on that a minute, bro."

"Come on, man. Le's do it like we ain't even came."

"Why y'all got to be so nasty?"

"I see. You gotta see about coppin' some white pussy, guess that's what you say."

"You is foul," Deke hissed. "Ain't goin' nowheres with your ornery ass."

"All right den." Howard made a brief fist. "In a minute." And headed for the door.

"Not even," said Deke maliciously.

Howard walked back up the street toward the Star. What Deke had said might very well be true, that Train would be there, and that he would want to be paid. "Deke ain't shit," he mumbled to himself. He did, however, consider, as he walked, taking the bus home, the night having been such a disappointment. He made no connection between this and his possible fear of Train. Although he checked his pockets, then, on the possibility that he'd forgotten his money for the cover charge. He had not.

He reached Grand River and stood in the splashes of sign lights, car lights and street lamps. A bus grumbled up and rocked to a stop with a screech. Its doors sucked open, disgorging passengers, then broke audible wind and wheezed away, black fumes from blackened exhaust grates hanging in the air like clouds of anger in a comic strip.

Until the last moment he debated with himself about going in, but finally entered Leroy's Star Bar, reservedly casing it, affecting the distracted air of one who had better places to be. And though he had no quibble with the music, he loitered by the bar without speaking to anyone, nursing a gin and tonic. Howard leaned his back against the bar, stretched his legs, self-satisfied. He told several women who passed within earshot that they stimulated his mind. By all appearances he had not done the same for theirs. He looked for familiar faces, for anyone. No one. And he hadn't seen Train. He stretched.

But Train had stationed himself in the crowd along the aisle to the front door. And when Howard moved in the file of people leaving, it was not until he was nearly abreast of Train that he saw him. Train stared, implacable, into Howard's eyes. Train with hard Milk Dud irises, taller than Howard, larger in every respect, a Jamaican beaded top opened on a chest that seemed, however implausibly, to be blacker than his midnight face. A corruption of bread invaded the strop of his jaw like a chickweed and his nose was interrupted by a smooth detoured creascent of lighter, dead tissue under a nostril. It sometimes shone like a paint splotch.

"Happenin'," said Howard, so taken off balance he failed to put a look on his face, though at least he succeeded in not betraying his dismay. By the changing lights it was hard to tell, but Train may have nodded. He may have said something too, but the music was too loud for him to tell. Train looked like a tall Joe Frazier with a terminal dose of Ugly-Dumb.

Just when Howard thought he would pass without a hitch, the line held up. Train blew smoke into his ear. Howard watched back at him, warily, but cool enough that he could manage an expression of vague displeasure. Train put the cigarette to his lips again, inhaled, teeth showing. "Seem we ain't talked about something I need." No smoke. Must have swallowed it. Thus absorbed, Howard said nothing. The line was completely stopped; apparently, there was a commotion outside the door.

"Where my money?"

"Don't owe you, Train. You know that." Trembling, Howard fixed his eyes ahead, attempted an abstracted look, as if contemplating moving to the front of the line to straighten things out.

"When I gettin' it?" Train's voice was too low for anyone else to pick up.

"Told you man, don't owe you nothin'."

"Where my money?"

"Maybe y'all got a hole in y'pocket. Call the police." Always mouthing. Couldn't resist.

The plum softness of Train's big nose pressed into Howard's hair and fingers wrenched shut on his forearm. "I am the polices, silly mutherfuck, you know dat?" Howard heard Train's teeth come together. "I ax you did you know—answer me punk!"

It took a second to get the tone right, like he might not answer, then Howard croaked. "Hear you."

"All-of-it. Right?"

Howard nodded.

"Be sweet, mutherfuck." Howard resisted rubbing the arm. Outside, the commotion earlier had been caused by a woman—still standing and stamping around in her blue sheer dress—fronting off her man. He stood apart, utterly indifferent. The exiting bar patrons and stragglers in the street sagged with her, as she stomped about, in a loose circle like a cell wall. The dude withstood her rage stolidly, lips compressed but his eyes, quite possibly, amused. "Anybody fuck w'me get they ass shot off," she screeched, out of control and pointing at him.

"Slap that silly bitch," one brother said. "Tear'm up, mama," said someone else. "Say what you do," another; "Oww, do it." Laughs, heads nodding, trying to see.

The man, imperturbable, said something to her. His arms remained folded.

"Tell me shit ..." she started away arms flailing.

Howard's leg hurt. Standing still in the milling circle of onlookers, he tried to will it away. Burning into his thigh. He put a finger there to scratch, but with self-restraint, though it stayed like a needle. Without removing his widening eyes from the woman, he held the pant leg away. The pocket burned a knife point into his skin. His teeth clenched. In one hysterical jerk he thrust his hand in, burning his finger, trying frantically to act calm ...

"Ch'all lookin' at?" The woman wailed at them all. "Who you laughin' at?"

The pocket flew inside out, an explosion of change on the sidewalk and the solitary butt of Train's still burning cigarette.

"Somebody throwin' money around."

"Axim do he got some foldin' money!"

The woman shouted, "Hit on me when you goin' with Marlotte," stumbling, rickety on her heels. "I don't be playin' that shit."

Howard saw him. Across the circle, Train held a pack of cigarettes toward Howard, eyes innocently congenial.

Howard's scalp itched.

With a sickening crumple, the woman racked up against the bricking of the bar front, slid over and was caught again by an uppercut before she was all the way down, head snapping up and hair blowing to one side. She carried out with this, seeming then to awaken from the first blow, unable yet to believe. And then her bleeding face cracked down on the cement and she lay moaning at the man's feet, moaning through her nose and weeping both, as one would who was being chased in a dream by terrible shadows. A few of the women called the man names, but other than that, no one closed in on him. The consensus moving from the periphery behind was that it had been his woman; no reason to get shot over some bitch. Howard could only concur. Like bored spectators at a construction dig, they began crossing Grand River. Some returned to the bar, new conversations already starting.

The man bent over the woman, shouted hoarsely for her to get up, but the louder he demanded, the louder she howled. She was missing one shoe, her hands crawling over her eyes and mouth, arms and dress powdered with grains of the sidewalk. She was conscious, quieter when he quit demanding, seemingly sober again. She cried tears into her fingers.

Bogue. Howard caught up with some others, walking away from where Train had been, without conceding to himself the truth of his motivation. He swiftly cut in ahead of the crowd departing the bar and heading for their cars in a lot adjacent to the building, keeping just a-head. He put on a step, walking on the gravel of the lot and letting his eyes wander up at each of headlights and roar of ignition, obstinately persuaded that he was not going to let a crazy nigger run him down. He slowed his walk on that account.

Ain't no swishy punk.

He walked then down a sidestreet parallel to, but three or four blocks east of where he had been with Deke at the party earlier. He had no intentions, really, of returning. Nor had he speculated about the direction he had taken, unless it was away from the beating. "Can't stand niggers don't maintain and got t'be loud and shit," he'd told Deke before. Fool enough, the woman had to be talking on her man in front of people. "But the dude extremely uncool, put his shit on Main Street," Howard murmured. The block was too dark. He reminded himself not to talk out loud. He tried to see ahead to any buckles in the sidewalk that might take off one of his heels. Because there were no driveways and there was a row of parked cars between himself and anyone approaching in a car, he felt confident he could make the run between the houses. Not that he would have to.

He paused to slip out his smokes and pinch one out. When he lit it, he looked back up the street where he had been and, sighting down the tunnel formed by the canopy of trees, thought he glimpsed a silhouette intruding on the glare of the neon and traffic of Grand River. At that distance, he could not tell whether it was approaching or retreating. Only a little he stepped up his pace, still undecided about where to go. He turned the corner left, into the sidestreet, generally in the direction of Billy Charles' flat. When he looked back over the hedge, however, he had lost the backdrop of Grand River as the lines of oak and ash shut off the lights. But he could hear the footsteps. Not Train. He had a Mark and would have come after him in the car.

Rather than use the sidewalk and make noise, Howard used the grass strip all the way to the corner, then turned right and walked north again. He held up for a few seconds. The figure turned onto the same sidestreet and clicked up the sidewalk.

It was hard to remember. Something about niggers acting like fools. You had to maintain. Play like flamboyant (sounds of steps) . . . whatever . . . "Hit y'woman you deserve lookin' like a fool . . ."

He inhaled deeply of his smoke; concentrated on his stride, letting the smoke out smooth. He took another draw and flicked the spiraling stub off on a lawn. He might have been overheard talking to himself.

Have to stop that shit.

Like a yacht riding into dock with the engines cut, the Mark IV swept up with its lights off. It never occurred to him to run, even when the three of them jumped out and strode over to the sidewalk ahead of him. Then he heard the running behind. He stopped, took his hands out of his pockets to avoid being misunderstood, and backed off the sidewalk a little against a tree, cool as if he had been expecting them.

Train stopped running, huffing a bit, and walked up to him. It was too dark to see, but he knew the other three by their size, especially the small one in the Godfather hat. He stared with a belligerent curiosity, hands shaking as he took out the cigarettes. The Mark idled like a muted vacuum cleaner.

"This the nigger, Train?" said the shrimp.

"Got cigarettes, Howard?" Train took the pack. "Mind if I ha'one, do you?"

"Long's you don't put it out in my pocket."

He squeezed the package into a ball. "Shut up, boy, 'less you want me t'slap the taste out you mouf."

"Fuck this trick up, Train." One of the others said it, but Howard tried keeping the little one in sight. The balled cigarettes hit him on the shirt front. Howard's stomach muscles tensed. He was sure they hadn't seen him flinch.

"Whup 'is dumb ass."

"Sick of it Howard. You know, like I been cool about it."

"Can you get t'that, brother?" said one of the three. Howard kept his eyes on Train.

"You know, like I ain't said shit about y'all bein' into me fo' money. That's the truf now, ain't it?"

"Hey Train, like that honky stiff y'all, not me. I don't say that's cool, ain't at all, but it was me, I say, 'Damn'—"

"Shut the fuck up, dumb fool punk," the little one shouted suddenly.

Couldn't resist. "You the seventh dwarf, ainchoo? Dopehead?"

His reaction was late and Train's fist caught him high on the side of the head, followed by a glancing kick on the shoulder as he fell, stumbling on a raised knuckle of tree root. He was on all fours, trying to stay off his pants, numbed, resignedly taking the kicks and punches in his ribs and on his head.

"Put my foot knee-deep in y'ass." Train chased him about the

lawn. With another sense Howard could hear the others making re-
marks: "Sorry ass." "Don't hit me please, suh," said another in a
high, teasing voice. "Please, kine sir." Howard scrambled up, expecting someone to come out on one of the porches. No one. His face and
the back of his neck humming with adrenalin, he breathed through
his mouth. There were a couple spots, above his right eye and below
the shoulder blade, where the muscles, though he couldn't feel pain,
tightened like a tissue harder than skin. He couldn't lift his arm. His
lip itched, but in a place that seemed a little off the face. He stood,
hands on hips awkwardly, appearing strangely disapproving, as if they
were taking his time. "Let's do it, punk."

"I ain't fightin' you, Train." A flash in his eyes. Howard got up.
"Ain't." He said this unevenly, trying to get his breath. He felt like a
bitch for the found of himself. His vision blurred.

"Play me fo' some okeydoke?" The slap jogged his head like a
wooden thing, like a camera. "Huh?" Again the impact and his sight
jumped. He could not feel.

"Fight!" shouted the little one.

Howard was suffused in a great calm, dabbing with his fingertips
along his upper lip, his heart racing but his movements settled and
thorough. With great concentration, he inspected the fingers.

"Ain't this a bitch?" said one.

"I seen sorry muthufuckas befo, but 'is one—"

Train came up to Howard's face. "Want m-money, boy."

Howard heard himself say, thickly, "Like, that's beautiful. But I
ain't got it right now. My management o'funds is like in serious jeop-
ardy."

"Thass deep, thass deep."

"He playin' a humble, Train."   ˚

"Fuck him up."

Train struck again. Howard went to his knees; got up immediately,
brushing them off. "Huh? You just talk, ain't you, punk?"

In utter despair at the uselessness of it, Howard said again that he
couldn't produce what he didn't have. A bubble of blood formed in
one nostril.

"Tell you, boy, you in a bad town t'be front'n up."

Dulled, Howard blinked several times. "Ain't front'n, Train."

"He playin' y'shit fo' the cheap, Train."

Like dogs, Howard thought. Done brought his simple dogs.

"Who got it, Howard?"

"Hey, I can get it, few weeks probably."

"You get a loan."

"Can't get no credit, man. You gotta be somebody and shit."

"An' you nobody."

"Dig that."

"This ain't nowhere to be nobody, Howard." Levelly Train said it, and Howard stiffened, expecting the blow. But a car came. When the lights caught the Mark everyone turned to the street, Train in front of him, a tall dude on the right, one near the sidewalk and the little one to Howard's left. Which was where he ran when the car horn sounded, dipping his shoulder and in one motion following through with a fist in the fool's throat, the Godfather flying away, already by him and putting on a kick of speed over the lawns toward Grand River . . .

"MUTHUFUCKER—HEEYY . . .

. . . wind cold on his forehead, feeling the dried blood of his nose like a skin of bubble gum, faster than the punks, than anybody, like it was a beating he was administering—come-own now muthufucka, you in my game now, showing them how, shuffle and cut, prancing his legs out like Walter Payton, broken field—come-own—gone moving down the sidestreet, then cutting down the street where the party had been.

Halfway, he saw they weren't coming; slowed down to a walk. Again he started running. He looked back. Then he stopped. He glanced up and down the block. He considered going down to Grand River, but could see the shirt was ripped. He walked toward the party, trying to catch his breath—Ain't played roundball so long! Down the other end of the block as he approached: headlights coming up the sidestreet. He shot between the houses, hopping a backyard gate without using his bad arm, and slunk behind the house. By the sound of the engine he knew. The Mark. It idled, the sound enlarging suddenly in the corridor between the houses. Howard's heart percussed against his throat and rib cage and he pressed, ready to run, against the cinder roughness of the imitation-brick asbestos. Letting his breath out of his mouth, slowly, when it had gone.

A dog.

It sniffed his hand. If it could do that, if it was that large, it might be a shepherd, or a Doberman. In this city, it might be a rat.

Carefully putting his feet ahead without bending the knee. Dog came too. He couldn't see in the darkness, not wanting to make a sound, easing around the corner of the house. He could not outrun it. To the fence.

He burst forward with two measured high-jumper strides, and met the ball of the fence post with a foot coming over and with an unrestrained howl went sprawling to the other side. A dog nose lethargically prodded the fence mesh.

"Muthufuckin' dumb-ass shit dog, you ain't shit, you my shit all crazy—" rubbing his pants and limping slightly.

With a peremptory snort, the dog nose backed off and the dog vanished, its outline swallowed in the blackness of the yard.

Howard had only gone a hundred feet or so before another car came and he had to slip between two houses.

When finally he arrived at the corner brick house where Billy Charles' party went on, he first tried the doors of Deke's car. They were locked. Skirting the glare of the corner streetlight, he hurried across to the house itself. He would wait for Deke on the steps beneath the small shingled overhang. He sat feeling his facial bruises, touching the proud flesh of his lips and the bulb of his eyebrow. His back ached. And worse, the shirt was ruined. The Gatsby's, though dirty, were still cool, which was something.

It had to be late. Deke would be along soon. The lights of a car startled him. He stooped around the side of the house, crouching, frog-hopping under the cover of some large bushes that ran close to the house and parallel to the sidestreet, in the sheltering darkness of a lawn tree blocking most of the streetlight.

The car passed, yet he remained in his uncomfortable stoop for some time. He listened to the city, to far off buses, brothers wheeling down the streets with the jams playing full, gunshots. No matter how similar the sound to the distant rattle-clap of semis banging heat-buckled pimples in the street or to a backfiring engine, still he knew some fool was shootin' his piece. Neighbor used to go drinking every Friday, get so sloppy and, ready for sleep, he gone out the front lawn, fire off a couple rounds and yell, "Salute mother fuckers." Then off to bed.

Before long, rain pattered in the leaves overhead, popping and snapping on the sidewalks and in the street. He waited in a kind of compromised catcher's crouch, electing this over the risk of getting his pants any more dirty than they were. Listening to the thump of the music from the party above, entranced by the rain on a piece of inter-section visible from his hiding place. When he

saw Train again, be dancing on his ass. He pictured himself shuffling smart, riffing jabs off Train's square fool head, backpedaling,
slipping wild punches, shooting the left, toying with him. (Just
goofin' the punk tonight cause he be with them other guys.) Pick
away, talk on him. "This what you like alone?" Cranking up the
bolo for the crowd, watch him in a circle. Do what you do, brother.

A man, coming up the street. Howard saw him only when he
passed through the shed of the alley vapor lamp. He heaved along
with a spastic's compensating jerky lurch, shoetoe set down, then
heel, toe then heel, leaning, stamping flat-footed every fourth or
fifth step.

He staggered.

When he got into the light at the corner, Howard guessed him
to be about thirty-five or forty, not any more, certainly. He wore
patent leathers, gray sans belts, a print-in-white shirt. He carried a
burgandy sportcoat under his arm. Howard was tickled. Dress like
a ole gashead.

Then the man danced in place, stumbling. Making choreogra-
phic sweeps of his hands, he skipped forward ('Temptations':
"Never met a girl who made me feel the way that you do ..."),
turned on one foot and smacked the other down. He snapped his
fingers on the beat.

Out came a sweet baritone that stunned. It had a deeper reach
and could fly, imploring.

How can you say that I'm
Cheating you of your time?
Tell me darlin' now—

No edges. He sang the loves betrayed, always, by a woman's
wiles or impatience. He sang the sad parts with an awesome loss
and grief, cracking on the pain words—

What can I *do* to make up to you
the *hurt* I have started?
Love *cannot* be charted.
Only the broken-hearted
Can make it improve, *baby, baby, baby* ...

He danced with it, dipping, shaking his head in disbelief, weakened, but not in his soul. Pointing at his heart and his eyes, he found the voice to admonish, moaned, softly, of deception. He knew, brother knew what must come to pass. Indicating the sky, he entreated heaven to witness it, and the anguish of his begged understanding was transformed. It moved through him to his feet and his chest, too good to bear, gonna be right—gotta be right—because he was staying on.

> Faith of the strong don't easily end,
> Columns of steel ain't apt to bend
> in the wind, darling—

The darkness began to show out through the drenched shirt. When he swung his bearded face back, water flew. Howard tried to remove himself from the fantastic sight. Still, absorbed in it, dude wasn't bad, had to admit that, crazy as the muthafucka be.

To avoid him, another car had to inch by, for he was dead in the middle of the intersection and wouldn't budge, nor did he interrupt his singing. He pivoted with it instead, calling on another unappreciative lover—

> I don't mean to be abrasive
> but lately you've been evasive
> Could it be someone else is filling your hours?

The same songs, old 'Temps' and 'Four Tops' and Jerry Butler. Everybody else either into some deep jass or they discomanic.

But this was soul, pure brother—singing like you teach yourself to do on the school field or walking with bloods. It made Howard still. Songs, same ones of blame-placing and pure want transcended by the music of hope, the repetition of chant. Not gospel singing. Maybe testimony. At times they could shame him, the lyrics so simple and alike, even anger him. Just like niggers, sing that silly boo-shit. It could anger him, seeing the man out there alone, but mostly it was the urge to cover him with something and take him into the darkness of Howard's own cover. But he wouldn't. Because what the brother did, he had to do, put into the air what don't do you no good nowheres else. Nowhere to be nobody.

In his spectacular delusionment, the man bowed three times, left, right, then forward, the last most ingratiated and deep, the longest hold of them all. Then he strode off into the rain and the darkness, soaked to the skin, heels spraying puddles.

Howard shifted his position to get out his joint, at the same instant realizing he had lost his glasses. Muther. Fuck.

Laughter and clapping and talk, above from the window of Billy Charles' apartment. For positive, he heard someone say, "Love it."

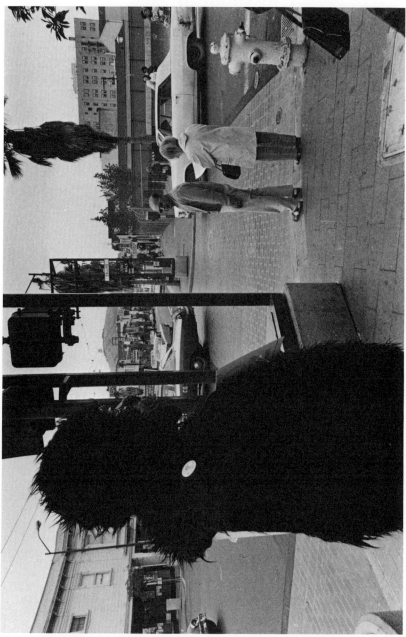

photo by Wilfredo Q. Castano; *Second Coming*, Vol. 10, Nos. 1 & 2—1981
A.D. Winans, Editor

Donna Brook
THE SHOOL OF PAIN

Hanging Loose, No. 42–1982
Dick Lourie et al, Editors

No one comes here to learn
what we teach.

They all want to be better off for it,
to know its applications, to grow
from the experience, to go through
just once.

What we offer
is the fact that it hurts
and is not the same as pleasure.
We've found

anything else, or less, or more
is not pain.

detail from painting by John Biggers; *Callaloo*, No. 5—1979
Charles H. Rowell, Editor

Jim Barnes
DOG DAYS 1978

Mississippi Mud, No. 26–1982
Joel Weinstein, Editor

An affliction so general you find no name
to cover the pain: dog days in Missouri, same
low dull sky, the repetitive gray that clouds
every window, every pond, the very clods

in fields that die into a memory of autumn.
Dog days linger. The fire of frost to come
hardly attracts you at all, at all, so strong
is desire coursing your blood, in this long

time. Daily you look for words, but what you
always see is the cryptic flight of blue-
black birds against the gray, the invisible
script you are never fast enough or able

to read. And so. And so the days hang above
you, meaningless as the adolescent love
among the weathering stalks of corn. You mourn
these days, and every day you end with pain,

with desire swollen within that will pass
only with the season, the first death of grass,
of the stalks of corn, among which the farm girl names
her quick pain and the boy knows the power in his name.

Brandon Kershner
3 DIALOGUES

Modern Poetry Studies, Vol. XI, No. 3–1983
Jerry L. McGuire & Robert Miklitsch, Editors

A

so I say what the hell could it matter
if he doesn't come back, he pushes her
in your face like half a grapefruit and says
lets all be friends and she says real quiet
but I dont think I can make it and I
say thats a lot of crap and you know it
and she pushes this ashtray around the table
like its too hot to let sit and I grab
her hand and her chin and tell her real
slow in the face you dont have to take
this

B

Im lying there looking at her
room which is smaller than I thought
and trying to remember her name which
I cant at the moment and the door
gets kicked open and this hawaiian
shirt comes in and he walks over
stifflegged and says you motha get
up you motha and she grabs the
sheet and says esteban and I
think I know this movie this is a
bad movie and hes crying and pulls
out a knife and says get up motha
and I think I get killed in this
movie what the hell is her name
anyway and he throws the knife
into this poster over the bed I
never noticed and squats
on the rug and rocks back and
forth still crying and he
says susan susan

C

she says hows bachelor life
you sonovabitch and I say
great just great I get a lot
done and theres a pause and
she says you sound funny
and I say little debbie and she
says who and I say I had
twelve little debbie cupcakes for
dinner tonight and she says
jesus christ and I hear her
palm on the phone and some
other noise and then she says
what about my casserole and I
say I was gonna have it tomorrow
but Im thinking about fasting
and she says alright you bastard
but you leave the minute youre better

Andrea Carlisle
DON'T IT MAKE YOU WONDER

Calyx, Vol. 6, No. 2–1982
Margarita Donnelly et al, Editors

for Rachel MacMaster Lowrie

A woman in a long cotton coat was waiting for a bus. She wore a small round felt hat, rust brown. Her shoes were black flats and her lean legs stockinged. She held a black envelope purse with a gold clasp. In an hour she would be at work, sitting in front of the switchboard at the telephone company, legs dangling from a high stool, elbows on the smooth ledge in front of the board. There would be phone numbers and area codes typed on yellow strips of paper in narrow slots above her head. The snug fit of the headset would feel good, shutting out the day, locking her into the black space of numbers, pleases, thank yous, and nothing else except the buzz of other operators in the background. Sooner or later she would shut that out too, even with one ear free she could escape that and enter the blankness, the waiting, the lights flashing red on and off in front of her. There would be busyness. There would be a hum of voices strolling into her ear naming cities: Minneapolis, please; St. Paul? Thank you. Redfield? Thank you very much. There would be that tunnel of voices and nothing else for four hours, a short break, then another four. She would have something to do with her hands. She would pull the narrow plugs out and pop them back into holes, out and in, in and out, into darkness, out again, and the voices themselves, holes in her ear, opening, closing, numbers, cities, pleases, thank yous, and so on.

No one else was at the bench under the bus stop sign. That was good, she thought. That was fine. If somebody should happen to come along, she could get up and walk down to the next bench a few blocks away. Maybe she would have to flag the bus if it caught her between benches but that would be all right, that was better than pulling some phoney conversation out of the air and having to play around with it while simply waiting for a bus. Was that cruel? Was she becoming sarcastic? Had she always been sarcastic? She wondered about it. No. No one had accused her of that before.

She looked down at herself. Her body was covered by the beige coat except for a narrow opening at its hem that revealed a cluster of white dots on the smooth dark blue of her dress. She was annoyed. It might have been Friday that she had worn this same dress and not a day or

two before. Images of herself standing arms straight down at her sides
pushed each other one by one along the front of her mind. Monday:
brown and yellow jersey. Tuesday: print skirt, green blouse. Wednesday:
gray felt skirt with strawberry pockets, red blouse. Thursday: white
dress with green stripes. Or was that Friday? No, it was Thursday, so on
Friday . . . her forehead pulled itself into a painful fold. There was nothing, no Friday image. Her eyes closed. She chewed her bottom lip. Nothing.

"Damn," she said.

A station wagon went by. Someone waved. The woman at the bus
stop waved back.

"Damn small town," she said to herself. "Can't even wait for a bus,
somebody sees you." Then she rolled her eyes and closed her mouth.
"I'm talking to myself. I can do that. It's okay to do that. Everybody
does. I just have to remember to keep my mouth closed when I do it."

She emphasized this point to herself with the jerking up and down of
her chin. When she brought her head away from the disappearing station
wagon to once again look for the bus, she saw a blonde child with big
blue-rimmed glasses seated on the bench, staring at her.

"What's your name?" The child's voice was bold.

The woman noticed that the little girl's hands were crusted with mud
and stickiness. Koolaid or snot, she thought. Who knows?

"Helen," the woman said, surprised at her automatic answer.

"Hi, Helen, I'm Elspeth. I live right over there." She pointed to a blue
cottage tucked into heaps of shrubbery.

Helen stood up and brushed off her coat. "I have to go," she said. "I
have to go to work now."

"How come?" said the child. "How come you have to work today?
Nobody else does. It's Sunday."

Helen slowly seated herself again on the bench. Her hands felt sweaty.
She did not like this child.

"What did you say? It's Sunday? Are you sure?"

"Of course I'm sure. I went to Sunday school this morning. My mom
went to church, my grandma called at exactly one o'clock long distance
and I have to go back to school tomorrow and keep going until vacation.
Those are all Sunday things."

Well, it was possible. It certainly was possible that this was Sunday.
How many days had there been in between? Oh yes, there was Friday
and on Friday she had worn this dress with white dots, yes, she remembered. But wearing it again today might have been all right, just barely
all right if this were Monday. But here it was, the wrong day. Why hadn't
the Bests told her it was Sunday instead of just waving at her as she stu-

pidly sat waiting for the Sunday bus? There was no Sunday bus. There was only this awful child. Well maybe the Bests hadn't really noticed and would not tell her father how they had seen his oddball daughter Helen sitting on a bench waiting for the Sunday bus. They would all have a good laugh over that. If it had really registered with them, that is. She hoped it hadn't.

"Want to come and see my hamster?" Elspeth had one of those faces that Helen hated, an unpretty child, a child with glasses, a crooked smile, and sort of a desperate look about her. You couldn't treat one of these the same way you could treat a cute child. With a cute child all you had to do was smile and comment on their looks. They did the rest. This type, though, they were harder.

"No, I can't see your hamster. I told you I have to go to work."

Helen stood up. "And I'm going to walk. I'm not going to wait for the bus anymore."

"Good thing," said Elspeth. "There's no buses on Sundays. But please, before you go, come and look at my hamster. At least come and look at his grave."

"Grave?"

"Yeah, I made him one. In case he dies. My mom says those things always die on you. We went to the Ben Franklin dime store and we were looking around and I saw a turtle and I wanted it but she said it wouldn't live until we got it home and then I wanted this hamster and she said oh, those things always die on you too, but I said I wanted it and I started to sort of cry and she said oh, Elspeth, stop it. And then she bought me that hamster and now I've got him a grave. Just in case. Come and see."

She grabbed Helen's hand and pulled her into the street. Helen pulled back, glancing quickly around her, but the child caught her uncertainty and pulled harder. In a moment they were across the street and through the hedge, then down a narrow brick path alongside the house and into a tiny back yard full of pink flamingoes bolted to the earth, their heads thrust in the direction of a cement deer which, in a similar graceful pose, gazed vacantly at the yard. There was also a small birdbath. It was beneath this that Elspeth had dug a small hole.

"Put your hand in!" The child commanded.

Helen shrank back.

Elspeth insisted. "Aw come on. Jeez! Put your hand in. It's only dirt."

Helen peered into the hole. She lay her purse on the lawn and examined her nails. Two were broken, not one was adequately covered with polish.

"What the hell?" she said, and put her hand deep into the moist cool earth. She felt clumps of dirt, squeezed them, pushed them deep into the hole.

"I cleaned it out good, huh? It's almost a perfect square."

Helen looked up. The child was proud.

"I measured it so it's eight inches by eight inches. That's a square, right? I dug it eight inches deep too. I don't know why." She shrugged, smiling.

Helen put her other hand into the hole and pushed the walls of the grave. It had been a long time since her hands had touched earth, since she had knelt down and even smelled it. Other scenes, garden scenes, fell in front of her eyes. Her mother, planting, the big flopping straw sun hat over her eyes, the planting apron with its pockets of seeds, and the bees. Both of them would shoo the bees away while her father pulled weeds out of the earth. Her mother, sweating, would bolt into the house every few minutes for iced tea with liquor poured into it.

"Just a drop of booze," she would call to Helen's father who kept his back turned. "Just a drop, Thomas. A little inner strength against this damned heat."

And then Helen saw herself burying something, a dog. She remembered its name was Patch, a little white puppy with a black spot over one eye. There was something odd about the way she was remembering the day of the burial. It was because, she realized, she was up high, looking down. She could smell the earth but she felt as though she were in the air hovering over herself, her mother and father, the little dog curled into the hole in the ground.

"I *said*," Elspeth had put her face two inches from Helen's ear, "I said did you ever have any pets?"

"Yes, I did. I had a puppy once, just after we moved here to Haines from Minneapolis. It was just a little puppy and it died. My parents and I, we buried it in the yard."

"You got a mom and dad? How old are you anyway?"

"Twenty." Oh why was it this child could pop questions and pull out answers so quickly. "None of your business," Helen said.

"Too late, now I know. You're twenty. God that's old. My mom isn't even twenty-five yet, really."

"Oh, listen Elspeth, I have to go." But Helen found her hands still in the hole, still fondling the small lumps of soil, smashing them and dropping them to the floor of the grave.

"Oh wait, can't you just wait? It's not hurting you to be here and don't tell me that stuff about having to work. I don't believe you and anyway you'd be late by now if you did go, and you'd be fired so you might as well just forget it."

Suddenly Helen recognized a new smell. She turned and saw a large bush with clusters of lilacs next to the cement steps leading to the back door.

"How long has it been," she wondered aloud, "since I've smelled anything? It's really summer again. And there are flowers."

"Well it's spring," the child corrected, "but it's hot. Want something to drink?"

Helen nodded and the child disappeared behind her. The screen door banged. Dark clouds tumbled into the patch of sky over the yard. Then a rumble and they broke, pinging first the flamingoes and deer, then Helen.

"You better come in!" Elspeth called from the window. Helen jumped up and turned. There was the child motioning her to come to the house. Helen picked up her purse and went to the back door.

"I can't come in now, Elspeth. I have to go. I have to go home."

Elspeth pushed open the door and put her hands on her hips. Her brown eyes were narrow and stern behind the blue glasses. "Oh yeah, first you gotta go to work and now you gotta go home and I'll just bet then you have to go see a movie. Come in, you're getting all wet." She reached for Helen's hand and tugged on it. Helen went in. The screen door whispered shut behind them, then another door closed over that and they could barely hear the rain outside.

Elspeth sat down at a round wood table. In the center stood a glass jar filled with daffodils. "Sit down here," the child ordered, pulling a chair close to her own.

They each had a glass of lemonade. Each screwed up her face and smiled at the first sour taste, as though the drink were playing a pleasant joke on them.

"Well," said Helen, eased, cooled. "Well, where's the hamster?"

"Oh you don't really have to see him. It's okay. We'll do something else."

"No, listen, I'd like to. Honest. I've never seen one close up before."

"You mean you've just seen hamster pictures?" Elspeth laughed.

"No, well, no," Helen laughed too. "Of course not." She sighed and looked around. The kitchen was very neat, like the one at home, large, gleaming. Pots on walls, counters cleared, sink shining. And it was all darkened by the rain storm sliding past the window. Helen felt as though she and Elspeth were caught inside the shadows of the room. She shivered and pulled her coat around her.

"Cold?" asked Elspeth. "I can't see how you'd be cold. It's so hot today. I can't see why you even wear that old coat."

"Oh," Helen looked down at the coat. "I just do," she said. "I just usually do." Her voice drifted off. Was there some place she was supposed to be? She remembered the telephone office, the stools and yellow sheets of numbers, the sandwiches in waxed paper. No, she did not have to be there. She felt the tightness in her stomach ease. She really did not have to be there because it was Sunday and on Sundays she just slept in or did the ironing or, what? Was there something else? Was her father expecting her to do something? He would be up by now and sitting in his brown leather chair by the radio. He would say, "Helen?" And she would say, "Yes, Papa?" And he would say, "Why didn't you..." or, "You should have..." Yes, that sort of thing happened on Sundays. Conversations about all she hadn't done during the week.

"Talk to me." Elspeth's voice was soft for the first time. Helen looked at her. Was this child sad? Oh God, would she have to do something to cheer her up? Would there be something like a game or a story? But no, this wasn't babysitting. Her father had made her stop babysitting years and years ago because she always came home crying. This was just a child from a bus stop with a hamster.

"Talk to me," Elspeth said again, almost whispering. "Tell me things."

"Where's your mother?" Helen was suddenly nervous. She looked around. "Not here?"

"No, you know that. She ain't here today. She's at my grandmother's."

"I thought your grandmother lived far away. You mean your mother is in another town and you're alone here? Where's your father?"

"No, no," said Elspeth, shaking her head. "No, I don't mean *that* grandmother. I mean the other one. That's where Mom is. She's visiting her own mother, see? I didn't go because I don't like wearing dresses and my mom says Grandma loves me in a dress and anyway she's sick and it smells bad in her room. My daddy won't be home for another week." She looked seriously at Helen. "He's in sales."

Helen nodded, half smiling at Elspeth's last words.

"Anyway," said Elspeth, "I can take care of myself but I get tired of talking to myself to say something."

"Ummmm..." Helen bit her lip and looked intensely at the girl. She frowned and twisted her mouth around. "Ummmm ummm ummmm," she said again, "and besides that," she laughed, "Humph!"

Elspeth looked at her, startled, then smiled. "You'll make a good friend, Helen."

Suddenly they both felt nervous. They turned their empty lemonade glasses round and round, spinning them, until they started to tip, then each caught her glass and stopped. Their dark corner grew silent. The rain brushed the screen on the kitchen window. For an instant they both caught the sound and smiled, then let it go. The rest of the house was absolutely still.

"Don't it make you wonder?" Elspeth said.

Helen turned and looked at the dark patch of wet green on the other side of the window.

"I said don't it make you wonder?" the child repeated, touching the sleeve of Helen's coat. Her voice was a whisper now.

"Yes," Helen whispered back, "yes." Then, urgently, turning toward the girl, "yes, yes, yes."

There had been the seeds and then seedlings. Her mother had taken her outside to see them and talked about plants growing into food in one part of the big back yard and then, walking across to the flower beds, talked about seeds growing into flowers and being just for prettiness. Helen had skipped along and nodded and asked questions and planted seeds of her own. Her mother's face shined with sweat even though she wore the big hat to protect it and it was pale from lack of sun. Her father told her sun caused a person to sweat but her mother's face would often glisten with perspiration, even inside the house, her lipstick smudged red around her soft, moist mouth. She would point to the things in the garden with clumsy white gloves over her soft hands and then she would remove the gloves and shake her long thin fingers and grab Helen and lift her, then laugh; or sometimes shake her, just slightly, and then laugh in a different way, a nervous way, as though the laughter were an afterthought.

"Yes," said Elspeth, "me too."

"Well!" Suddenly Helen's mind was occupied and frantic. There must be a way to get away from this child and go home. What was she doing anyway, sitting in a strange house, talking to this pushy girl? This couldn't be right. This would be something they would say about her now, how she went to this house and, and what? And had some lemonade? No, it *was* all right, she insisted, trying to catch the notion and hold it. Yes, it was all right to go somewhere and have lemonade and talk to a child. That had to be okay.

Helen looked at Elspeth. "Do you think I should be here?"

"Yeah, I think it's okay." Elspeth started to pick her nose, pushing her forefinger into it and goosing it around until the nostril was stretched to one side.

Helen smiled. Yes, this is right. This is a child and it's raining and she has a hamster and parents and it's a Sunday. She took a deep breath and whistled.

"What was that for?" asked Elspeth.

"Everything," Helen said.

"Well, I'll tell you something, Helen, I like you and I hope you come back again. Really." She pulled her finger out of her nose and looked at Helen from behind her blue glasses with positive sincerity.

"That's real nice, Elspeth." Helen was more comfortable now.

"And my mom will like you too. I just know that. She's going to come home soon and we'll all play Scrabble or something together. She'll give you coffee."

"No." Helen stood up. "No, I don't want to talk to a grown up person. I don't want to get to know your mom."

"Don't you like grown ups? I know what you mean. Sometimes I don't either. Sometimes they're very, very mean and they hurt my feelings. I get really mad."

Helen went to the kitchen window and looked outside. There were the wet flamingoes, the shining deer. The rain had stopped. "I don't like them, no, Elspeth, I don't. I never have liked them except for my mother and she's not ..."

Elspeth crossed the room and looked up at her. Helen wanted to cry. Who was this awful child and what did she want? Was there something she was supposed to tell her? Was there anything she could say to a child, to anyone? If it were only Monday, if only she could be sitting safely inside the headset going down into the tunnel of numbers. Elspeth tugged at her. "Come on, Helen, you're getting all sweaty and twitchy again."

"Well my mother is gone!" Helen turned and yelled into the little face, yelled into the wide open floating eyes. "My mother is gone!"

"Do you mean," said Elspeth softly, "gone like when grownups talk about somebody who's dead is gone, or do you mean just gone?"

There was the hat on the peg inside the back door, the straw hat with the long green ribbon around the band, and there was the garden apron and the trowel on the counter. All the dishes in the kitchen were smashed and the gleaming sink was covered with blood. On the stove was a package of razor blades. There was an ambulance that came and went and Papa who went with it and left her with the Bests and there was a long time of not going to school and not seeing her mother, and then there was seeing her mother again. She came home, bandages on her arms. She didn't work in her garden again. And then she was gone. She had a suitcase and she had packed it and left a note for Helen saying she would be back some day to get her and that Helen would understand all of this when she got older. That had been ten years ago.

"Do you mean dead?"

Helen looked outside at the birdbath, full of rainwater now, and the little hole next to it. She thought there would be a little puddle inside it now, and it would smell mudwet and rich. There would be worms on the sidewalks.

"Yes, I mean dead," she said slowly.

Elspeth turned away. There was a long silence. At last she spoke, "Helen, I don't have a hamster."

Helen looked at the child who was looking out the window. "I don't have a hamster," Elspeth repeated. "I had one and it died and my mom threw it in the garbage, so I just decided to make a grave today. You know, just to make a grave, I guess." She didn't shift her gaze. "My hamster died last week. I asked my mom if we could go the the Ben Franklin and get another one but she said that one was enough trouble and maybe when I'm older I can get a dog or something. A cat maybe. So anyhow I just made that grave, just today, just before I went out front and saw you sitting over there at the bus stop."

Helen took Elspeth's hand. "I'm going to go now," she said softly.

Her father would be in the chair, his feet propped on the green hassock, a beer sitting in the ashes of the big tray on a stand beside the chair. He might be listening to the radio and talking along with it, asking questions, laughing and answering them, or maybe watching television. Maybe Mr. Best was there talking about the world news or the time his son got stung by all the bees. Silly Willy Best. And her father might look up at her as she came in the door and ask where she had been and then not listen to her answer. Later she would make him dinner and do the dishes and look out at the back yard, at the flowerbed, empty now, and the garden, overgrown. The cool spring night air would come hushed against her face, would come whispering to her through the window, blowing open her collar, pushing the hair back from her brow. Her hands would be covered with hot soapy water. When she was finished her white long thin fingers would be completely clean. There would be no trace of the earth she had touched that day.

Elspeth was talking to her. "Well I just hope you can come back sometime." She slid her hand against the smooth porcelain on the sink, smudging the gleaming surface. "I just really do." Her voice had become very small.

"Thanks," Helen said. "I might, but I have to work, you know. I really do have a job. That's the truth."

The child's eyes looked into Helen's for a moment. Then she turned her head away, and down.

"Damn you Elspeth," Helen shouted. "Don't pout now. Don't get all funny like a kid or I won't come back, not ever. I mean it!" She felt her foot slam hard on the linoleum. Fragments of the hardness seemed to fly up her leg toward her heart. She put her hand to her chest. Tears streamed silently down her cheeks. She couldn't make a sound. Elspeth leaned against her and, for a few moments, Helen allowed herself to absorb the warmth of the girl's body. Then she sighed and went to the back door and walked slowly down the cement steps into the smell of lilacs.

She turned around once, wanting to beg for forgiveness, to cover those last harsh words, but Elspeth was smiling, already forgiving. Her small hand was raised to wave goodbye.

"Thank you for the lemonade, Elspeth, and for . . ." she paused.

"For everything," Elspeth finished for her.

"Yes," Helen smiled, "for everything."

And she smiled as she carefully carried herself along the wet narrow brick path, between house and overhanging shrubs, and she smiled as she thought of herself waiting at the bus stop on a Sunday and the Bests driving by and waving, their station wagon packed with their grandchildren, their Sunday toys and plans. When they told her father they would speak in a concerned whisper. He would listen, frowning, and nod, and aim his ashes toward the big ashtray but hold the cigar back, just far enough, so the ashes would miss and hit the floor.

Wooden, life-size figures have been around awhile in all sorts of forms and for all sorts of purposes. Their history goes back at least as far as the 17th century in which painted, wood *tromp l'oeil* figures called "dummy boards" were placed inside houses. A bit of the old "lived-in" feel, one could suppose. Or maybe cheap companionship.

Jim Pallas makes cut-out, life-size figures out of plywood. He calls them *Hitch Hikers*, which is exactly what they do. Painted to be "realistic at 50 m.p.h.," Jim's figures express his fascination with the concept of risk and chance. As with their human counterparts, just about anything can happen when they're on the road.

Basically the project works like this: After selecting a subject, Pallas has him/her look at his notebook which documents this series as a whole. The subject must promise that within one year s/he will write a note on the back of the *Hitch Hiker* and set it on the road to a destination of choice.

Of the ten or so *Hitch Hikers* that have been created, perhaps the "highest profiles" have been mail artist Ray Johnson and Detroit weathercaster/movie MC, Sonny Elliot.

Sonny, in particular, has been bouncing around town on his way to the current museum director at the Detroit Institute of Arts. He's been to the P.R. department of television station WJBK, and then on to WDIV, another Detroit station and later on to "stand-up" appearances during the local public television auctions. He was last seen in the arms of a guard at the Detroit Historical Museum across the street from the Institute of Arts. As any hitchhiker knows, the wait to get to where you're going can be incredible sometimes.

Other of Pallas' *Hitch Hikers* have had more direct travels. One wound up at his destination in Waltonville, Illinois, leaving from Michigan and arriving by way of Florida. Some that have been set out on the roads have simply disappeared. Pallas declares his *Hitch Hikers* "not art works," encouraging people to have fun with them and not to worry about theft or damage. However, he also asks people that give a lift to his figures to write their names and addresses on the back, stating how and when they offered a ride. Later, if and when the *Hitch Hiker* gets to a destination and Jim gets word of it, he will send all who participated some documentation of the travels.

Facing page, top: Jim Pallas as Hitch Hiker *arrived by thumb at Detroit Focus Gallery for* 48222, *a mail art show in 1981.*

Bottom: Hitch Hiker *Ray Johnson thumbing on I-94.*

painted plywood cut-outs by Jim Pallas; *lightworks*, No. 16—1983
Charlton Burch, Editor

Dan Thrapp
GRAVEDIGGER

Puerto Del Sol, Vol. 19—Fall 1983
Kevin McIlvoy, Editor

I used to work by myself. For ten years since I quit farming. But then came this trouble with my back. It won't go away though sometimes it seems to. The doctor wanted me to quit, but I didn't want to. If I quit, it won't be for that. It'll be because I can't feel good about it anymore.

My daughter was the first to say I should get someone to help, so in the winter I got a local boy to help sometimes. Then he went off to the army. That's when this boy from the college came along. His mom had seen my daughter's note in the laundromat. At the beginning of the summer he called up and said he wanted to work. I had a burial to do in the town north of here, so I picked him up at his house in the morning. He was skinny and glum and long-legged. His eyes drifted around and wouldn't look at me directly. He wouldn't have been bad looking if he had cut his hair.

"This is pretty weird," he said. "A job like this posted at the laundry." He didn't say much else at first. Then he wanted to know about the money, even though I'd told him before, so I told him again how it was sixty dollars for each one we opened and closed. I told my joke. "One dollar to open, fifty-nine dollars to close it again." But he only wanted to know if he would get half. That's what occupied his mind.

I would pay him fifteen at least, I said, and when he got the hang of it and could do his share, he would make more.

I remember how he didn't like that. He liked to use obscenities, and I don't mind that much, but he tossed them around like they didn't mean anything. He used obscenities even when he wasn't mad, though this wasn't one of those times. In fact, he didn't actually say anything, but that's the way people are when they first meet. Even those who swear all the time don't do it at first. I remember just how he was, sitting down in the seat with his knees up on the dashboard, wearing that funny little tweed cap he always wore, the brim pulled down to cover his eyes. And he didn't say anything, but in his mouth was a cigarette which he took out to examine like there was something wrong with the filter, and that little thing let me know what he thought. He didn't think much of the deal. I knew it was going to be trouble. It put us at odds.

And sure enough, after a while he started in. He said he hadn't expected me to be so old. "Older," he said like there was a difference.

"What's old got to do with it?" I said.

He gave me that glum look of his and shrugged. "I just thought gravedigging was hard work," he said.

I told him I was sixty-three years young and didn't say anything else. After a minute he sort of whistled out his smoke and pulled the hat down further. "I figured that's why you hired me," he said.

I didn't tell him about my back. I tried not to show it, but that's hard. Whenever the weather is damp, it is. That's why my daughter worried. She thought the digging was nothing but bad for me, but she didn't understand how I've always liked the digging, and I always looked forward to it. The feel of it, the way the blade slips into solid earth, the precision of that, the smell of the earth at the back of my mouth. It's a good feeling. It's a good thing to do when it's done with that feeling. I never minded the work at all, but this boy never liked it.

On our way down there on that first morning I tried to tell him how a grave is dug. I wanted him to know how to do it right because if you do it right, it's not hard work. You learn little things from doing it. You learn to put your shovels in oil to keep the blades clean of rust. You always use your own shovel. You try to do everything as well as you can. I told him that to dig a grave is like digging one hole four times, one after the next. You dig one and then clean it out as though it was the only one you had to dig, but then you dig another and clean it out and then another until you've done four, and then the hole is just as deep and square and right as it should be.

I showed him how to use sharpshooters, these shorthandled shovels with long, narrow blades for reaching down sixteen inches. I showed him how to chew out a small hole first and then how to kick that blade all the way down and always leave one edge out so that it will act like a wedge and break the earth free in a solid piece. He acted like I was wasting his time. He stamped his feet around and put his hands on his hips.

"How the hell can you pick up anything with it?" he said. "It's like eating with chopsticks."

He wanted a reason for everything. Why we had to clean out so carefully on every level. Why we had to use such "weird" shovels. He wanted to know why the hole had to be so wide, so I told him all about concrete vaults. The casket is always placed in a concrete vault. That's what I told him, that it was state law, and that's why we dug

the grave so wide, and he thought it was a dumb law and said what difference did it make after the casket was in the ground where nobody
could see it. That's the way he thought. I also told him about the vaults
they used to make, the ones that were just slabs of concrete wired together, and how the wire would rust out and the whole thing collapsed.
He thought that was funny. He called it a coffin sandwich and thought
he was clever. A lot of things I never would've guessed, he thought were
funny. He liked to say that he made his in-come on people's out-go. I
didn't think that was funny. He thought it was funny that we had to put
the topsoil to one side so that it could go back in last, and when I explained that it was important, he said, "It's still weird then." That was
his word for anything he didn't understand.

He said cemeteries were funny places. "Wasted space. What good is
it?" They could take the bodies, he said, and figure some way to keep
them stiff and sharpen them in a giant pencil sharpener and use them for
fence posts.

He thought that idea was real funny, and I said, "Is that what you
want?" No, he was going to be cremated or else donate his body to sci-
ence.

I didn't care what he did, but it got on my nerves how he talked. I
didn't really listen after awhile because he wasn't worth listening to. I
shut my mind and concentrated on what I was doing. I can do that. It
can be good, pleasant work with the cemetery quiet, the green lawn, the
bright flowers, white clouds passing over, the rows of clean stones all
sharp edged and definite. I've dug hundreds of graves in ten years and
never tired of it. All the cemeteries in this county, I've worked them. All
of them, nice places. I never minded working alone even when my back
was trouble. It wasn't trouble, not really.

The first helper I had was good, and I guess I liked him, and he liked
the work, but this boy disliked it, and that made all the difference. He
only wanted to get it done. That's why he wouldn't listen to me. On
that first burial I let him wear himself out awhile. He fought with the
shovel and didn't let it work for him. He couldn't keep up with me and
got so frustrated with his sharpshooter he was mad enough to spit and
swore all the time at it and said he couldn't use such a stupid shovel. He
just didn't know. I suppose he got kind of belligerent, but he did see it
through, out of stubbornness more than anything, and so I showed him
how to boost the shovelful up with his knee because he was using his
arms, and I explained how to shift the work from legs to back to arms
so that different muscles could rest. And by the fourth level, he was getting that somewhat, but he had already worn himself out and had to
take a rest every few minutes. When we were done and waiting for the

truck bringing the vault, he stretched out flat on the lawn and didn't even smoke another cigarette, and when we closed after the funeral, he was already getting stiff and just piddled at it. I did most of the work.

I thought that was that and he would quit after the day, take his fifteen dollars and go find something else he thought was easier. But he didn't quit. I hoped he would, but he said to call him when there was another to do, and I have to give him credit, he called me twice, so I took him on the next one, and he did better. But he complained about the money again, and wanted to know when I would up his share. I said maybe on the next one.

Right away he started to figure on it. "When I get my share," he said, "I'll work my share. I'm getting the hang of this. I'm getting in shape." He figured if we could do a burial in under three hours, we could make more money. "We could do two a day, and that's sixty apiece. Eight per week? What's that? Two-hundred-and-forty apiece."

He had big dollar signs in his eyes, but I said, "Where are you going to get all those burials? You want to bury half the county in one summer."

He hadn't thought of that, but he wondered right away if we couldn't dig all the holes ahead of time. Even he knew that was utter foolishness, but I said there was another reason too. He was hoping people would die, and that was wrong. He laughed at that. He laughed at me for saying it. That made me mad. "There's something else too," I said. "You'll make twenty when you earn it, but I doubt you'll ever make thirty."

He looked like I'd hit him with a double whammy, and he got real sour then, and I thought he might quit after all. But he didn't. I kept him on, and he was young and had energy, so I started paying him twenty, but he kept after me all through June, saying I was an unfair employer and saying I was greedy. I should've let him go then, but I finally gave in instead. I decided he was working as hard, he just had a lazy attitude. The money didn't make any difference. I told him that. But I wanted to keep things right. Equal money didn't mean equal vote.

He said that was alright with him, and maybe we did get along a little better for awhile, but then he started in with ideas to "streamline the operation." Finally he said he was thinking of expanding. He thought we could hire another crew to work the other end of the county. He said that he could oversee one crew and I could oversee the other, and then we wouldn't have to work at all and still come out with twenty dollars per burial.

We were working when he said it. Usually I just ignored his talk, but this time I stopped and sat on the edge of the hole and looked at him.

"Well, what's wrong with that?" he said.

"Nothing except we aren't going to do it," I said.

"Why not?"

"Because I want the job done right."

"That's all you ever want," he said. "But you don't even know what right is. You just make up rules. Just to suit yourself. All these stupid weird rules for how to dig a hole in the ground."

"That's how it is," I said. "You can take it or leave it."

He still didn't leave. I guess he found out the other end of the county had its own people. And all the churches at this end contracted with me. He called it a monopoly, but he stayed. He liked the money too much. I should've let him go, but I didn't have any grievance against his work, and he had said he was going back to school again in the fall, so I thought I could hang on. But he wore at me all summer, and I thought about not calling him, but my back would hurt, and so I would call. And if I didn't have anything for a few days, he would call me.

Then it got to be August, and that's when this final thing happened that makes me wonder how I can keep on. I guess it was a pretty weird month. During the whole first week there were none to do, which isn't normal. People usually die more in August in the heat or maybe just with the thought of another winter. But there weren't any burials for a week. And he called a few times and probably thought I was cheating him. So when there was one to do in a little cemetery down south, I called him. I didn't want to though. I wanted to work it myself. It's the oldest cemetery in the county, and it's a quiet place, a nice place with a little white church on one side of the hill and the cemetery on the other, overlooking the river. You can see clear down the valley to the high, interstate bridge, and you can see trains worming along the tracks that follow the river. It was a place I wanted to work alone, but it had rained during the night, and my back gave me trouble, so I called him in the morning and picked him up as usual at his house.

The sky was still overcast, and mist steamed out of the fields the way it does, and the ditches were full of pink water, and the air was heavy. But some spots were poking through the clouds. I thought it might clear up, but then we topped a hill and way down to the southwest there was another stormfront moving in, you could see it. The sun had rolled up red and was cutting under the overcast. It made the stormfront look like a wide slug of pink metal, like a welding bead stretched all the way a-cross from north to south. We should have gone back to phone and see if they had postponed the funeral, but we didn't. It wouldn't have made any difference. They never know in advance.

He slept on the way out and didn't wake up until we got there. The rain had carved out ruts and spread a delta of mud where the drive emptied out, and my truck slipped sideways getting up the grade, and that woke him. "Having fun, Earl?" he said.

We made it up past the little Baptist church and over the hill, and when we came down the slope, we could see that off to the south, a part of the front was already beginning to roll down into the valley, and you could see a ragged curtain of rain, whiter than the rest of the cloud. We found where the caretaker had placed a stake to mark the plot. The stone was already in place, a double monument. Husband and wife will do it that way, and here the husband had died already, so there was his name and his dates and then below that her name and a place for the date they hadn't engraved yet. And this was a problem. The names weren't side by side. The man had died and been put there over twenty years ago. We didn't know on which side.

I sent the boy up to the church to see if anyone was there. I stayed and looked the situation over, and there were other stones to the right side, but this plot was the last one, so to the left was open lawn. And it seemed right to think that he had been put to rest on the left, so I cut the sod on the right. The boy came back and said there was no one around the church. Then I thought maybe we should wait a bit, but he didn't like that.

"Stand around?" he said. "With that rain coming like it is?"

I suppose it's one of those situations. You think how you've been careful for so long. You think that you deserve a chance, that it's owed to you. I wanted to get it over. The whole summer over and done with. I didn't want to argue and fight and have one of those days. I wanted to go home and rest my back. So I said we could go on and dig a little. The vault would come in a few hours, and there needed to be a place for it. We couldn't ask that man to wait. And I said that if we went in on the wrong side we would surely strike the old vault soon enough, and he said sure, that was good thinking. Even if it was one of those old, wired-up vaults, he said, we'd strike that concrete lid first. We could fill in again and cover our mistake by piling dirt from the new hole on the old. He was hot to get to it. He liked the odds.

And then there was a little sun breaking through, and the grass around us brightened, and that seemed like a good sign. "Hell, it won't even rain," he said. So we started digging, and then it wasn't two minutes before the breeze died down to a whisper, the way it does before a storm, and then the air got heavier than it had been, and then the shadow of the overcast went spreading like a stain across the hillside again.

We dug that first level, and I took the first turn cleaning out. But the pain down my back was like molten metal, and when we got started on the second level, suddenly it just wouldn't work any more. "That's great," he said. "You sure pick the best days to break down." But he saw that it hurt, and he as much as made me get out and go sit on the tailgate where I could lean way over to make it feel a little better. He said it was alright with him as long as he got all the money, and he went on, digging fast and not doing the best job, but I didn't say anything. I could always make him clean up the sides later. I only asked him to take the shovel and thump the bottom of the hole to see if it sounded hollow, but it didn't.

He went on and finished the third and got going on the last level, and for awhile the storm seemed to be holding off. But it wasn't. Down where the river turned, the trees were black and the ridge beyond had disappeared in haze. The cloud was coming in smooth as pillows. You could see the contours bulge and roll under and deform as it moved. And except for the sound of his boot knocking the shovel down each time, it was so quiet you could hear crows down in the valley. And I was sitting there, hunched over, watching him break out the dirt and straighten to swing it up and out, and all of a sudden, when I saw that brick of dirt land and break apart on the pile, I knew it wasn't clay. It was topsoil.

"Stop," I said. "Hold up, Steve." And he stopped and looked at me, irritated. I got over there to the pile of dirt, on my knees.

"What now?" he said.

The dirt was dark loam, just a little clay laced through it. I started breaking it up with my hands, and it didn't take me long to find a metal uniform button, and then there was some bits of wood, and then a silver casket handle all crusted over, and I guess we found a bit or two of everything there was left. I don't know if I'll ever feel like I felt right then. Nothing is worse than causing something awful. All I could do was look at him, and I saw he didn't even know what we had done.

"Can't you see?" I said. "We've dug into the old grave. We've dug up the remains of the man."

It took him a minute. Then all he said was, "What happened to the vault?"

I didn't know. I couldn't think at first, but then I had the answer. The man had died so long ago there was no vault. I hadn't even thought of that.

Well, it was sad, and I thought he would understand, but he only laughed at the whole idea. "How about that," he said. "We sure blew it." And then he was for keeping the silver handle. He wanted to poke round for more souvenirs. To him it was something to brag about.

But I said, "You leave it all alone. You don't tell no one about this. You open your mouth, and I'll put a shovel in it."

I guess I got mad at him. But I thought it was his fault, the way he had pressured me all summer and worn me down. And it was more than that. I was thinking about the work and the rain and everything. I didn't want to fight with him. I didn't want to start over. For the first time I only wanted to get the job finished. I knew that, and then I didn't feel anything anymore. It all just went out of me.

He knew it too. He couldn't help grinning at me because he knew. "Don't get upset, Earl," he said. "I'll take care of this. It'll be a little shallow, but no one will ever know." He stood there another minute, waiting for me to say something or make some sign, but I wouldn't. Finally he said, "I'm not digging this grave over again and that's that."

And that was it. I sat and watched him. I let him do what he did, and I let them come and place the vault down like nothing was wrong. And after the funeral he took care of everything, even putting all the flowers on top. It still hadn't rained. Only a few heavy drops spotted the truck. The storm didn't start in until we were on our way back.

He was quiet for awhile. Then he said, "There wasn't nothing left anyway." That was the only excuse he could think of.

I guess my mind was finally made up on the way back into town. At the corner of his block, I stopped the truck and sat looking at him for a minute, and I thought how he wasn't to blame, but he wasn't a good boy either, and I told him so. I said someday he would know that. I told him I didn't want him working with me anymore. And I paid him sixty dollars.

He didn't say much, only that he was quitting anyway to go back to school. He said it was an experience digging graves with someone like me. And as he was getting out, he turned back and said he would keep it under his hat. That was all.

I went home and sat at the kitchen table, and my daughter said I didn't look well. I didn't tell her what had happened. I said I felt tired and my back was troubling me.

That night I got up like I sometimes do, and it was still raining steadily. I stood at the kitchen door with the porch light on and watched the way the drops of water exploded in the mud of my wife's flower beds.

Somebody turned on a light in the house down the street, and I knew it was another old man like myself lived there. For awhile I wondered what had gotten him up in the middle of the night, and I even thought I would walk down there and tell him. But it was raining, and I didn't. There was nothing really I could tell him. I stood at the door and thought about it all, and I watched until his light went out again.

When she was alive, my wife used to go to the Methodist church, but I never did. She's in their cemetery now, and I suppose that's where I'll go.

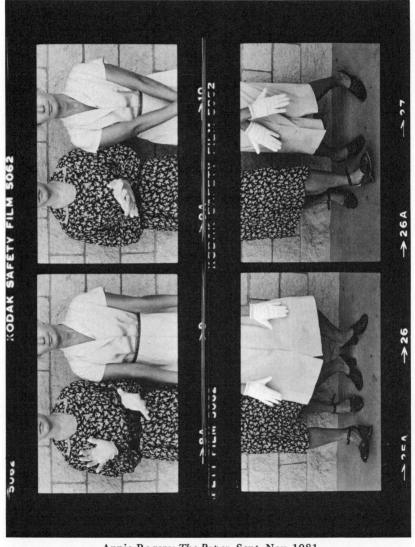

Annie Rogers; *The Paper*, Sept.-Nov. 1981
Pat Matsueda, Editor

Richard Grayson
THE FACTS ARE ALWAYS FRIENDLY

Cumberland Journal, No. 15–1981 ("Disjointed Fictions" issue, by R. Grayson)
George Myers Jr., Editor

On December 21, 1972, at 11:48 p.m. Eastern Standard Time, the sun entered the sign of Capricorn and winter began in the Northern Hemisphere.

On December 22, 1972, at 11:49 p.m. Eastern Standard Time, Kevin Miller stopped to kiss Ronna Berkowitz on a deserted beach and told her that he loved her, a statement to which Ronna responded, "It's been awfully hard without you lately."

OnDecember 23, 1972, Kevin Miller and Ronna Berkowitz attended a showing of the film "Sunday, Bloody Sunday," a film in which the actress Glenda Jackson speaks the following lines of dialogue: "I'm sick of all this bullshit that anything is better than nothing.... Sometimes nothing has to be better than just anything."

On December 14, 1972, Avis Feintuch read a letter to the editor of *The Village Voice* written by her friend Kevin Miller, a letter which read in part: "... Is the world so depressing a place that there's never anything good to report? Maybe we should just chuck the whole thing...."

On December 25, 1972, following Christmas dinner with her father and stepmother, Ronna Berkowitz asked Kevin Miller if he ever got angry, a question to which Kevin responded, "Not as often as I would like to."

On December 26, 1972, Avis Feintuch heard a ripping sound and knew that this meant that Alan Karpoff was tearing the wrapper off a lubricated rubber prophylactic.

On December 27, 1972, Avis Feintuch told Kevin Miller that Alan Karpoff treated her so nicely she couldn't believe what was happening: "I'm so used to being shitted on" were Avis' exact words.

On December 28, 1972, Ronna Berkowitz went to the college library to do research on a term paper about bird symbolism in Yeats, only to find the library closed due to the national day of mourning for former President Harry S. Truman.

On December 29, 1972, Kevin Miller unsuccessfully attempted to write a "statement of purpose" on an application for admission to graduate study in the Department of Government at George Washington University.

On December 30, 1972, Kevin Miller and Ronna Berkowitz, on their way to dinner, encountered Scott Koestner, the former boyfriend of Avis Feintuch, who informed them that Avis was "having a nervous breakdown over her term papers and calls me three times a day," a statement which Kevin later suggested might be wishful thinking on Scott's part.

On December 31, 1972, at 11:50 p.m. Eastern Standard Time, Ronna Berkowitz refused a marijuana cigarette which had already been smoked by Avis Feintuch, Alan Karpoff, Kevin Miller and several other persons attending a New Year's Eve party at Alan Karpoff's house.

On January 1, 1973, at 4:24 a.m. Eastern Standard Time, Ronna Berkowitz asked Kevin Miller if he had ever been in love with his friend Avis Feintuch, a question to which Kevin replied, "It doesn't matter now, does it?"

On January 2, 1973, at 3:19 a.m. Eastern Standard Time, Kevin Miller fell asleep while typing up a research paper comparing the Liberal Party of the United Kingdom with the Free Democratic Party of the Federal Republic of Germany.

On January 3, 1973, Avis Feintuch made the statement, "I wonder what Scott Koestner wants from my life," a statement referring to the fact that her old boyfriend Scott had sent her an empty package of Benson & Hedges cigarettes in the mail.

On January 4, 1973, Ronna Berkowitz asked Kevin Miller if they could go back to the beach again during the coming weekend, a request to which Kevin responded affirmatively.

On January 5, 1973, Scott Koestner telephoned Avis Feintuch and asked if he could see her, a request to which Avis responded negatively, telling him that she would be spending the weekend mountain-climbing with Alan Karpoff.

On January 6, 1973, Scott Koestner told Kevin Miller that Avis Feintuch had become, in his words, "a real bitch," a statement which Kevin denied in silence.

On January 7, 1973, Ronna Berkowitz, in replying to a question from Kevin Miller wondering how long it would take for them to start having quarrels, said, "God, give us a few weeks at least."

On January 8, 1973, Scott Koestner had a nocturnal emission during a dream about Avis Feintuch.

On January 9, 1973, Scott Koestner said to Kevin Miller after they saw Ronna Berkowitz get on the B-36 bus, "Finally you've got a girl I approve of," a statement to which Kevin responded, "Yeah, but I'm waiting for the balloon to burst."

On January 10, 1973, Avis Feintuch and Alan Karpoff lay in the back seat of a 1968 Pontiac, fogging up the automobile's windows.

On January 11, 1973, Ronna Berkowitz took a short break from studying for final exams to have coffee with Scott Koestner, to whom she confessed that she had for some unknown reason become depressed lately, a statement to which Scott responded, "Do you and Kevin see much of Avis and that mountain-climbing jerk?"

On January 12, 1973, Leo Wolfson, novelist and professor of English, told Ronna Berkowitz that he found a great deal of anger hidden in the short stories which Ronna had written for his Advanced Fiction Writing course.

On January 13, 1973, Ronna Berkowitz called Kevin Miller in great distress following an argument with her mother, who had told Ronna that she was just as selfish as her father, Mrs. Berkowitz's former husband.

On January 14, 1973, Kevin Miller stayed in bed all day, feeling ill and depressed, wondering if he was doing the right thing in getting involved with Ronna Berkowitz, and wondering if he really loved her or if their relationship was a neurotic one.

On January 15, 1973, Scott Koestner asked Kevin Miller if he would accompany him on a trip to Fort Lauderdale, Florida, during their intersession vacation, a request to which Kevin responded negatively.

On January 16, 1973, Alan Karpoff asked Avis Feintuch if she would accompany him on a trip to Atlanta, Georgia, during their intersession vacation, a request to which Avis responded enthusiastically.

On January 17, 1973, Avis Feintuch's parents informed her that they would no longer continue to support her financially if she went ahead with her scheduled trip to Atlanta with Alan Karpoff.

On January 18, 1973, Ronna Berkowitz told Kevin Miller that his illness might be a way of avoiding something.

On January 19, 1973, Kevin Miller began to feel better following a session with a clinical psychologist, Dr. Elayne Porter.

On January 20, 1973, at 2:43 a.m. Eastern Standard Time, Alan Karpoff, while waiting on Interstate 95 just outside Dunn, North Carolina, for representatives of the American Automobile Association to arrive to repair his broken-down car, gave Avis Feintuch a look which she mentally described as one "that could kill."

On January 21, 1973, Scott Koestner had sexual intercourse with a seventeen-year-old girl in a motel room in Fort Lauderdale, Florida.

On January 22, 1973, Avis Feintuch had sexual intercourse with

Alan Karpoff in the bedroom of a friend's house in Atlanta, Georgia.

On January 23, 1973, Kevin Miller attempted to have sexual intercourse with Ronna Berkowitz, who protested that she was not yet ready to do so.

On January 24, 1973, Kevin Miller registered for twelve credits for his last semester as an undergraduate, "pulling" two courses for Ronna Berkowitz, who, as a lower junior, would not legally register for two days.

On January 25, 1973, Scott Koestner, noticing Alan Karpoff and Avis Feintuch walking hand in hand on the college campus, sarcastically asked Kevin Miller, "So when's the wedding?"

On January 26, 1973, Kevin Miller, while breathing hard and lying horizontally on top of Ronna Berkowitz, said jokingly, "Gee, I really appreciate your doing this, especially since I know it's not any fun for you," a statement to which Ronna replied laughingly, "Who have you been talking to?"

On January 27, 1973, a ceasefire of all hostilities in the Viet Nam conflict went into effect as provided by an agreement signed in Paris by Henry Kissinger and Le Duc Tho.

On January 28, 1973, Scott Koestner phoned Avis Feintuch, who earlier in the week had told him that they could do something together that weekend provided Alan Karpoff went mountain-climbing; Scott said, "So Prince Charming's away?"—a statement to which Avis replied, "Look, do you want to do something or not?"

On January 29, 1973, Avis Feintuch's mother called Avis "a slut."

On January 30, 1973, Avis Feintuch asked Kevin Miller about the criminal penalties for matricide.

On January 31, 1973, Kevin Miller told Avis Feintuch that he could be happy seeing Ronna Berkowitz "twenty-four hours a day."

On February 1, 1973, Ronna Berkowitz dreamed that Kevin Miller left her to sleep with Avis Feintuch.

On February 2, 1973, a groundhog in Punxsutawney, Pennsylvania, almost saw its own shadow.

On February 3, 1973, Ronna Berkowitz came down with influenza.

On February 4, 1973, Alan Karpoff climbed to the summit of a mountain just outside New Paltz, New York, while Avis Feintuch had sexual intercourse with her old boyfriend, Scott Koestner, regretting the act even as it was happening.

On February 5, 1973, Avis Feintuch fell asleep during a Classics class, an 8 a.m. lecture course entitled Women in Antiquity.

On February 6, 1973, Kevin Miller felt uncomfortable as he noticed the great tension between Scott Koestner and Alan Karpoff, who were sitting on either side of him in Hamilton Hall.

On February 7, 1973, the United States Senate voted 70-0 to establish a special committee headed by Senator Sam J. Ervin of North Carolina to investigate what had become known as the Watergate affair.

On February 8, 1973, Kevin Miller told Ronna Berkowitz that he had never seen Avis Feintuch looking happier than she did in Alan Karpoff's presence that afternoon at luch at the Golden Roost.

On February 9, 1973, Ronna Berkowitz opened a note she had received from Kevin Miller in that morning's mail, a note which told Ronna that Kevin loved her even though she was paranoid.

On February 10, 1973, Avis Feintuch told her father to tell Scott Koestner, who was on the telephone, that she was not at home.

On February 11, 1973, Scott Koestner got into a fistfight with another student over a parking space, a fight which resulted in a cut lip on Scott's part and no damage whatsoever on the part of the other student.

On February 12, 1973, Kevin Miller asked Ronna Berkowitz if she would mind if Scott Koestner, who had been very depressed of late, came over to Ronna's house with Kevin, a request to which Ronna acceded, though rather reluctantly.

On February 13, 1973, at 1:41 a.m. Eastern Standard Time, Ronna Berkowitz kissed Kevin Miller at the door of her apartment and said, referring to Scott Koestner, who was already downstairs, "Next time leave him home."

On February 14, 1973, Avis Feintuch gave Alan Karpoff a Valentine while they were sitting on a Castro convertible couch, eating navel oranges and watching the Marx Brothers' film "A Night at the Opera" on television.

On February 15, 1973, Alan Karpoff gave Avis Feintuch a Valentine, apologizing for not getting one earlier and stating that he did not realize "those kinds of things" were important to her.

On February 16, 1973, Scott Koestner asked Kevin Miller why Avis Feintuch was ignoring him.

On February 17, 1973, Kevin Miller asked Avis Feintuch why she was ignoring Scott Koestner.

On February 18, 1973, Alan Karpoff had lunch at the Golden Roost with Ronna Berkowitz because there was no one else around, a lunch during the course of which Alan wondered several times what Kevin Miller or anybody could see in someone like Ronna.

On February 19, 1973, Scott Koestner received a letter notifying him that he had been accepted for admission to the Law School of the University of Pennsylvania.

On February 20, 1973, Scott Koestner received birthday cards from several people, among them Kevin Miller and Ronna Berkowitz, but he did not receive one from Avis Feintuch.

On February 21, 1973, Avis Feintuch wondered why she had missed her menstrual period.

On February 22, 1973, Scott Koestner was fired from his part-time job as an assistant manager of a store owned by a large pharmacy chain because he had been trying to organize the store's employees into a union.

On February 23, 1973, Kevin Miller was awakened following a disturbing dream in which he had enjoyed sexual relations with Alan Karpoff.

On February 24, 1973, Kevin Miller found Avis Feintuch sitting on a bench outside Hamilton Hall, looking upset because she had been waiting twenty-eight minutes for Alan Karpoff, who was apparently not going to appear as scheduled.

On February 25, 1973, Ronna Berkowitz returned from her kitchen with two cups of rosehips tea to find Kevin Miller asleep on the floor in front of the television set, which was broadcasting the third episode of the Public Broadcasting Service's cinema-verite documentary series, "An American Family," which dealt with the day-to-day lives of William and Patricia Loud of Santa Barbara, California, and their five children.

On February 26, 1973, an x-ray photograph would have shown a fetus in the uterus of Avis Feintuch.

On February 27, 1973, Ronna Berkowitz told Kevin Miller that she was thinking of spending the summer traveling in Europe with two girlfriends, a statement which upset Kevin a great deal, though he successfully attempted to hide it.

On February 28, 1973, Scott Koestner wondered if Kevin Miller and Ronna Berkowitz actually had sexual relations together.

On March 1, 1973, Kevin Miller told the clinical psychologist Dr. Elayne Porter that "sex makes a person defenseless and vulnerable" and alluded to various hurtful experiences he had had in the past.

On March 2, 1973, Avis Feintuch consulted Dr. Steven Polk, gynecologist and obstetrician.

On March 3, 1973, Scott Koestner told Kevin Miller, while they were drinking from a pitcher of dark beer in the Golden Roost, that "Life sucks," a statement with which Kevin did not agree or disagree.

On March 4, 1973, Avis Feintuch, while smoking a marijuana cigarette, told Kevin Miller that she felt all of her neuroses were coming back because she was so busy with her Classics homework and her part-time job in a lingerie store, and because Alan Karpoff was always so busy with his mountain-climbing that they rarely saw each other anymore.

On March 5, 1973, Avis Feintuch cried continuously for fifty-one minutes.

On March 6, 1973, Avis Feintuch saw Scott Koestner during a crowded passing between classes and smiled and waved to him, gestures which Scott did not respond to or acknowledge.

On March 7, 1973, at 3:45 a.m. Eastern Standard Time, while spreading Deaf Smith Peanut Butter across a slice of whole wheat bread, Ronna Berkowitz told Kevin Miller for the first time, "You know I love you, don't you?"—a statement to which Kevin responded with a smile and a nod of his head.

On March 8, 1973, Avis Feintuch told Kevin Miller a secret.

On March 9, 1973, Kevin Miller told Ronna Berkowitz a secret.

On March 10, 1973, Ronna Berkowitz, Kevin Miller and Avis Feintuch sat in chairs in Avis' kitchen debating whether they would tell the secret to Alan Karpoff and/or Scott Koestner.

On March 11, 1973, Ronna Berkowitz took Kevin Miller's hand as they witnessed Ronna's cousin breaking a glass under a wedding canopy, thus confirming the sacrament of marriage in the Jewish religion.

On March 12, 1973, Scott Koestner had sexual relations with two different women, neither of whom was Avis Feintuch.

On March 13, 1973, Alan Karpoff failed a geology midterm.

On March 14, 1973, Alan Karpoff and Ronna Berkowitz debated the merits of various films and performers who had been nominated for Academy Awards.

On March 15, 1973, President Richard M. Nixon, in a policy statement on the use of executive privilege, barred staff members and former staff members from testifying before Congressional committees.

On March 16, 1973, Avis Feintuch slept over at Ronna Berkowitz's house following a dilation and curettage to remove the fetus from her uterus.

On March 17, 1973, Alan Karpoff could not understand why Avis Feintuch's mother had told him Avis was spending a few days at Ronna Berkowitz's house since Avis and Ronna were not particularly good friends.

On March 18, 1973, Scott Koestner, after a 10 a.m. Political Theory course, told Kevin Miller that Kevin's life-style was "self-satisfied-ly neurotic," a statement to which Kevin did not respond.

On March 19, 1973, Ronna Berkowitz began writing a short story featuring fictional characters who were based upon herself, Kevin Miller, Avis Feintuch, Alan Karpoff and Scott Koestner.

On March 20, 1973, at 7:07 p.m. Eastern Standard Time, the sun entered the sign of Aries, thus ending the season of winter in the northern hemisphere.

W. C. Morton
DAFNEY'S LAMENTATION

Chase Avenue Press; *A Chain Of Lakes* (1983), by W. C. Morton
W. C. Morton, Editor

Dafney parades her resentment of this city
under the accusation of cultural sterility,
past the mannequin lovers
the foam filled women
past the human beings along the avenue.
She murmurs incantations
to those who will listen
"Philadelphia, San Francisco"
and that one most powerful
"New York".
Her mind has given these names
to perfection
and she treasures them
like the names of lovers
who brought her to combustion
and melted her down.
Her song is sweet and cloudy
like my uncle's wine
and lets me dream too
about places where people
are better and more alive.
We dream along, passing the bottle,
and I never drink too deeply,
knowing what's at the bottom
of Dafney's lamentation.

Hilda Morley
"EPIDAURUS"

Matrix Press; *What Are Winds & What Are Waters* (1983), by Hilda Morley
Kathy Walkup, Editor

Epidaurus:
> you loved it

We should have stayed there
> perhaps

forever: & you grown healthy
in your love of the place
> The amphitheater,

form of a seashell,
> no bigger

it seemed at a little distance than a
man's hand
> Your own had a

curve you recognized in
that semi-circle
> & the voices,

the human voices   sounding
on that stage were sheltered
in the level they reached for: their timbre
a precision,
> not a vibration

missing
> You should have

stayed there—
> Aesculapius, god of healing,

whose shrine it is
might have said Yes to you
> to whom

finally, from a great distance
he said: No

Jaroslav Seifert
"IT WAS AFTERNOON OR LATER"

The Spirit That Moves Us Press; *The Casting Of Bells* (1983), by Jaroslav Seifert
Morty Sklar, Editor

It was afternoon or later,
A meal under the oak,
Difficult to remember.
The maid happily spread the wash in the yard
Shaking each piece with both round hands
And as if this had defied the flat sky above
A rain, as short and ridiculous
As a child's piano with twelve keys,
Began to cool the air.
The clothes hung limp and would not dry.
And from behind the river's mist
The round white moon rose suddenly.

Someone must have noticed
When she swam in Machov Lake
The floating shirts impatiently against her...
Of that I could sing,
But not now.

—tr. from the Czech by Paul Jagasich & Tom O'Grady

Patricia Rahmann
HEATHEN WAYS

Confrontation, No. 24–1982
Martin Tucker, Editor

When Daddy was assigned to the 4th Infantry and we moved to Fort Missoula, Mother decided to put us in a Catholic school. I think I know the day, possibly the moment, when this notion first occurred to her. It was the day Etta, our nurse and laundress since I was a baby, left on the bus for South Carolina. "To be with her own people," Mother explained to us, alternately weeping over the loss and raging against Etta's ingratitude at a time when she was needed. "Most needed!" The violence of Mother's emotion and the shame of Etta's betrayal subdued us. Timmy and Beth went outside to play, and I moped around the house while Mother haphazardly instructed the new cook (who didn't do laundry) on what her duties would be.

By lunchtime Mother didn't feel at all well. She had bouillon and soda crackers on a tray and made a long distance telephone call to her old friend, Mrs. McFarren. Though Daddy complained about the phone bills, she never hesitated to make calls. They always picked up her spirits. I heard her laughing with Mrs. McFarren and then gasping for breath, say in her high party voice, "You know how it is, Dodie darling. We're not Catholic, just careless." This, I think, was the moment when the Catholic school idea started. It was also the moment I realized, without understanding exactly why, that Mother was pregnant. I was nearly ten, intensely interested in adults and knew that Mother's jokes were often the best clue to what was seriously on her mind.

She glanced up from her talk, replaced the bouillon cup in its saucer, and putting a hand over the receiver, said to me in her level voice, "Go outside with the other children and run and play and have a good time, damn you." She did not approve of children listening to adult conversation so I don't know what else they said, but by evening she had come to her school decision.

Bathed, powdered, negligeed and half-way through the elaborate business of preparing for an evening at the Officers Club, she sat before her oversized dressing table ready to do her face. I, with rare permission to watch, sat with Peter, our cocker spaniel, on the foot of her chaise lounge. We lived by the rule that children should be seen and not heard, at least on most occasions, and this, I sensed, was one. "Tim," she called, raising her voice for my father through the open door to his room. Daddy snored so they always had separate bedrooms. "Tim, are you listening?"

"I hear you."

"Don't you think nuns must make excellent teachers?" He didn't answer. "They must be very patient women," she continued, smoothing lotion on her arms. "They'd have to be in that kind of life."

My father appeared suddenly in the doorway, stripped to the waist, face lathered, razor poised, his English setter, Jack, by his side. She turned halfway on her bench to face him, and with a burst declared, "Tim, we're putting the children in a Catholic school!"

"What are you talking about?"

"It's the perfect solution."

"To what?"

"To everything." It seemed obvious to her. "There are so many advantages over the public school. The girls can take sewing lessons. Embroidery. Some sort of needlework. I'm sure nuns teach that."

Daddy frowned and cocked his head. The firing range had caused some deafness in his left ear which was most apparent when he was faced with the unfamiliar. "Needlework?" he repeated.

"Yes." She was joyful. Strange, I'd never seen my Mother sew on a button. "And cooking." Cooking? She never cooked, except to help Daddy fix partridge or some other game on the cook's night out. She wouldn't really cook until her inheritance was used up and they would be reduced to living on army pay. Now Etta was gone; my mother was pregnant; world war seemed imminent, and, I suppose, sewing lessons for Beth and me were a precaution, a hedge against the future. "And," she continued, "I can arrange for them to have a hot lunch with the boarding students." For my Southern mother a hot lunch was an important consideration in getting us through our first Montana winter.

"Goddamn it, Isabel, you shouldn't go ahead on a thing like this without consulting me." But he sounded mild.

She went on to tell him that she had talked to a Mother Superior and that they would take Timmy in first grade. "He's big for five." Daddy was proud of that. And there was no objection to our not being Catholic. "They're looking for recruits." He was sure of that. But cathechism was required. "Well, a little religion around here wouldn't hurt," he conceded, and returned to his shaving followed by faithful Jack.

"I'm sure they are dedicated teachers." Mother spoke more to herself then. "They'd have to be strict. After all, they've no outside interests, nothing to distract them." Her voice trailed as she leaned into the mirrored tryptich, head up, offering her face to its reflection, lips parting in anxious, suffering adoration. Her dark nipples gleamed through the silky material, and she brought her shoulders slightly forward to examine her tanned cleavage through the blur of lowered lids. From where I sat she seemed to be reflected in triplicate to infinity. I looked away and waited. A Catholic school. The thought made me shy and excited. Finally, I

319

ventured quietly, afraid of breaking a spell or violating a code, "Mother?"
"Unh?" She applied mascara, her tongue curling in concentration.
"What dress are you going to wear?"
"The midnight blue."
I loved the midnight blue. It was chiffon with thin spaghetti straps
and flared below the thigh in white organdy cut in jagged curves like a
flame curling up about the knees. I sorted through the overflow of her
closet, heavy with perfume and her own distinct odor, to find it. It needed cleaning so she wore the forest green instead.

Clearly the nuns had an excellent laundress. The white coifs and bib-like
scapulars over their black habits were immaculate and stiff with starch.
Their shoes were shined. Being accustomed to uniforms, I accepted, as a
matter of course, individual differences beneath the garb.
    Timmy's stout old nun looked like a broad-backed Labrador waddling
over her litter. Beth's Sister Anne Marie was graceful with the second
graders on the playground—laughing, her skirts swinging when she whirled about in games. She had a face like an angel.
    My teacher, Sister Claire of the Cross, had a face like a walnut. A bare
inch taller than Arnold, the biggest fourth grader, her black habit apparently concealed nothing more than bird-bones and stringy tendon. She
seemed fleshless, except for surprisingly full, dry lips. There was a faint
trace of lysol about her, and everyone said that she was the strictest teacher in school, therefore (according to my mother) the best.
    She orchestrated the seating arrangement in rows of dark blue, make-
shift depression uniforms, alternating good pupils with bad. I sat across
the aisle from Arnold who must have been the most ragged child to ever
set foot in Saint Francis Xavier School. His home-cut hair was matted.
His grin revealed pitted teeth which I think hurt him, because sometimes
he would hug his head to his desk as though in pain until told to sit up.
He wore shoes only in the coldest weather, and they were men's, sizes
too big.
    On her Monday inspection of fingernails and ears, Sister Claire rou-
tinely ordered him to turn up his palm, which she would then slap with
her ruler. After the shock of the first time, the class anticipated this
weekly event. Drawing in away from her skirts as she worked her way
down the aisle, holding still, we waited for the crack. He never cried out.
Nor complained. Never. Just a quick sucking in of breath. I admired him
for that, and secretly thought he could be handsome. But it wasn't only
his dirty fingernails or shoeless condition that Sister Claire didn't approve of. She didn't approve of anyone who said "ain't" or "she don't"
or "my brudder, he."
    She had pets. Rose Ellen, with ruler-straight bangs who knew the
multiplication tables through twelve the first week, was the smartest.

But I, by being the best behaved, would become her favorite.

The first day of school she called me up to her desk, complimented me on my new uniform, and plucking a speck of lint from my front, asked where I got it. "Mother had it made. Her dressmaker," I replied. Then lowering her voice and drawing me closer as though we were conspirators about to share some dread secret, she moistened her perpetually dry lips and asked what sect my family belonged to. I didn't know what sect meant. "Your form says Protestant." She tapped papers on her desk. "Which Protestant church?" I didn't know. Her faded eyes enlarged by steel-rimmed glasses were grave with concern and her next words so low that they were more mimed than spoken. "Have you ever gone to church?" I remembered being in a big white one once when Timmy was christened. But, no, I didn't know the name. Could I find out? "Yes, Ma'am," I answered. "Yes, Sister," she corrected. "Yes, Sister," I repeated, and standing in the privileged sanctuary of space behind her desk, aware of the class watching, I was filled with shame and craven gratitude for her solicitous attention to me.

The next day while the class worked on spelling I was called up to make my report. "Episcopalian," I whispered. Then drawing a chair up next to hers, Sister Claire taught me the Hail Mary. When she was satisfied that I knew it perfectly we knelt together on the floor behind her desk. "Blessed art thou among women and blessed is the fruit of thy womb..." I was grateful to be hidden for that intimate moment from the eyes of the class, but, of course, by then they knew I was not Catholic.

The following Monday the whole school knew. It was evident for all to see, because Mother sent Beth and me to school dressed in red farmerettes—overalls with a pinafore top she had ordered from Best's in New York. I protested that I didn't think pants were allowed, but Mother was already annoyed (Daddy amused) by my making the sign of the cross before every meal. "I'm not interested in your opinion, Miss Priss." She pulled the brush through my snarled hair. "All I require from you is unquestioning obedience." It was a quote from an old commanding officer she admired and thought witty.

"But Mother."

"Never mind." She softened. "Be grateful for what you have. They're new and pretty. I say you can wear them." It was useless to argue with her.

Still, from the moment the soldier lowered the tailgate on the army truck that delivered us to the playground, we felt humiliated. Girls clustered around to ask why we were dressed like that. Boys hooted. Arnold chanted, "You're gonna get it." Surprisingly we weren't punished, and since there was no way to send us home without making elaborate arrangements, we remained conspicuously in school for the day.

But Sister Claire did have one of her low-voiced conferences with me during spelling. I promised to explain to Mother that pants were not allowed, pretending that she was innocent of this information, praying that Sister would not interpret my being dressed in farmerettes as contempt for their rules, but simple ignorance on our part.

With drinks before dinner, Mother and Daddy laughed at the scandalizing of the nuns. Beth stuck our her lip and declared that she hated overalls and would never wear them again. "Think of all the little girls in China who would be glad to have anything from Best's." Daddy rubbed his aging setter's balding chest. "Especially snazzy red pants." He winked at me.

"Oh, Daddy." I was coy because it was expected, but felt miserable because I was afraid my parents might not ever really understand how serious the situation was. Then Timmy burst into tears, wailing that he didn't want sisters who wore red pants. Mother pulled him to her lap and planted a lipsticked kiss on his forehead. "Daddy just likes to tease the girls." She wiped his nose with her cocktail napkin. "Stop it, Tim."

But after that I took nothing for granted. I was always letter perfect in catechism, and grimly determined to make up for Mother's and Daddy's heathen ways. I knelt longer than anyone on the hard prayer benches in church every Friday afternoon while the rest of the class filed one at a time into the confessional and then out to the playground. Sister Claire would enter the booth last, leaving me alone in the dim church to wonder what sins she could possibly commit that took so long to confess. I would lower my eyes in pious concentration or raise them to stare at the agonized figure of our Lord on the cross—willing myself to share his suffering for all sinners, but most especially for my parents whose sins were blatant and Sister Claire whose sins were strictly between her, the priest, and God. When she finished, we would genuflect toward the altar together, and—crossing ourselves with holy water—leave by the side door.

On one of these occasions, she paused on the steps to ask if, when I was old enough to make the choice, I would become a Catholic. "Yes," I answered, though I had never thought of it before that moment. "Yes, Sister, I will."

"You will have to be strong."

"I will be." We were solemn, and at some point it became a tacit understanding between us that I, like Sister Claire, would someday join the Holy Order of The Sisters of Charity.

In the Spring Mother gave birth to a five-pound girl named Caroline, and Daddy left with the 4th Infantry for Alaska. The men would be under canvas for the summer while putting up the first Quonsets at what would become, within eighteen months, an enormous base at war with Japan.

Women and children were left behind, but, by the first of May, Daddy called to tell us that a new hunting pal had wrangled the only available housing in Anchorage for us—the offices of a closed fish cannery. Mother thought this "hugely funny" and, when telling Mrs. McFarren about it on the telephone, laughed until she cried uncontrollably.

I offered prayers of thanks that our family would be reunited, then mooned about, wondering if there would be any spiritual guidance at all in a wilderness so remote that people had to live in canneries. Was there a Catholic school? "I don't know. I don't know about the school." Mother suddenly lost all patience. "Stand up straight, you little fool, and *remember who you are!*"

She scribbled notes in her pointed handwriting, informing our teachers that we would not be returning to St. Francis in the fall. To underline the message, she sent us to school dressed in matching peach colored shorts. It was our first breach of propriety since the red farmerette episode.

During spelling, I stood behind Sister Claire's desk while she read and re-read Mother's note. Her heavy lips were loose, but she seemed smaller and more wizened than ever. She said nothing about the shorts. She crushed the note in her yellowed fist and, opening her drawer, took out a pink glass rosary. "This is for you." She lowered it bead by bead into my palm, then her hand closed over mine and held it in such a strong grip that the tiny cross bit into the flesh at the base of my thumb.. Her watery gray eyes—immense through the thick lenses—regarded me steadily as she reminded me that we must all endure many trials in this life. "Yes, Sister," I acknowledged obediently. Her face came closer. "Will you write to me?" Then unexpected emotion in her frail old-woman's voice alarmed me. I'd never heard her ask for anything. Ever. Sister Claire instructed, ordered, demanded, told. She never asked. "Will you?" she whispered. I nodded dumbly. "Every week? Faithfully?"

"Yes, Sister," I murmured. We knelt for a final Hail Mary. She added a special request for my safety, and I returned to my seat.

Immediately Arnold leaned across the aisle. "Wha'd she say?" I knew she was watching him. "About your pink panties?" I opened my speller and pretended not to hear, but unable to contain himself, he reached over and poked my bare thigh with a finger. "Hey...wha'd she say?" I shook my head to warn him. Too late. Sister Claire flew down the aisle —swift, silent, terrible. With a vicious wrench of his ear, she dragged him from his desk to the floor at her feet. He gasped, then was quiet. Her Lysoled presence enveloped us. "How dare you." Her low tone was terrifying. "Apologize." Silence. She tightened her grip. His face twisted up; his eyes rolled past her to the ceiling; his lips drew back over the pitted teeth. On one knee in a classic posture of the martyred or the damned, he refused to reply.

"Please," I barely breathed. "Please, don't. He didn't mean..." But she dragged him from the room, leaving us so cowed and frightened that no one asked me what he had done.

In Seattle, Mother went off to arrange for the dogs to be shipped to Anchorage and to buy a new coat at I. Magnin's. She left instructions with the nurse (who had already given notice) that we were to order lunch through room service and then could play in the lobby while the baby was put down for her nap. We would simply have to be trusted to behave ourselves without supervision. There was no choice.

I sat at the desk in the corner of the lobby and took out the hotel stationery folder. Beth and Timmy wandered off to the fountain in the center of the room. "Dear Sister Claire," I wrote in my best Palmer Method. Timmy was dangling his yoyo in the fountain. Was that allowed? I wasn't sure. "Dear Sister Claire," I rewrote on a clean sheet, feeling a bit anxious about the waste. But what could I tell her? I could think of nothing. I had never spoken to her without being spoken to first, never volunteered anything except for those few words on Arnold's behalf which she didn't hear. Refused to hear. Beth had snatched Timmy's yoyo and was running around a potted palm. He might cry. I folded the unwritten letter and put it in an envelope in my purse. Aware of my new suit from Best's, I walked up to the tall wide desk and addressed the man behind the counter. "Would you please tell those children that they are not allowed to run in the lobby?"

He gazed at me for a long moment while he adjusted the handkerchief in his breast pocket, then said, "You take care of your business, young lady. And I'll take care of mine."

We had been forbidden to leave the hotel, but I pushed through the revolving doors, walked around the corner of the building out of sight of the doorman, opened my purse and took out the little pink rosary I'd carefully wrapped in tissue paper and the unwritten letter to Sister Claire. I quickly dropped them through a grate in the pavement before I turned my face to the wall and sobbed.

Roger Bower
ON DOOR JAMBS

Pudding Magazine, No. 6–1982
Jennifer Welch Bosveld, Editor

Time passes for me in inches
marked on the jambs
of country houses—
city houses—
short wavy lines
by chewed,
stubby pencils
on top layers
of chipped enamel.

My children strain upward;
feet flat on the floor,
backs tight against the jamb,
pushing past the last marker.
And the marks climb.
And time is growing up toward me—
line by line,
in inches, marked
on the jambs of doors
children pass through;

they pass through.

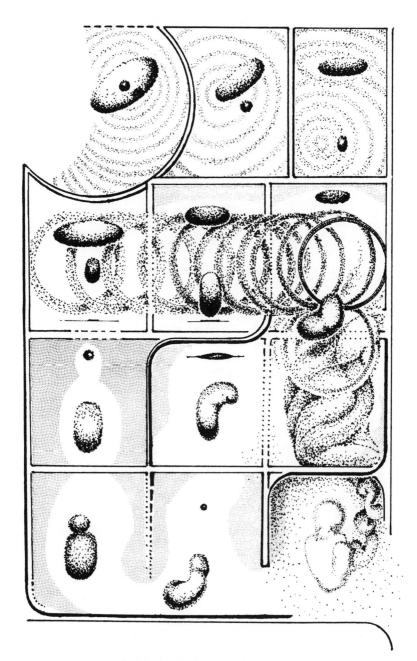

Jurek Polanski; *Telescope*, Nos. V/VI—1983
Julia Wendell & Jack Stephens, Editors

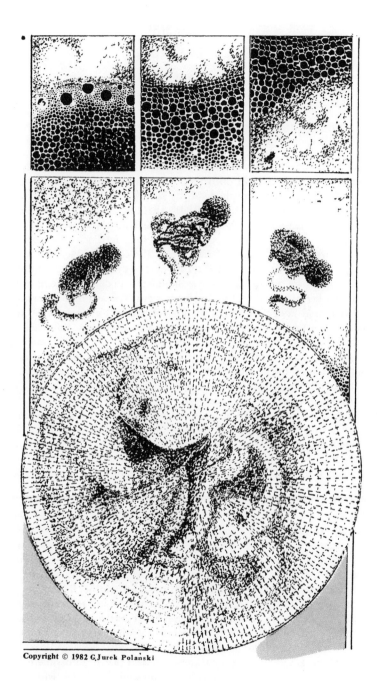

D.E. Steward
PIERRE

Gargoyle Magazine, Nos. 20-21 ("Fiction/82")—1982
Richard Peabody & Gretchen Johnsen, Editors

In the early morning frosts of October you wrapped your lower legs in sheepskin before going out onto the hoarfrost on the slopes and to the icy rocks high up on the south lee of the Massif de Larize where there at the big spring you had a hut. You built that hut the summer you were fifteen and when you cut the poles for the overhang you even made an attempt at a gambrel roof to get more cover for your flock that most of the time was large enough to badly crowd the covered space. You put that hut on the foundations left in the ruins of the sheep shed that had been there before, against an immense boulder, with one of the end walls being another high boulder that butted in tight. You had four other huts that you used in cycle through the grazing season but that one in the rocks on the Larize south lee was the one you liked best. You tried to be there every spring equinox and then back again on the autumnal in September because on the equinoxes, when the West was clear at sunset, from the top of the boulder that made the hut's end wall the sun went down directly on the Pic de Fontfrede and you enjoyed sitting there to see that symmetry.

When they questioned you on good and evil in Pamiers at the end, you gave them the example of the way the sun set at the equinoxes on the Pic as something unassaultably good, and the Bishop, who was not posing the questions, leaving that to the bench of priests from Carcassonne and Toulouse, coughed loudly but you went on and he coughed again and then when you began to laugh at the way he tapped his crozier on the floor and glared at one of the priests from Toulouse who took his cue and told you to stop blaspheming and recessed the court, you were free again to go back out into the yard with your guard and squat in the sun watching the chickens pecking across the cobblestones. It was late February then, already warm enough for you to be sure that the snow up on the Col de Puymorens, the pass you had taken back and forth to Catalonia, would be thawing so that you could get another flock through if you had to. But only with the right dogs, you would tell your guard, who had been brought up polishing harness and routing out stables there in Pamiers and so did not know sheep or the mountains or anything about what it might be like to be somewhere else. With the right dogs you told him, because one thing you knew well was that it is possible to do almost anything with sheep, even run them up a cliff, with the right dogs.

You trained your own, bred and raised them so that there were always one or more bitches with their litters bouncing after you and the herd dogs out on the point. You had no trouble selling your pups down in the sheep markets because even before your beard began to grow everybody said that you had the best herd dogs in the Plantaurel. There were times with your spring lambs gamboling along the slope below like pot lids popping off a stove and the latest litter of eight or ten pups not yet whelped tearing around in the dirt around you where you sat on a milking stool in front of a hut, when you felt sure that the whole purpose of the universe, of good and bad, right and wrong and everything else, was to allow the short season of being young, or at least to set all of us up at one time or another to see, and even if only for those few minutes, to understand, first cause.

Standing under the tribune of the Bishop and his priests, you wanted to describe some of this to them, but loudly like crows around the wet afterbirth of ewes they came down on you for assuming anything about any first cause, shouting that God, only God could know first cause. And the Bishop, who was a local, your age and someone who had crossed paths with you before and knew about you and wanted to get you and anybody else he needed to get in order to eventually become Pope and be able to build the grand palace of the grand schism at Avignon with his garden facing east, then, when he was trying you long before all that, he pointed his crozier at you in all the flurry over first causes and called you arrogant. Later sitting outside in the sun against the wall your guard asked you what the word arrogant meant and you answered laconically that you thought of it as being the smugness of people who had never seen fit to get up out of the valley to see what was up in the high country. That put off your guard for a while and he went back over to the doorway to stand with his lance, leaving you sitting alone in the February sun picking your teeth and imagining in slope by slope detail exactly how much snow really would be left up on the Col de Puymorens with warm weather coming so early that year. Below in the cell it was still winter cold and you wished that you had more than one sheepskin with you through the nights and on Sundays when the inquisition was in recess, and when they brought you food you chewed it thoughtfully.

When you were working for the landowning woman at Montaillou, that night if the wind had not blown the icicles off the eaves outside your window to clatter dryly down the roof against the sweeping sound of the blowing rain you might not have gotten up to go outside. Collecting a cloak at the front door where dinner smell still hung in the room from the hearth with the embers the only bright color you had seen for days of heavy gray weather that had laid in all week until the winds had begun just before dark that evening, you closed the door carefully and walked up toward where you could see the fold from the first ridge and

heard the bawling and knocking of hocks and rumps crowding back against
the palisade before you had come to the lip and could look over and see.
They made no noise at all killing, it was the panicked flock crowded back
and banging into the slats waiting for one more wolf to come in and take
one more of them out by the neck that you heard. But when you came
down into the basin winging rocks and screaming and thudded one of them
hard enough in the ribs, a hollow sound like the icicles careening down the
roof, so that it yelped away first out of the hole they had broken through
the reed and oak slat fence, there were growls, and after you drove them all
out away from the blood and the six dead and dying sheep, they came around behind again fast on the icy grass, flat and dead that thawing night,
the first March wind and rain.

You knew they were going to come back in for you and you had rocks
sailing out of there as fast as you could pick them up and a long fence pole
ready. They were weaving fast, one crossing, another crossing down in front
of it, another crossing again closer each time, and you wondered how you
were going to do it because you had never had to fight wolves at night like
that before and you were not going to be able to get up on anything because the rush roof of the fold surely was not going to hold you. But then
she came over the lip of the basin up from the farm having heard the wind
herself or you going down the stairs or your bellowing when you had come
up on it and was letting go with rocks and calling back down for help every
time she bent down to pick up more. Then the whole of the household
came up and helped the two of you fix the fence before you all went back
down and had hot wine before going back to sleep.

They were her sheep after all, she owned the land. When you met her by
chance on the Barcelona road at an inn in Vich later that year after she had
come over the mountains herself because of the rumor that the Churchmen
in Pamiers were going to send the bailiff and his men after her since by then
they were arresting everyone who had ever had a Cathar in their household
or entertained the hint of Catharism in their lives, you stayed together for
a while. You kept a flock near Vich most of that summer and she would
come up into the hills to meet you in the day bringing food from down
below. Until you contracted to drive a Catalonian flock to Valencia, she
was peevish only when she talked about why you had not seen fit before
when you had been living at the same farmstead, her place, for the two
winters past back in Montaillou, but both of you joked about that and you
would ask her why if she had not liked your performance when you were
working for her she had bothered to come up after you and save you from
the wolves that night. When you did leave with the contract flock you both
talked about her coming along but you had promised to be back before
winter and she stayed in Vich. You saw her once more when you got back
to Catalonia over a year later but she was with an officer of the Court of
Barcelona then and so later you paid a scrivener set up near the Barcelona
port to write her for you that if you both ever got back home you would

like to work for her again. Eventually she bought a house in Vich and had children by the officer, one of whom, who looked just like her mother, did go back to Montaillou after the Inquisition to throw the squatters off her mother's land and hire shepherds to run sheep again.

In October, the month before you finally left Montaillou, when they came for your brother and his wife and the bailiff's men slammed your father hard against the wall of the loomshed and broke his shoulder, you were out with the flock on the hut on Mount Fourcat below the Pic de Saint Bathelemy and got the news only a day later from a peddler coming out your way. He said that your nephew had started up to tell you the afternoon it happened but had gotten lost and came back out of the mountains at dark crying all the way down the street with everybody in Montaillou afraid to come out to him after what had happened to the Maurys, your brother and his wife gone under guard off to Pamiers, your father flat on his back with his shoulder and nobody left to do anything except your nephew, all eight years of him, and his younger sisters and brothers.

The peddler came up the switchback shouting as he spotted you on the rocks after you yodeled to him and beginning even before he finished telling you, you threw your sheep into an old rock and brushwood fold down the draw and pulled out leaving them with the dogs and were down in two hours running all the way to find that there was nothing you could do except listen to your father talk it through.

No warning, they had come in the middle of the afternoon with an order for the arrest of the couple named Maury, five of them, not local men but from Foix. When he had tried to hold them back at the door of the loom shed from coming in for your brother, one of them had head-butted him in the stomach with a lance's shaft shoved against his windpipe and taken him down and kicked him, the kick being how they broke his shoulder, while another one was dragging your sister-in-law out from the house.

You went to Pamiers to try to do something and stood around outside the keep looking up at the oriel at the back of the room where the trials were being held in camera but all you managed to do was bribe a guard to take in a message to your brother which, when having just handed the guard the money as you were standing there below the bridge talking in the dark with him with the river sluicing past, you had a hard time composing because there was nothing to say except that they had broken your father's shoulder. After that you went home to Montaillou but were back outside the keep again three days later to pick up what rumors you could and stand around some more, and then home again to get the flock down because it was already turning cold and the first snow could have come anytime, although it did not that year until late November after you had left. Up at the hut on Mount Fourcat you found the neighbor boy and your oldest nephew with the flock and the three of you brought it down in just a day and then you went back into Pamiers to wait outside the keep some more.

Two days after the first cold day of November it was finished inside and they handed them over to the bailiff again and the next morning you saw your brother and his wife and seven others burned in the market square. He had seen you when they brought them out but her head was down with her hair across her face and she had not looked up. You shouted toward the stakes when the flames went up and your voice carried over everybody else's monodic wails and sighs to meet the screaming coming from inside the sparks and smoke. You thought you could see your brother's stake moving, some succusion of mirage or perhaps his back and arms had been strong enough to shake it for a while something like a herd dog shakes a marmot killing it, but slower, throwing against the stake with his shoulders and his thighs, only it was fire and the deathness of it was taking him, took him and the rest of them quickly. Then you went home where you found your father pushing his apprentice so hard, standing there by the carding table shouting with his arm and side all trussed up, that the apprentice came to you that night outside and asked you if you would say something to your father for him.

Your brother and his wife had been *credentes*, professed, and most people in Montaillou knew that. Your father was not, off and on he went to mass. But he told you, that night of the day they died as you sat with the children and the apprentice already upstairs talking over the little guttering cresset on the table between you throwing the shadow of your mugs and the demijohn of poire dancing crazily every time one of you leaned over toward the other speaking the sorts of things that you had not talked through together since you had been an *auditore*, a listener to the Cathars many years before, that he himself had once been an *auditore* and that he wanted to have the *consolamentum* from one of the Perfects before he died. He made you promise that you would do that for him and when you got up to leave him sitting there you went over to his side of the table and kissed him before going out the door to make the frosty climb toward the Trois Seigneurs before the sun came up. You got there before it did, to your friend's cave on the west side of the Roc de Querqueou facing the little lake, the Etang d'Artax, on which ice was already freezing out from the reeds that you watched going gray from black before the open water in the middle like virga disappearing from a bank of clouds as you sat there on the rocks waiting for him to come out. When he did, the two of you ate at the bread you had brought up to him, pine nuts and each one of the apples that he had and then both of you went down to the lake to wash and drink.

You were together long into the morning and he was garrulous, as most eremitic people are with the occasion. While you sat there outside the cave on the kindling block picking your teeth asking questions now and then when he lost you in his enthusiasms, you realized that you were still an *auditore*. He talked and that is what you had come up there for because you were still seeing your sister-in-law stumbling with her dirty hair over her face and your brother looking through the throng for you and then finding you and then with the wild, mild eyes of a steer, glancing ahead at the bank of fagots and then back at you before he lost you in the crowd. Your friend the Perfect patiently told you how much worse it had been in the Plantaurel when the Catholic crusaders had come down from Dijon to pick through the villages and towns looting as they took hundreds off without even summary trials before burning and how they, those who were what the Church called the Albigensian Crusade, had captured the fortress community of Perfects at Montsegur and burned them all because that was the vindict of the Albigensian Crusade and the Bishop of Pamiers' Inquisition. He told you how when Raymond Roger, the Count de Foix, had been accused of Catharism before the Albigensian Crusade was launched that he had gone in front of the Lateran Council in 1215 with all his children trailing behind him as proof that he followed the tenets of the Church and how even so he had been denounced once more and went home to his chateau high on the promontory above Foix to brood out the rest of his life disgraced and isolated. And how then, in your times, it was left to Bernard Guy, the Grand Inquisitor, to root out what Catharism remained in the South and that this was what was happening, begun nine years before in 1308 and allowing careerists like the Bishop of Pamiers to make their names by executing *credentes* like your brother and his wife.

You listened, pushing the pine splinter you rolled in your fingers into the hole in the crown of the bad tooth in the back of your jaw contemplating the pain of it while wondering what all your friend, a Perfect who had so far survived, was telling you you had to do with the excitement you had felt when you heard the Perfects for the first time, what all those horsemen down out of Burgandy had had to do with the way people felt about something not right about eating meat and what was wrong, as the Perfects said, with people being fundamentally good, not bad as the Church insisted. You probed at your bad tooth and then threw the splinter away as you realized that this was what made people like your father want the Catharist *consolamentum* to be given to them at the end, they wanted to believe that they were good and not irrevocably bad.

When you left the Perfect that day you went down and across the valley and climbed back up the other side to do some hut work over on Mount Fourcat. You wanted your huts to be in shape for your nephew or whoever else might use them in the spring. Rumors about another visit from the bailiff's men from Foix were strong in Montaillou when you came down to the valley again. So you stayed at your father's house only one night and left in the morning, behind your sheep for Catalonia.

Author's note: Written after having read of the Fournier Register but before reading Le Roy Ladurie's Montaillou (Gallimard, 1975).

Tony Hoagland
THE QUESTION

Luna Tack, No. IV—1983
Dave Duer, Editor

"we are what is missing from the world"

Some questions have no answers.
Raised, they hang there in the mind
like holes, or jokes whose punchlines
you've forgotten.
The great Portugese poet, Pessoa,
said that the idea of happiness
is what makes men permanently sad.
The body, imagining the soul,
looks ugly to itself.
A man hears the word, and the world
becomes a place that he misunderstands.
So he climbs high into his life,
ashamed of all he doesn't know,
and refuses to come down.

If you could coax him out again,
you could tell him, say,
that anything can be explained.
The shape of apples, for example,
by their love of travel.
Or that the sky is blue because
it's an easy color on the eyes.
These theories may be wrong, of course,
but there's a lot of sanity
in trying to make sense.

Even the dog, chasing his tail
has, temporarily, a center.
Even the bird disappearing
into its hole, knows
that the world goes on without it.
And Pessoa, that eminently healthy man,
that artist, wore a blue wool hat
even on the hottest summer days.
Simply to toss at strangers on the street.
He liked to see them catch it,
and grow immediately less strange.

Harley Elliott
FOR FARMERS

New Letters, Vol. 49, Nos. 3 & 4 ("Reader I")—1983
James McKinley, Editor (David Ray, at time of nomination)

Surrounded by broken
pots and arrowheads
I walk the space where
earth dome houses stood.

The Kingdom of Quivira
neolithic farmers
tattooed arms beneath the stars
and a sight named Coronado
winding through the smoky hills

in a dazzle of crosses
and weapons on animals
with stone hard feet.
Gold squash and pumpkins shudder.

The man of metal
speaks of seven cities
made of gold
streets made of gold
gold temples clothes
and shoes of gold
gold idols rings
coffins plates the very
gutters made of gold.

The farmers stare
off at the sky
a high-pitched blue above
where wind and stone remain.
"We hear you stranger.
sit down
eat drink.

That which you
desire is just
a little further on."

Dick Bakken
HOW TO EAT CORN

Poetry Flash, Oct. 1983
Joyce Jenkins, Editor

My grandfather ate squash, ate corn. He ate corn
like this, lifting the ear, saying
You eat corn like this, when you eat corn
eat like this. And I pulled shuck and silk away
and saw the worm. On and on
as grandfather lifted ears and spoke and showed
his teeth and the yellow sun passed again and again,
the worm was curled under my thumb
only a shuck-width away, saying
This is how I eat corn. Like this. Like this.
I eat corn like this. When I eat like this
I am eating corn.